ROUTLEDGE LIBRARY EDITIONS: LIBRARY AND INFORMATION SCIENCE

Volume 2

A KALEIDOSCOPE OF CHOICES

A KALEIDOSCOPE OF CHOICES
Reshaping Roles and Opportunities for Serialists

Edited by
BETH HOLLEY AND MARY ANN SHEBLE

LONDON AND NEW YORK

First published in 1995 by The Haworth Press, Inc.

This edition first published in 2020
by Routledge
2 Park Square, Milton Park, Abingdon, Oxon OX14 4RN

and by Routledge
52 Vanderbilt Avenue, New York, NY 10017

Routledge is an imprint of the Taylor & Francis Group, an informa business

© 1995 The Haworth Press, Inc.

All rights reserved. No part of this book may be reprinted or reproduced or utilised in any form or by any electronic, mechanical, or other means, now known or hereafter invented, including photocopying and recording, or in any information storage or retrieval system, without permission in writing from the publishers.

Trademark notice: Product or corporate names may be trademarks or registered trademarks, and are used only for identification and explanation without intent to infringe.

British Library Cataloguing in Publication Data
A catalogue record for this book is available from the British Library

ISBN: 978-0-367-34616-4 (Set)
ISBN: 978-0-429-34352-0 (Set) (ebk)
ISBN: 978-0-367-42595-1 (Volume 2) (hbk)
ISBN: 978-0-367-42603-3 (Volume 2) (pbk)
ISBN: 978-0-367-85381-5 (Volume 2) (ebk)

Publisher's Note
The publisher has gone to great lengths to ensure the quality of this reprint but points out that some imperfections in the original copies may be apparent.

Disclaimer
The publisher has made every effort to trace copyright holders and would welcome correspondence from those they have been unable to trace.

A KALEIDOSCOPE OF CHOICES: RESHAPING ROLES AND OPPORTUNITIES FOR SERIALISTS

Proceedings of the
NORTH AMERICAN SERIALS
INTEREST GROUP, Inc.

9th Annual Conference
June 2-5, 1994
University of British Columbia,
Vancouver, B.C.

Beth Holley
Mary Ann Sheble
Editors

The Haworth Press, Inc.
New York · London · Norwood (Australia)

A Kaleidoscope of Choices: Reshaping Roles and Opportunities for Serialists has also been published as *The Serials Librarian*, Volume 25, Numbers 3/4 1995.

© 1995 by The Haworth Press, Inc. All rights reserved. Copies of this journal may be noncommercially reproduced for the purpose of educational or scientific advancement. Otherwise, no part of this work may be reproduced or utilized in any form or by any means, electronic or mechanical, including photocopying, microfilm and recording, or by any information storage and retrieval system, without permission in writing from the publisher. Permission does not extend for any services providing photocopies for sale in any way. Printed in the United States of America.

The development, preparation, and publication of this work has been undertaken with great care. However, the publisher, employees, editors, and agents of The Haworth Press and all imprints of The Haworth Press, Inc., including The Haworth Medical Press and Pharmaceutical Products Press, are not responsible for any errors contained herein or for consequences that may ensue from use of materials or information contained in this work. Opinions expressed by the author(s) are not necessarily those of The Haworth Press, Inc.

The Haworth Press, Inc., 10 Alice Street, Binghamton, NY 13904-1580 USA

Library of Congress Cataloging-in-Publication Data

North American Serials Interest Group. Conference (9th : 1994 : University of British Columbia)
    A kaleidoscope of choices : reshaping roles and opportunities for serialists : proceedings of the North American Serials Interest Group, Inc. : 9th Annual Conference, June 2-5, 1994, University of British Columbia, Vancouver, B.C. / Beth Holley, Mary Ann Sheble, editors.
       p. cm.
    "Has also been published as The serials librarian, volume 25, numbers 3/4 1995"–T.p. verso.
    Includes bibliographical reference and index.
    ISBN 1-56024-742-8 (acid free paper)
    1. Serials control systems–United States–Congresses. 2. Serials control systems–Canada–Congresses. I. Holley, Beth. II. Sheble, Mary Ann. III. Title
Z692.S5N67 1994   95-3013
025.3'432–dc20   CIP

A Kaleidoscope of Choices: Reshaping Roles and Opportunities for Serialists

CONTENTS

Introduction   1
Beth Holley
Mary Ann Sheble

PRECONFERENCE PROGRAM: INTERNET TOOLS AND RESOURCES: AN ELECTRONIC BUFFET

GENERAL SESSION

Issues in Information Policy and Access   5
Birdie MacLennan

The Internet, Client-Server Computing, and the Revolution in Electronic Publishing   11
Birdie MacLennan

BREAKOUT SESSIONS

Tunneling Through Cyberspace in Search of Adventure: An Introduction to Gopher   17
Betty Landesman

Digging Your Own Den in Cyberspace: A Gopher Construction Kit   21
Birdie MacLennan

Come into My Parlor, Said the Spider: World Wide Web and the Mosaic Interface   27
Birdie MacLennan

Communicating with Lists: A Beginner's Guide to Listservs
and ListProcs 33
    Leslie Knapp

(Almost) Everything Else You Ever Wanted to Know
About Listservs and ListProcs 39
    Betty Landesman

PLENARY SESSION I: OVERVIEW OF CHANGE

Technological Change and Its Influence on the Practice
and Role of Information Management 43
    Czeslaw Jan Grycz

The Future of Publishing 55
    Robert Weber

Reshaping the Serials Vendor Industry 65
    Dan Tonkery

Changing Focus: Tomorrow's Virtual Library 73
    Naomi C. Broering

PLENARY SESSION II: AN INTROSPECTIVE VIEW OF CHANGE AND CHOICE

Getting Past the Rapids: Individuals and Change 95
    Linda Moore

PLENARY SESSION III: CHOOSING CHANGE: NEW PRODUCTS AND NEW SKILLS

Electronic Chemistry Journals: Elemental Concerns 111
    Richard Entlich

Adventures in Information Space: Biomedical Discoveries
in a Molecular Sequence Milieu 125
    Mark S. Boguski

Grabbing the Bull by the Tail: Holding on During Change ... 133
    Marjorie E. Bloss

CONCURRENT SESSIONS: A KALEIDOSCOPE OF CHANGE

CONCURRENT SESSION I:
MANAGING ORGANIZATIONAL CHANGE

Managing Organizational Change: The Harvard College
   Library Experience   149
      Mary Elizabeth Clack

CONCURRENT SESSION II:
REPORTS FROM THE FRONTIERS OF CHANGE

Wanted: Information Manager: New Roles for Librarians
   and Vendors   163
      Sharon Cline McKay

From Earth to Ether: One Publisher's Reincarnation   173
      Susan Lewis

Library Cultures in Conflict: Exploring New Roles
   for Librarians   181
      Johann A. van Reenen

CONCURRENT SESSION III:
PROFESSIONAL ADVICE ON HANDLING CHANGE

Understanding Transition: The People Side
   of Managing Change   193
      Judy Clarke

CONCURRENT SESSION IV:
REAL PEOPLE AND VIRTUAL LIBRARIES

At Ease in Liberspace   203
      Susan A. Cady

The Human Side of the Virtual Library   213
      Marion T. Reid

CONCURRENT SESSION V: FROM CUTTER HANDMAIDS TO CYBERSPACE GUIDES: THE FUTURE OF CATALOGERS

Tools for a New Age: An Overview — *Regina R. Reynolds* — 223

Getting the Expert into the System: Expert Systems and Cataloging — *Paul J. Weiss* — 235

Standard Generalized Markup Language and the Transformation of Cataloging — *Daniel V. Pitti* — 243

NASIG WORKSHOPS

Rethinking the Workforce and Workplace: Alternative Ways of Getting the Job Done — *Fred Hamilton* — 255

The New World Order: Serials Management of Electronic Resources and Document Delivery — *Marla Edelman* — 261

Negotiating Contracts for Electronic Resources — *Nancy Gibbs* — 269

"Keep Them Doggies Rollin'," or, Using Series Authority Records to Improve Cataloging and Processing Workflow — *Kristine A. J. Smets* — 277

To Be Continued? Or, The Birth of a Series — *Steve Oberg* — 283

Integrating Documents Processing into Traditional Technical Services — *Judy Chandler Irvin* — 289

Ethics in Action: The Vendor's Perspective — *Heather Miller* — 295

Cost Accounting for the Serials Librarian: Making Financial Decisions in Tight Times *Barbara Shaffer*	301
Serialists on the Front Line: New Opportunities for Serials Professionals in Reference and User Education *Katy Ginanni*	307
Who Needs to Know What? Essential Communication for Automation Implementation and Effective Reorganization *Rita Broadway*	311
Document Delivery: Staffing, Technology, and Budgeting Implications *Lucy Duhon*	319
Methods for Collecting, Processing, and Providing Access to Electronic Serials *Paula Sullenger*	327
Is It Tweaking or Cataloging Enrichment? Choices in Reshaping Serial Cataloging Copy *Phoebe Timberlake*	333
The Journal Pricing Season: The Publisher, Subscription Agent, and Librarian's Viewpoint *Debbie Madsen*	339
... And Then It Happened: Effect of Changes in the Serials Information Environment on the Small-to-Medium Size Academic Library *Elaine Jurries*	345
Workstation Ergonomics and Computer Calisthenics *Amira Unver*	349
Problem Solving Workshop Based on Total Quality Management (TQM) Principles *Lawrence R. Keating II*	353

Job Hunter's Workshop: How to Find and Land the Right
Job, and Survive the Transition 357
    Carol MacAdam

Ninth Annual NASIG Conference Registrants, University
of British Columbia, June 1994 363

Index 381

Introduction

The theme of the ninth annual conference of the North American Serials Interest Group (NASIG) was "A Kaleidoscope of Choices: Reshaping Roles and Opportunities for Serialists." The conference was held from June 2-5, 1994, at the University of British Columbia, Vancouver, B.C.

Several of the conference plenary sessions addressed the impact of technology on libraries, scholarly communication, vendors, and the publishing industry. Other plenary sessions focused on the skills required to manage the many changes in the library profession that are consistently created through rapidly evolving technology.

Speakers in the concurrent sessions brought many of these ideas to the day-to-day level though discussions of their experience with organizing to manage change, managing the virtual library, the roles of the vendor and publisher in providing access to electronic information, and innovations for the bibliographic control of electronic publications.[1]

Eighteen workshops covered a diversity of concerns, ranging from tactics required to negotiate contracts for electronic resources to the use of series authority records to improve cataloging and processing. The conference was preceded by a program on Internet tools and resources.

NASIG's ninth annual meeting drew close to 600 attendees. A large North American contingent was joined by participants from Europe and Asia. Attendees represented all areas of the serials spectrum.

This volume includes papers from the plenary and concurrent

[Haworth co-indexing entry note]: "Introduction." Holley, Beth and Mary Ann Sheble. Co-published simultaneously in *The Serials Librarian* (The Haworth Press, Inc.) Vol. 25, No. 3/4, 1995, pp. 1-2; and: *A Kaleidoscope of Choices: Reshaping Roles and Opportunities for Serialists* (ed: Beth Holley and Mary Ann Sheble) The Haworth Press, Inc., 1995, pp. 1-2. Multiple copies of this article/chapter may be purchased from The Haworth Document Delivery Center [1-800-3-HAWORTH; 9:00 a.m. - 5:00 p.m. (EST)].

© 1995 by The Haworth Press, Inc. All rights reserved.

sessions, along with summary reports of the preconference and conference workshops. We hope that these papers will provide readers with ideas for managing the challenges of new technology and the rapidly changing information environment.

We would like to thank our NASIG Board liaison, Constance Foster, for guiding us through the editorial process, and Robert Persing for preparing the index. We also acknowledge Karen Garrison for her expert secretarial help, and the University of Alabama Libraries for their support of the project.

Beth Holley
University of Alabama Libraries

Mary Ann Sheble
University of Detroit Mercy Libraries

NOTE

1. The editors regret that a contribution from Pieter S. Bolman was unavailable for inclusion in the conference proceedings.

*PRECONFERENCE
PROGRAM:
INTERNET TOOLS
AND RESOURCES:
AN ELECTRONIC BUFFET*

GENERAL SESSION

Issues in Information Policy and Access

Nancy Hannum

Workshop Leader

Birdie MacLennan

Recorder

SUMMARY. The federal governments of Canada and the U.S. are the largest producers of information in North America. This presentation offers an overview of current Canadian and U.S. climates in the development of new technologies to provide access to government information and the ongoing debate in working toward a national policy for equitable and affordable dissemination of and access to this information.

The Legal Resource Centre of the Legal Services Society of British Columbia is a government-funded program with a statutory

---

Birdie MacLennan is Serials Coordinator at the University of Vermont, Burlington, VT.

[Haworth co-indexing entry note]: "Issues in Information Policy and Access." MacLennan, Birdie. Co-published simultaneously in *The Serials Librarian* (The Haworth Press, Inc.) Vol. 25, No. 3/4, 1995, pp. 5-9; and: *A Kaleidoscope of Choices: Reshaping Roles and Opportunities for Serialists* (ed: Beth Holley and Mary Ann Sheble) The Haworth Press, Inc., 1995, pp. 5-9. Multiple copies of this article/chapter may be purchased from The Haworth Document Delivery Center [1-800-3-HAWORTH; 9:00 a.m. - 5:00 p.m. (EST)].

mandate to provide legal information and advice to the citizens of British Columbia. Legal information needs and government information as a whole play an important role in shaping a democratic society. The belief that democracy requires an informed public and that an informed public is fundamental to a free society was espoused by Thomas Jefferson and others in the 18th century, and has since become one of the basic tenets of librarianship. In this opening preconference presentation, Nancy Hannum, director of the Legal Resource Centre of the Legal Services Society of British Columbia and member of the British Columbia Library Association's Task Force on Information Policy, offered an overview of current Canadian and U.S. climates in the development of new technologies to provide access to government information and the ongoing debate in working toward a national policy for equitable and affordable dissemination of and access to this information.

The Canadian and U.S. federal governments are the largest producers of information in the information-producing sector of North America. In recent years, the federal governments have realized that the ability to sell information represents potential for substantial sources of revenue. The basic assumption that citizens of a democratic society have "a right to know" and thus should have equitable and affordable access to government information is being overshadowed, in many instances, by a shift in assumptions that view information as an economic commodity. Several examples of this trend were noted at both the provincial and federal levels.

The British Columbia Library Association's (BCLA) Information Policy Task Force was formed in 1991, as the provincial government began working on Freedom of Information legislation. One of the documents that emerged from the government was "A Policy on Tradeable Information," which would have allowed the government to sell information that was not necessary for the enactment of government programs. The BCLA and others argued that a government's function is to maintain government and enact programs; therefore, most of the information would not be "tradeable." The proposed policy was defeated.

At the federal level, constituents from the Canadian Library Association, the information technology industry, and the federal government met in Ottawa in December 1992 to discuss national information policy. As government and business discussed potential for new technologies and efficient methods for collecting information and packaging it for sale to the private sector, librarians voiced concern about the future of government depository programs, copyright issues, and the increasing cost of government information.

In Ottawa there is an inter-departmental working group on database industry support with a mandate to work for quick release of government information to the private sector. There is currently no estimate of the cost of creating the information, the proposed sale price, justification for its release through private vendors, or an assessment of the impact on public access to this information. There is no comparable coordinating government agency to assure that information will be distributed to the public.

In the meantime, British Columbia has privatized the government distribution arm of the Queen's Printer and the government is in the position of having to buy back government materials to make them available through library depository programs. Products from various government sources continue to rise in price.

Similar trends were noted in the United States, where various government agencies have privatized information. This has resulted in higher costs of the information to end-users and the government has been placed in the position of having to buy back its own information to make it available to the public.

In October 1993, concerned members of the government information library community met in Chicago. They were responding, in part, to a bill in the U.S. House of Representatives which would transfer the position of the Superintendent of Documents and the Library Depository Program to the Library of Congress. Their meeting resulted in a document entitled, "Reinventing Access to Federal Government Information: A Report on the Conference of the Future of Federal Government Information." In their report they noted that "the need for provision of timely, equitable, and no-fee access to government information requires a cooperative network of producing agencies, participating libraries, and a central coordinating government authority." A major concern is that, as government is taking initiatives to sell and/or privatize information, the essential principle of public access to information is getting sidelined and, in fact, the information is becoming less accessible and more costly.

Hannum drew an analogy from Herbert Schiller, a communications economist at the University of California, who, at the 1992 BCLA Information Policy Conference, remarked on a steady shift of power from public interests to private interests since World War II and noted that the shift was particularly troubling in the cultural consciousness sector of society (e.g., schools, libraries, museums) in that it leads to a "production of consciousness." The analogy was taken a step further in considering the perspective of Ursula Franklin, professor emerita at the University of Toronto, who remarked that the development of monoculture in the agricultural sector, or the planting of fewer, rather than more, kinds of crops for profitability in mass production is similar to what is occurring in today's information sector.[1] The advent of the profitability factor in the production of agricultural crops and/or of information resources means fewer possibilities in the realm of biodiversity or "food for the mind."

What is the role of librarians in the current information policy climate? They are the experts on information and have a responsibility to become involved in the discussion and debate in order to ensure that their users will have timely and equitable access to information. Hannum quoted U.S. science fiction writer Bruce Sterling, who noted that, "Information is not power. If information were power, librarians would be the most powerful people on the planet."[2] If information is not power, information *has* power, and librarians have an obligation to learn about the dynamics of power, while advocating for the rights of their users in having equitable access to information.

In closing, Hannum commented on ways in which librarians have been getting involved in making technological advances work for library-related and public sector interests. The FreeNet movement was discussed as a free public access community computer network that provides a wide-range of information and services to the community it serves. The FreeNet movement started in Cleveland, Ohio in 1986 and has grown steadily since its inception to include some thirty-three sites in four countries. In Canada, FreeNets are being started in at least eighty communities, with three sites currently in operation in Ottawa, Victoria, and Vancouver. Services offered by FreeNet include healthcare, education, government, recreational information, community calendars, and electronic mail for direct communication and public discussion. The Vancouver FreeNet was recently launched by an active set of committees that work together to focus on information content and technological planning. Librarians and many other representatives from the public community sector have been involved in planning and implementation.

The presentation concluded with the National Public Telecommunications Network video, "If It Plays in Peoria," which describes the Heartland FreeNet's origins and implementation in Peoria, Illinois.

NOTES

1. Ursula Franklin. Private conversation with Nancy Hannum.
2. Quote of the day, *Globe and Mail*, 1 June 1994.

The Internet, Client-Server Computing, and the Revolution in Electronic Publishing

David F.W. Robison

Workshop Leader

Birdie MacLennan

Recorder

SUMMARY. With the broad-based implementation of client-server computing on the Internet that we see today, a number of applications are appearing and becoming very popular among network users. Most notable among these applications are Mosaic/World Wide Web (WWW) and gopher. These applications make electronic publishing easier for both publisher and reader. Publishers have begun to take advantage of this new environment, and readers and libraries are not far behind.

The client-server computing model is the basis of most of the major Internet activities, including electronic mail (e-mail), telnet, file transfer protocol (FTP), gopher, Wide Area Information Server (WAIS), World Wide Web (WWW), and other applications. Through client-server technology, new paradigms in electronic publishing

---

Birdie MacLennan is Serials Coordinator at the University of Vermont, Burlington, VT.

[Haworth co-indexing entry note]: "The Internet, Client-Server Computing, and the Revolution in Electronic Publishing." MacLennan, Birdie. Co-published simultaneously in *The Serials Librarian* (The Haworth Press, Inc.) Vol. 25, No. 3/4, 1995, pp. 11-16; and: *A Kaleidoscope of Choices: Reshaping Roles and Opportunities for Serialists* (ed: Beth Holley and Mary Ann Sheble) The Haworth Press, Inc., 1995, pp. 11-16. Multiple copies of this article/chapter may be purchased from The Haworth Document Delivery Center [1-800-3-HAWORTH; 9:00 a.m. - 5:00 p.m. (EST)].

© 1995 by The Haworth Press, Inc. All rights reserved.

and dissemination of scholarly information are emerging. In this presentation, David F. W. Robison, educational documentation specialist at NorthWestNet, offered an overview of the client-server computing environment and focused on some of the major applications for its use in electronic publishing. New models in publishing were discussed, as well as possible future scenarios in publishing and the implications for libraries.

In the client-server model, computing activities are divided between the client and the server, and separated between a local and a distant location. The client typically resides on a local computer. "Local" could be a local host, such as a Unix machine, or, increasingly, clients may reside on a desktop computer. The server resides at a remote location. It could be across the city, across the country, or around the globe. Information requests are sent from a client, using special software from a local computer, to an information server at a remote location. The server receives the request, processes it, and responds by sending the answer back to the client.

Examples of client-server applications in electronic publishing include: e-mail, gopher, and WWW. In the e-mail model, electronic publications are sent to an e-mail server (i.e., an e-mail account on computer host) and e-mail software acts as a client in retrieving individual publications as they are distributed to an account. In the gopher model, local gopher client software (e.g., Turbo Gopher for Macintosh, WinGopher for PC's, or Unix Gopher through a terminal connection) is used to connect to a distant server to read or retrieve information from that site. In the WWW model, Mosaic is probably the most popular client for retrieving multi-media materials (e.g., text, graphics, sound, motion pictures, etc.) from Web servers, although other clients are available, such as Cello or Lynx. Local sites that cannot support a high-speed network connection may use Lynx clients to access text-only information from Web servers.

Advantages of client-server computing include greater flexibility in that many different clients can connect to a single remote server. It also allows for the mix or specialization of several different interfaces or search and retrieval protocols, whereby users may connect to a single source or site and link to other sources or sites using the same interface to retrieve information. For example, users can connect to the University of California's Melvyl system and from there, connect to other catalogs using a Z39.50 interface, which allows users to continue searching catalogs at remote sites using Melvyl's search protocols.

Disadvantages include the need to have more powerful computing resources to support client capabilities (i.e., preferably at least eight megabytes of memory and more hard disk space to accommodate larger files). Higher speed connections to the Internet are also necessary to use client-server applications to their fullest potential. Desktop configurations are becoming increasingly more complex to set-up and maintain.

Several client-server models of electronic publishing, using gopher and WWW applications were discussed. Gopher applications included: *The Federal Register, NetCetera,* and Electronic Newsstand™. WWW applications included: Global Network Navigator, *Palo Alto Weekly, 3W-Global Network News,* and *Wired* magazine.

The Federal Register is a U.S. government publication that is being made available on the Internet, with some value-added features, by Counterpoint Publishing. Interested persons may preview portions of this gopher service for free; however, access to full-text information and/or the full range of services is fee-based.

NetCetera is a weekly newsletter from NorthWestNet, which is mounted on the NorthWestNet gopher as well as distributed to NorthWestNet members. With the gopher version, not only are networked resources described, but the gopher menu structure also allows for direct link(s) to the original source. In this way, users are able to pick and choose from NorthWestNet's gopher menus to go directly to remote sources and services that are cited in the newsletter, and NorthWestNet is able to create a kind of interactive newsletter environment for their members.

The Electronic Newsstand™ is a service of the Internet Company, a commercial firm that works with magazine publishers to make portions of the publishers' magazines available on a gopher server, including an informational file about the publication, a table of contents, and one or two complete articles from each current issue. Similar information is also available for back issues. While users are able to browse selected editorial content, they also get information on how to order a subscription to the magazine. Thus, the Electronic Newsstand™ serves as both a browsing tool for users and a promotional tool for publishers, as the primary purpose of the service is to sell subscriptions.

Global Network Navigator (GNN) is a WWW application and one of its more popular services is a regularly updated Web edition of the "catalog" or list of network resources from Ed Krol's book, *The Whole Internet Guide and Catalog*. GNN also offers "meta-centers," where users can find information on travelling, businesses, etc., and a "marketplace" where commercial organizations who support GNN services place advertisements.

The *Palo Alto Weekly* is a free, full-text weekly newspaper from Palo Alto, California. Its Web server includes articles of local interest, classifieds, and information about the businesses in Palo Alto. It is a community-oriented newspaper with a commercial slant.

The *3W-Global Network News* is a magazine published in England specifically about the WWW. Information about the journal, including selected articles, graphics and information files, can be found on their Web server. The full-text of the issues is only available through a paid subscription.

The *Wired* magazine Web server, which recently received an award for best-designed Web site, includes information about the current issue and the full-text of most of the back issues. However, the full-text does not include all the graphics for which *Wired* has become famous or infamous. The Web site also includes some adjunct information about the journal. The readers of both the electronic and printed versions will find some articles on the Web server before the issue reaches print, particularly politically oriented articles about cyberspace, where *Wired* editors wish to get readers' response or reaction on articles or issues that are considered important or timely.

Robison presented three models, or "classifications" of electronic publishing that are prevalent at this time: (1) full-text publishing, which includes the full-text of an entire article or issue of a journal and also might include graphics; (2) "teasers," where publishers make selected examples of content-oriented information and/or services available in hope that users will be enticed into paying for the full range of services that are offered; and (3) catalogs, which are full-text versions of publishers' catalogs and provide descriptive information about publishers and the titles they offer.

In terms of publication itself, new pricing structures are emerging. Traditionally, libraries have paid for books or serials as a one-time payment, or as an annual subscription. In pricing structures for licensed databases, users pay annual fees and often have nothing to show for their fee at the end of the year. In some software licensing agreements, users might pay a set fee to purchase a one-time "monographic" version, or they might have the option to pay an additional fee if the monograph will be upgradable.

Where "continuously updated" monographs are involved, the lines may become blurred between monographs and serials, particularly if the publisher promises that every month an additional chapter or a new version will be issued. This is not so different from traditional print looseleaf binder materials. The electronic versions, however, may be more efficient because no one will have to go the shelves to file pages into binders. Instead, updates may be received by e-mail and their receipts may be recorded with a check-in system not unsimilar to check-in systems that are currently in use for printed materials. However, since group authoring is becoming a more common method for individual authors to publish an article on the network and to invite comments and/or revisions to the original work (perhaps for the next issue of the journal, or for a new version of the monograph) librarians will have to be ready to change and adapt. As Robison noted, "This stuff could be really crazy to try to keep track of." Rather than being overwhelmed by these new technologies and publishing models, Robison encouraged the audience to look at the current environment as something new and exciting, and as a positive way to think about doing scholarship.

Some concerns associated with electronic publishing were noted, including unresolved copyright issues, myriad pricing structures, and methods for publishers to collect payments for the information they are providing. There is also some concern about how to preserve the integrity and/or uniqueness of electronic documents since electronic information is easy to reproduce, edit, modify, or forge. Librarians need to be involved in discussing and influencing these issues because they have a role in helping people find information and in determining whether or not the information that is retrieved is reliable and/or of good quality.

In the future we can expect to see more electronic publications, publishing services, and publishing consultants. Because of the abundance of free and/or affordable commercial services offered on the networks, users may choose to bypass libraries to pay for viewing or faxing information that is readily available without the services of a library or librarian. Again, librarians need to maintain a visible presence and be involved in the action as archivers and servers of electronic publications, or as part of the new publishing models by collaborating with university presses, or by becoming their own publishers. Libraries can also be "virtual assistants" in that the library's choices for information can be made available to others through programs, including gophers, web servers, and other programs that locate specific information. In closing, Robison noted that he had no doubt that libraries and librarians can and will accommodate shifts and changes in new technologies and publishing.

This presentation contained citations to several networked sources, and included many slides and overhead examples of sources on the network. Names and electronic addresses, or Uniform Resource Locators (URLs) to the sources cited were presented to preconference participants as a handout, "Publishers and Publishing Efforts on the Internet." Members of the audience were encouraged to try out various addresses/sources at the Internet room, which was available to NASIG delegates throughout much of the weekend, for "hands-on" Internet access.

BREAKOUT SESSIONS

Tunneling Through Cyberspace in Search of Adventure: An Introduction to Gopher

Maggie Rioux
Workshop Presenter

Betty Landesman
Recorder

SUMMARY. A gopher is a virtual furry critter which tunnels through the Internet maze, finding information and bringing it back to your own computer. How does it work and what makes it so special? Some of the gopher resources useful to serialists, and gopher tools like Veronica and Jughead are discussed.

This breakout session was explicitly intended not as a "how to do it at the keyboard" tutorial but rather as an introduction to what

---

Betty Landesman is Coordinator for Systems Planning, George Washington University, Washington, DC.

[Haworth co-indexing entry note]: "Tunneling Through Cyberspace in Search of Adventure: An Introduction to Gopher." Landesman, Betty. Co-published simultaneously in *The Serials Librarian* (The Haworth Press, Inc.) Vol. 25, No. 3/4, 1995, pp. 17-20; and: *A Kaleidoscope of Choices: Reshaping Roles and Opportunities for Serialists* (ed: Beth Holley and Mary Ann Sheble) The Haworth Press, Inc., 1995, pp. 17-20. Multiple copies of this article/chapter may be purchased from The Haworth Document Delivery Center [1-800-3-HAWORTH; 9:00 a.m. - 5:00 p.m. (EST)].

"gopher" is, how it can be used, and what resources are available. The topic was clearly of interest to preconference attendees, with more than 100 registrants substantially filling a large breakout room.

"Gopher" is a menu-driven way of organizing Internet resources to assist users in navigating through them. Gopher software was developed at the University of Minnesota in April 1991 to assist students in answering their own questions and has proliferated ever since.

A key concept in understanding how gopher works is that of the client-server model. Part of the work is done on the user's local computer (the "client"), the rest on a remote computer (the "server"). The user needs software on her/his local computer and connects to the Internet either directly or by logging in to another computer with a client. Unlike telnet, where the user logs into a remote computer and stays connected until work is completed, the gopher client-server model operates using "connect-grab-release." The client goes out to the server, makes a request for information, disconnects, and displays the information for the user. The user is not using Internet resources while reading the information on the screen, and many more people have access to the server. The term "gopher" is loosely used to describe the software on the user's local computer, the server, or the whole system.

Gopher users see menu items which are "pointers" to other items: sub-menus, contents of files, telnet gateways that connect to another computer, search engines. Directories (other menus) are the most common item type and are often identifiable by a front slash ("/") at the end. The actual location of resources being pointed to can be anywhere in the world and is irrelevant to the user. Gopher brings information back from the server to the client using file transfer protocol (FTP) without the user's having to actually know how to *use* FTP.

"All the gopher servers in the world" is a standard item on every gopher menu. It provides a good starting point for finding a particular server if the institution that "owns" that server is known. Other common menu items on gopher servers are campus-wide information systems (including phone books and E-mail addresses) and library catalogs. "Gopher Jewels" provides pointers to most gophers worldwide, organized by subject instead of by location. LC Marvel provides access to the Library of Congress catalogs as well as information about copyright and government. NASIG has its own gopher server that provides members access to NASIG newsletters and proceedings as well as pointers to other gophers; this is not a publicly registered server.

There are some tools available to further assist users in navigating "gopherspace." "Bookmarks" are files of pointers to frequently-used resources that are created by individual users. This capability is available on local clients, i.e., gopher software loaded on the user's local computer, may or may not be available on a shared client where the user logs into a central computer with her/his own account, but is not available on public clients. "Veronica" is a keyword index to the titles of menu items on all publicly registered gopher servers. There are a few Veronica servers around the world; a directory of these servers is often found on a gopher menu under "Other Internet Resources." "Jughead" is an index to a predefined set of menu items, established locally on an institution's own gopher server.

Many of the questions posed by session attendees pointed out the many local variations in the ways individual users are connected to the Internet. People do not necessarily know how they are connected, if they have a client, or if they can telnet or e-mail a binary file. They sit at their local area network stations and follow instructions they were given or click on icons. The illustrations used during the session did not match what some users see on their computer screens at home. These questions in their own way showed why the focus of the session was not a hands-on tutorial, as it would be difficult to find a single configuration that would match many people's particular combination of hardware, software, and connectivity options. Users were encouraged to seek the technical people at their home institutions to find out what they have available and how to use gopher on their computers.

There was a question on the difference between Archie and Veronica. Archie searches actual file names on ftp servers; Veronica searches menu items on gopher servers. Another question pointed out a discrepancy between the talk and the handouts as to which university (Nevada? Utah?) had developed Veronica. The presenter admitted that she was not exactly sure, but that it did not really matter because like everything else in gopherspace it is all just "out there"–and the user does not have to know where s/he is actually going for information! Another question from a user not sure of where his client was resulted in the following definition: a client lives on a computer that the user can sit down and type "telnet" on.

Three handouts were distributed. *Interesting Gopher Resources* provides an alphabetical, very selective list of resources that might be of particular interest to NASIG members to try. The presenter noted at the beginning of the session that some of the information on this handout was already out of date–a practical illustration of the changing nature of the gopher universe! *Veronica: A Finding Tool for Gopherspace* offers some nuts-and-bolts instructions on how to use Veronica and Jughead. *Selected References for Later Investigation* includes books, online tutorials, and sources of gopher clients. These handouts will be made available via the NASIG gopher.

Digging Your Own Den in Cyberspace: A Gopher Construction Kit

Eric Celeste

Workshop Leader

Birdie MacLennan

Recorder

SUMMARY. A basic introduction to setting up and maintaining a gopher den (ahem, server) is presented. What kind of time and commitment does it take to establish a niche in gopherspace? What are the tools you need and where can you find them? Where do you get help and support? What are some of the difficulties you will encounter?

What kind of time commitment does it take to establish a niche in gopherspace? What are the tools that you need and where can you find them? Where do you go to get help and support? What are some of the issues, concerns, and difficulties you might encounter? In this presentation, Eric Celeste, head of the Serials Copy Cataloging and Record Maintenance Unit (SCARMU) of the MIT Libraries, answered these questions and others, while providing a basic introduction and framework for setting up and maintaining a gopher server.

Birdie MacLennan is Serials Coordinator at the University of Vermont, Burlington, VT.

[Haworth co-indexing entry note]: "Digging Your Own Den in Cyberspace: A Gopher Construction Kit." MacLennan, Birdie. Co-published simultaneously in *The Serials Librarian* (The Haworth Press, Inc.) Vol. 25, No. 3/4, 1995, pp. 21-26; and: *A Kaleidoscope of Choices: Reshaping Roles and Opportunities for Serialists* (ed: Beth Holley and Mary Ann Sheble) The Haworth Press, Inc., 1995, pp. 21-26. Multiple copies of this article/chapter may be purchased from The Haworth Document Delivery Center [1-800-3-HAWORTH; 9:00 a.m. - 5:00 p.m. (EST)].

© 1995 by The Haworth Press, Inc. All rights reserved.

Celeste began his presentation with a basic question: Why gopher? One of the key activities on the networks, or in cyberspace, is the creation of information. As Nancy Hannum had pointed out in the opening preconference session on information policy, there are several issues around who creates and owns information on the networks. Gopher servers are one of the ways in which individuals, institutions, and organizations can take advantage of networking technologies to publish, organize, and otherwise make available information.

There are several benefits associated with gopher technology. Once a server has been established and information has been mounted on it, that information is relatively easy for people to access. It is not necessary for systems administrators to set up individual accounts for people to be able to use gopher services. Also, navigational aids and/or direct links to other useful networked resources can easily be provided along with, or as part of the actual content of the gopher. Gopher servers are also very efficient because they allow for provision of information with a relatively small load, or set of demands on a machine. A unique feature of gophers and gopherspace is the Veronica indexing capability, which provides a method of searching information in multiple gopher servers. When executing Veronica searches, it is not necessary for users to know the address of a particular gopher server in order to be able to find information.

Celeste offered some thoughts on gopher technologies in relation to recent developments with World Wide Web (WWW) technologies. He noted that sites providing information via gopher servers are actually part of the WWW, in that Mosaic and other Web clients can read and process gopher information. While WWW offers more options in terms of being able to use multi-media resources and hypertext links to customize documents, gopher clients are more universally accessible than Web clients, which generally take more computer resources or machine power to be used effectively. Additionally, a number of popular Internet service providers, such as America Online and CompuServe, offer access to gopher servers, but are not quite ready to provide similar access for WWW servers. So, while more people currently have access to gopher servers than Web servers, gopher can still be viewed as a more universally accessible system. Celeste added that despite these differences, both Gopher and WWW were wonderful developments and useful tools.

How does a gopher server work? Gopher technology is based on the client-server architecture of the Internet. This can be characterized as an interaction of queries and responses. Queries are sent from a local gopher client to a remote gopher server, which responds by sending an answer back to the client. The underlying principle that gopher uses in its interactive sessions is the telnet protocol. The client actually telnets to the server's port (usually port 70) and the server opens a connection. The client (or information seeker) then sends the server an information request to specify what is wanted from the server. The server then checks the gopher file system for the requested material, generates a response, and sends the response back to the client. Because the gopher protocol is very sparse and concise, it does not require the server to use a great deal of computer resources in checking its files and sending back a response. As soon as the information is sent back to the client, the client-server connection ceases, but the client continues working to present the response in a useful and readable format on the local machine.

It is important for people who intend to set up gopher servers to understand the structure of gopher files and directories. There are several different platforms for setting up gopher servers (e.g., Unix, DOS, Windows, Macintosh) and the set-up will vary according to the platform. Celeste's presentation focused on the Unix environment, although he noted that no matter in which environment one is working, it is important to maintain a system that describes to the server specifically what information is provided. In the Unix environment, this consists of creating files and directories as gopher menu selections. It also creates and maintains ".links" files which describe gopher materials, or each menu item, to the server so that it will know how to process information requests. ".Links" files are not seen as gopher menu items but operate in the background as part of the gopher file structure to guide users to information sources on local and remote gopher servers. Information in some sample ".links" files that were presented included coding for the type of link or menu item (e.g., text file, directory, telnet service, index-search, graphics image, et al.); the "name" for the menu item (i.e., as it is to appear in the public view of the menu); the numbering sequence; or order of appearance of the item on the menu; the host name for where the item is stored; the port number; and the path to the actual source. Uniform Resource Locators (URLs) are also becoming more common as part of the link information. Celeste noted that some of the ".links" files examples he presented in a section of his handout might be useful references for anyone just starting to set up a server. He also recommended that anyone interested in seeing more examples of ".links" files go to any gopher server and key in an equal sign (i.e., "=" without the quotes) next to any menu item, which will display the ".links" file associated with the menu item.

Celeste also discussed some structural, organizational, maintenance, and political issues associated with developing a gopher server.

It is important to think about the structure and organization of the information that is being provided and to get people like catalogers involved in organizing gopher menus. There are some commonalities in gopherspace and cataloging that are useful for organizing and structuring information in gopher servers. A number of these were noted and discussed as part of a handout entitled "GARP's Good Gopher Guidelines," which was prepared by members of GARP (Gopher and Archie Review Panel) and the MIT Libraries Gopher Implementation Team, as they worked to develop the MIT gopher. The GARP guidelines include recommendations for:

- The creation of "About this Menu" files as opening menu item selections for information included in the menu, how it is organized, and who should be contacted for questions or comments;
- Name authorities in creating entries for author and/or title information;
- Eliminating initial articles—particularly for alphabetical listings;
- Including descriptive subject terms in menu items, since this will help Veronica searchers get directly to appropriate information and collections.

Maintenance issues are important to consider before beginning the process of setting up a gopher server. Setting up a server, although initially quite time-consuming, is not a one-time deal. It is only the beginning of the work. Much gopher information is dependent on remote sources and accessed at remote servers, via ".links" file information. There is usually no formal agreement with maintainers at remote server sites to guarantee that their link to the information source will be viable at any given time. Users may check an information source on a local server that was linked to a remote server last week or yesterday, and find that the information is no longer there or is no longer accessible. If the machine name, or the name of the file or directory of information changes, the link could be rendered unusable. Thus, it is important to think about finding some regular way to monitor ".links" information to ensure the integrity of the information source. There are tools, which are available from the gopher site at *boombox.micro.umn.edu*, that gopher maintainers can use to automate a ".links" verification process.

Since gopher menus will develop and change over time, it is also a good idea to create a "What's New" file or directory to keep users apprised of updates and changes. However, it is also very important to commit to maintaining a "What's New" file, because "What's New" files that are not updated regularly are not very helpful.

Software for gopher applications is continually being updated and changed. While it is important to use what works for any given environment, it is also important to stay in touch with new developments and to make decisions about updates and/or changes in the local environment based on the impact or feasibility of such developments.

Gopher servers often represent an image of an institution or organization, especially to people who approach information about an institution or organization through the Internet. It is useful to recognize that gopher set-up and maintenance crosses functional boundaries, and that involving people from different areas, such as systems, technical services, public services, and subject specialists, will work to create a gopher that is collaborative and represents the organization. It is also important to know that gopher development may take considerable investment of staff time. It is probably not something that can be done very well "on the side," since maintenance is ongoing.

Celeste offered the following suggestions for people who are considering creating a gopher server:

1. Get support from people as high up in the organizational structure as possible, preferably from someone who can facilitate communication and/or involvement with staff from many different areas.
2. Involve as many people as possible in the project. The MIT Libraries Gopher Implementation Team (GARP), involved staff from technical services, public services, systems, subject selectors, and some people from outside the libraries to help build a broad base of support and expertise.
3. Keep everyone up to date on progress, plans, and other key developments in the project. Let people know what information is available on the server, particularly as new information is added.

In concluding, Celeste noted that "it really is a lot of fun" to develop a gopher server, to create information links and menus, and to have the satisfaction of watching users log in to a server.

A very interactive discussion period followed the presentation. It included commentaries from audience members about problems and successes in setting up gopher servers, the need for better organization of information within gopher servers, and sources to look to for more information.

A handout included information about topics covered in the presentation, including: illustrations of client-server architecture, ".links" file information and samples, a checklist of important things to consider and/or do when setting up a gopher server, a list of sources to look to for finding more information, and "GARP's Good Gopher Guidelines" from the MIT Libraries Gopher Implementation Team.

Come into My Parlor, Said the Spider: World Wide Web and the Mosaic Interface

Ann Okerson
David L. Rodgers

Workshop Leaders

Birdie MacLennan

Recorder

SUMMARY. The World Wide Web (WWW) is an Internet access protocol. Along with the new user interface developed last year by the National Center for Supercomputing Applications (NCSA) called Mosaic, the Web provides its creator the ability to present information in an attractive format. Even better, it enables links within documents and between documents, files, sound and graphical (i.e., multi-media) formats. Items can be read linearly or the reader can move in a hyper-text/media manner among information. MOSAIC can be used as an interface for many kinds of Internet information accesses, but it is particularly useful with WWW, because it simplifies access to non-text forms such as images, movies, sound, etc. Mosaic is able to interpret the type of media being requested and to transparently open the tools the user needs.

What is World Wide Web and the Mosaic interface? In this preconference breakout session, Ann Okerson, director of the Office of

---

Birdie MacLennan is Serials Coordinator at the University of Vermont, Burlington, VT.

[Haworth co-indexing entry note]: "Come into My Parlor, Said the Spider: World Wide Web and the Mosaic Interface." MacLennan, Birdie. Co-published simultaneously in *The Serials Librarian* (The Haworth Press, Inc.) Vol. 25, No. 3/4, 1995, pp. 27-32; and: *A Kaleidoscope of Choices: Reshaping Roles and Opportunities for Serialists* (ed: Beth Holley and Mary Ann Sheble) The Haworth Press, Inc., 1995, pp. 27-32. Multiple copies of this article/chapter may be purchased from The Haworth Document Delivery Center [1-800-3-HAWORTH; 9:00 a.m. - 5:00 p.m. (EST)].

© 1995 by The Haworth Press, Inc. All rights reserved.

Scientific and Academic Publishing at the Association of Research Libraries (ARL), and David L. Rodgers, research scientist at the School of Information and Library Studies at the University of Michigan, set out to answer this and other questions by presenting an overview and demonstration of these relatively new and exciting developments on the Internet.

Okerson opened the session with an introduction to the World Wide Web and Mosaic. The World Wide Web (also known as WWW or simply "the Web") is a client-server based Internet protocol that enables users to employ multi-media formats in accessing information from various sites on the Internet. For a number of years, it was a protocol that had yet to achieve full potential. In 1993, the National Center for Supercomputing Applications (NCSA), at the University of Illinois, Urbana-Champaign, announced the development of a new Web browser (or client) called Mosaic, and made it freely available to the Internet community. With Mosaic browsers, it became possible for publishers and other information providers to use Web servers to present information to end-users in an easy-to-use, attractive, desktop format. Additionally, hypertext/ media links (e.g., text, graphic images, sound, or motion picture files) that are embedded within documents, or between documents (i.e., to information on Web servers at different locations) give users the option to read, view, or hear materials in a linear manner (as one would read a printed book) or to move, with the click of a mouse, back and forth between documents, files, and graphics that are connected or "webbed" through hypertext links.

Largely as a result of the Mosaic interface, Web applications have soared within the last year, and use of the Web continues to grow at an extraordinary rate. It is becoming increasingly common, when one follows various network discussion lists or newsgroups, to see evidence of a strong and prevailing Mosaic/Web presence. Regularly, information providers are creating new home pages, new documents, and new links, which may or may not be made public, while more and more Web users are discovering the powerful new capabilities of the medium.

In compiling the listing of journals and newsletters for the 4th edition (1994) of the ARL publication, the *Directory of Electronic Journals, Newsletters, and Academic Discussion Lists*, Beth King noted the existence of at least a dozen new electronic journals that had been developed and produced for the Web. She also found that approximately three dozen "traditional" electronic journals and newsletters that have been around since the early days of electronic publishing (i.e., approximately one to three years) now have their publications available on Web servers. Within a very short period of time–or in the year since publication of the 3rd edition of the *Directory*–a new category of electronic publishing, via the Web, had emerged.

What is it about the Mosaic/Web interface that makes it so popular? For starters, it is very easy to use, if certain conditions exist. First, a machine with a high speed Internet connection and a sizeable memory is required in order to retrieve files that contain graphic images, movies, or sound. Machines also need to be equipped with various client programs or "viewers" that Mosaic invokes to display graphic, movie, and sound files. Additionally, in order to find information or specific documents on the Web, users need to become familiar with HTTP (HyperText Transmission Protocol) addresses and Uniform Resource Locators (URLs), which are specific addresses and protocols needed to address files. Given all of the above, the World Wide Web/Mosaic interface had become the latest "killer application" of the 1990s. Once the interface is used at its fullest potential, it is difficult to image never having had it.

Following Okerson's introduction, David Rodgers presented an explanation of how Mosaic and the Web work together, and offered some perspectives on Mosaic/Web applications in electronic publishing. In referring to an excerpt from Web developers' documentation, he noted the official definition for World Wide Web as a "wide-area hypermedia information retrieval initiative aiming to give universal access to a large universe of documents." In Rodgers' own words, what the development of the Web has really produced is an "easy-to-use, consistent means of accessing a variety of media."

The Web has been used for many different kinds of electronic publishing applications, and Rodgers briefly offered some perspectives for strategic goals in online, or electronic publishing initiatives: (1) information should be accessible anytime, from anywhere;

(2) information should be reusable–that is, retrievable, editable, and manipulable.

There are a number of advantages of online publishing, which allow for completely new models in the dissemination of scholarly information. Online publishing allows for:

- Dynamic, rather than static information resources through updating, annotation, public commentary, and the ability for live-link, multi-media applications;
- Enhanced possibilities for collaboration;
- Knowledge dissemination that will be more timely and immediate in being close to the point of knowledge creation;
- Search and retrieval of information from large collections and in cross-disciplinary areas;
- Non-linear searching/browsing via hypertext links;
- Customized/personalized information resources.

The Web is based on the client-server architecture of the Internet. Rodgers described servers as places where information sources are stored, and clients as places where people with information needs reside. The client is the software interface between the user and the source(s) on the server. His points were illustrated by invoking a home page that had been developed as a demonstration for this preconference session, and by clicking on an embedded hypertext link within the home page that led to a graphical image/illustration of client-server architecture on the Internet. The "NASIG Demo" home page was discussed at some length later in the presentation.

The World Wide Web client-server environment has several components. Web server applications, are based on HTTP (Hyper-Text Transmission Protocol), which is a set of rules or conventions through which Web clients and servers communicate. Of Web client applications, Mosaic is the most popular for retrieving information, primarily because of its ability to process documents consisting of a mixture of different media. Once data have been retrieved by Mosaic, the client sends the information to helper programs, or viewers, that display results. For example, sound files are invoked through a sound viewer, movies are displayed through a video viewer, and graphics are seen through a graphical viewer. Mosaic poses many possibilities as a very rich environment for creating documents.

Other components of a Web system include HTML, the HyperText Markup Language, which is a tagset used to encode textual elements in documents (e.g., title, paragraph, footnote, etc.) as well as links to materials that are to be retrieved by the HTTP, or Web server protocol. HTML codes are embedded at the document level for retrieving and processing materials. Uniform Resource Locators (URLs), another important component of the Web, are pointers that specify a particular protocol that is to be used for retrieving the information, as well as the specific address, or network coordinates for location of the material. An important feature of URLs is that they support several Internet protocols, including gopher, telnet, FTP, and HTTP. Materials available through these various protocols are also available through the Web/Mosaic interface.

At this point Rodgers noted the URL for the home page that he and Okerson had developed for demonstration during their presentation:

http://e-math.ams.org/web/nasigdemo/nasig.html

The "http://" portion of the URL specifies the protocol that is to be used for retrieval purposes. In this case, it is HTTP because the server is a Web server. The rest of the URL is the machine's full-length path to the location of a file called *nasig.html,* which creates the home page. The definition of a home page is simply the Mosaic view of a World Wide Web document that is retrieved when one starts the application, or keys in a URL.

There are three distinguishing features of the Web: (1) *Multimedia*, which is text mixed with graphic images, sound, or video; (2) *Hypertext*, where links can be constructed between sections in documents (e.g., footnotes) or between documents (e.g., separate documents or files on different machines). Given a properly coded hypertext document and the proper viewer(s), users can seamlessly navigate the Web; and (3) the notion of *interactivity*, where forms can be invoked to specify transactions to be processed, and spots ("hot spots") within images, such as weather maps, can have interactive links.

There are also some limitations in World Wide Web and Mosaic applications. Web technologies make extensive use of HTML, which is of limited use for scientific information because it does not support mathematical expressions or tabular material. URLs also represent a significant number of limitations because users must know how to manipulate and to spell them. The situation for locating URL information is improving slightly, as more sites register URLs and research continues in the area of "Web Walkers," software, or know-bots that can look-up URL information. However, finding a better and more effective means for locating information on the Internet and integrating new technologies into the venue of digital libraries still has a way to go, and could extend to the next decade, or longer.

Mosaic's principle limitation is the layout capability. Although it will lay out HTML in a reasonably effective and attractive manner, it is not an infinite or flexible kind of style sheet. Mosaic has an unfortunate tendency not to deal with anything it does not understand. For example, users have been known to read documents through Mosaic in which large chunks of material are inaccessible because they do not conform to the client's understanding of HTML.

In looking at some of the benefits and limitations of the Web/Mosaic interface, it is important to recognize that we have embarked in a new process and that this is a time of experimentation and risk taking. While some network tools are not as robust or as general or as rich in capability as we would hope, it is already hard to imagine what life was like before some of the latest, greatest "killer applications," such as Mosaic and the Web, were developed. As time goes on, the process and the technology will continue to unfold.

At this point, Okerson and Rodgers demonstrated the home page that they had developed for their presentation, while fielding questions from the audience about various uses, applications, and set-ups for the Web/Mosaic interface. Rodgers and Okerson noted that the NASIG Demo home page included links to most of the sources that had been discussed in the presentation, as well as to a number of other resources where people could look for information in getting started with initial set-ups or HTML tagging. Users were encouraged to write down the HTTP address of the NASIG Demo and experiment with the Web/Mosaic interface.

http://e-math.ams.org/web/nasigdemo/html

Communicating with Lists: A Beginner's Guide to Listservs and ListProcs

Marilyn Geller

Workshop Presenter

Leslie Knapp

Recorder

SUMMARY. Listservs and ListProcs provide a framework for a geographically diverse group of people to send and receive information on a chosen topic. This paper introduces participants to the basics of joining electronic discussion groups, including how to subscribe to a list, how to determine options for receiving mail from the list, how to set mail options, and how to participate in discussions on a list.

In a preconference program at the ninth annual NASIG Conference in Vancouver, British Columbia, Marilyn Geller, serials cataloger at the Massachusetts Institute of Technology Libraries, described how to navigate Listservs and ListProcs to approximately thirty librarians and vendors.

She said that during her stay at the conference, she would be in

---

Leslie Knapp is New England Field Account Services Manager, EBSCO Subscription Services, Woburn, MA.

[Haworth co-indexing entry note]: "Communicating with Lists: A Beginner's Guide to Listservs and ListProcs." Knapp, Leslie. Co-published simultaneously in *The Serials Librarian* (The Haworth Press, Inc.) Vol. 25, No. 3/4, 1995, pp. 33-37; and: *A Kaleidoscope of Choices: Reshaping Roles and Opportunities for Serialists* (ed: Beth Holley and Mary Ann Sheble) The Haworth Press, Inc., 1995, pp. 33-37. Multiple copies of this article/chapter may be purchased from The Haworth Document Delivery Center [1-800-3-HAWORTH; 9:00 a.m. - 5:00 p.m. (EST)].

© 1995 by The Haworth Press, Inc. All rights reserved.

touch via e-mail with her children (ages fourteen, twelve, and nine) who already subscribe to bulletin boards and discussion groups. She observed that children with these very skills would become the students academic librarians will be serving in the not-too-distant future.

Geller stated that to use Listservs and ListProcs, the first order of business was to locate them. She recommended the fourth edition of the Association of Research Libraries' *Directory of Electronic Journals, Newsletters and Academic Discussion Lists*. It is currently available in hard copy only.

To find library related lists, she suggested Charles W. Bailey, Jr.'s *Library Oriented Computer Conferences and Electronic Serials* (revised more or less annually). Since this list is available only electronically, Geller showed the audience how to retrieve this file by sending a message that reads:

get library lists
to
listserv@uhupvm1.uh.edu

She noted that this particular list was specific to library science and that lists on numerous other subjects are also available.

Although she did not recommend it (because of its enormous size), she then outlined how to retrieve the "List of Lists" on Bitnet by sending a message that reads:

lists global
to
listserv@uga.bitnet

She also showed how to search for specific lists on the Bitnet LISTSERV by sending a similar message that reads:

lists global/[search word]
to
listserv@uga.bitnet

The example used was the word *serial*, which retrieved a number of serial related lists.

To retrieve lists from UNIX ListProc Lists, a message reading:

lists
should be sent to
listproc@[known UNIX server]

This command will retrieve a local file, specific to the named server.

One of Geller's main points throughout the program was that the message is always sent to the Listserv or to the ListProc, and not to the list itself.

She also explained that Listserv software and ListProc software not only serve the same functions, but also have similar command structures.

To subscribe to a list, a message must be sent to the Listserv or ListProc:

subscribe [list] Your Name

Once the Listserv or ListProc receives the first and last name, a message of welcome is returned. She noted the importance of saving all welcome messages because they included useful information for future reference, such as the name and address of the list owner, and options. She also mentioned that a copy of the request is usually sent to the list owner to notify him or her that there is a new subscriber.

Geller demonstrated how to check options by use of the *query* command, for which there is no ListProc equivalent.

Using SERIALST as the example, she discussed options requiring "yes" and "no" responses, including:

ACK: whether or not to have software acknowledge receipt of message
MAIL: whether or not to receive mail
INDEX: receive only daily index of subject lines
DIGEST: receive all messages strung together
FILES: ability to retrieve files from archives

She highlighted the importance of setting REPRO to "yes." This ensures that a copy of a message sent to a list is also sent to the original sender. She described *header* options and how answering "yes" to CONCEAL means that a subscriber's name is not shown on the list of subscribers, but that the list owner does know the name of the subscriber.

Geller also pointed out that at the end of a transaction like checking options, a reminder is displayed about the time and energy and resources used on the Listserv.

After reminding the audience once again of the importance of sending messages directly to the Listserv or ListProc, Geller showed how to retrieve lists of archived files by using the *index* command. She compared the responses to this command from the Listservs and ListProcs, namely, file names and types; and paths and names of files.

She then demonstrated how to stop mail and how a copy of the request to stop mail goes to the list owner.

Geller also noted that private lists like NASIG's usually require a password and that if a password is unknown, then the list owner must be contacted (another important reason to save welcome messages!).

She then discussed the pros and cons of unsubscribing to a list and how the message to unsubscribe is matched to the e-mail address. She said that in much the same way some print publishers follow-up when they lose a subscriber, some list owners send messages to subscribers, asking why they decided to unsubscribe.

Summarizing the handout, Geller described some common mistakes in navigating Listservs and ListProcs and how to avoid them. Using the analogy of the editorial and circulation departments of a newspaper, she admonished the audience to send actual messages to the list (letters to the editor for the readership) and administrative messages to the Listserv or ListProc (circulation department). She advised the audience against sending personal messages to the list!

In response to audience questions, Marilyn suggested that it was probably better to stop mail rather than to unsubscribe, or simply to set the MAIL option to index only, especially when planning to resubscribe.

She reported that list owners are eager to please, approachable, and usually delighted that people want to read what is on their lists.

She also noted that forwarding messages should be done only with permission from the author.

Finally, Geller made the audience aware of a list which actually lists new lists. She recommended that this list be monitored routinely. She gave the group the address:

NEW-LIST@NDSUVM1
or
NEW-LIST@VMI.NODAK.EDU

and reminded the audience how to subscribe to it–BY SENDING A MESSAGE TO THE Listserv!

(Almost) Everything Else You Ever Wanted to Know About Listservs and ListProcs

Marilyn Geller

Workshop Leader

Betty Landesman

Recorder

SUMMARY. Listservs and ListProcs provide their subscribers with a wealth of information beyond the daily discussion messages. This paper tells how to search for and retrieve information from a list's archives, how to use the information in list headers, and how to find new lists.

A morning session had covered finding lists, subscribing to lists, finding out available options on lists, setting options, and getting indexes and files from list archives. This session focussed on hidden information in Listservs. Some thirty-five registrants were encouraged to ask questions at any point during the presentation.

The list header is information that the Listserver software uses to administer the Listserv. The user can make use of this information. A reminder-never repeated too often!-was issued to users to make

---

Betty Landesman is Coordinator for Systems Planning, George Washington University, Washington, DC.

[Haworth co-indexing entry note]: "(Almost) Everything Else You Ever Wanted to Know About Listservs and ListProcs." Landesman, Betty. Co-published simultaneously in *The Serials Librarian* (The Haworth Press, Inc.) Vol. 25, No. 3/4, 1995, pp. 39-42; and: *A Kaleidoscope of Choices: Reshaping Roles and Opportunities for Serialists* (ed: Beth Holley and Mary Ann Sheble) The Haworth Press, Inc., 1995, pp. 39-42. Multiple copies of this article/chapter may be purchased from The Haworth Document Delivery Center [1-800-3-HAWORTH; 9:00 a.m. - 5:00 p.m. (EST)].

© 1995 by The Haworth Press, Inc. All rights reserved.

sure that they send administrative messages to the Listserv, not to the list. A message sent to the Listserv to "review" a list (e.g., "review serialst") shows the requester the list header. Additional options for reviewing a list can also provide all non-concealed subscribers to the list, or subscribers sorted by country.

The list header shows the full title of the list, who can use it, how it is used, and when. Who can look at the archives? [PUBLIC = anyone; PRIVATE = subscribers only.] Who can subscribe to the list? [OPEN = anyone; BY OWNER = only owner can subscribe people to list; CLOSED = only people who are subscribed can be subscribed.] Where are replies automatically sent? [LIST = to list; SENDER = to original sender of message.] What kind of archive is available for the list [NOTEBOOKS or not], how often is it compiled, is it accessible, and by whom? [PUBLIC = non-subscribers can access archives.] Who can send material to the list? [EDITOR = list is moderated, messages go to editor who in turn puts messages through to list; PUBLIC = anyone can send message to list.] How is the digest created and delivered? ["digest" is a way to get mail from the list in groups.] Who are the list owners?

The above information is available from a Listserv. Unix ListProc software provides a version of this information via a message to the ListProc using the "information" command with the name of the list, e.g., "information unix-listproc." This returns whatever information the list owner put into the file and is not as complete as the "review" command for Listserv software. On NASIG-L we do have committee lists, and we are beginning to put in the charge to the committee, its membership, and the name and e-mail address of its chair. Therefore, if people cannot find out a great deal about the administration of the list, they can at least get information about the various NASIG committees.

Searching of archives also differs between Listserv and ListProc softwares. Specific instructions for searching a Listserv in batch mode and for searching a ListProc archive were reviewed. In the case of ListProc, all that is retrieved is one line in each message in the archive that contains the search term, without any context or how to find the item in the archive; while searching itself is easy, the data retrieved is not very helpful. In the coming year we should be seeing improvements in searching Unix ListProc.

How can a user tell if a list uses Listserv or ListProc? The "release" command sent to the Listserv/ListProc provides the release number and type of software. Often a response received from the Listserv/ListProc will indicate where it is from, e.g., a Bitnet Listserver. Some information is available from list headers. Anastasios Katsikonis is the developer of Unix ListProc; Eric Thomas is the developer of Listserv software. Both of these products have recently become commercial, available on the market for a fee; while they will cost more for administrators to run, they will also be more competitive.

Some options for Listserv mail were reviewed. One option is to set mail to "index": instead of seeing each message one at a time, the subscriber will receive a periodic index (e.g., daily) which lists the messages sent that day including date, size, author, and subject. Specified items can then be requested and received from the list. There are very few Unix equivalents for ListProc. Another Listserv capability is to send a message to any Listserv node, giving all the options desired for a series of lists. The node will forward the messages to a backbone server which will find the appropriate hosts for each list and send the messages on. There is no equivalent capability for ListProc.

The session concluded with a summary of "good housekeeping tips" for lists. Subscribers should keep a record of all the lists they subscribe to. Print out the "scope and purpose" message that lists send out periodically; this is a reminder of the available commands and options, what the purpose of the list is, and acceptable practices on the list. Set lists to suspend mail while away, or mailboxes will fill up. If there is an "on vacation" message capability available as a response to incoming messages, this should only be used for personal e-mail and not for lists. Lists should be set to "no mail." If an individual's e-mail address is going to change, s/he should unsubscribe from all lists before the change occurs and then re-subscribe from the new address. Otherwise the only way to unsubscribe from an old address is to contact the list owner.

If it is too difficult to keep up with all the lists that seem relevant, one technique is for people to share lists. The responsibility for monitoring specific lists and sharing useful information from those lists with colleagues is divided up. This technique works in small groups of three to four people who talk to each other about their interests, and who are in agreement about what to forward and what to filter out. Individual systems provide some filtering capabilities, but this is not a function of Listserv software as a whole. Some versions of Listserv allow filtering by keyword topic, but this is not widely implemented on most lists. The "topics" area of the list header will indicate whether or not a list provides this capability.

One handout was distributed. *Internet Tools and Resources: An Electronic Buffet* includes information on finding lists, summaries of Listserv and ListProc commands, guidelines on effective use of lists, and instructions on searching Listservs in batch mode. The same handout was distibuted at both Listserv sessions so that attendees at this afternoon session who may not have known all the particulars covered in the morning one could use it as a reference.

PLENARY SESSION I:
OVERVIEW OF CHANGE

Technological Change and Its Influence on the Practice and Role of Information Management

Czeslaw Jan Grycz

SUMMARY. When one considers the building blocks of scholarly communication, it is possible to see historical trends forcing them apart into relatively specialized and isolated roles. Today, the entities that are most concerned with professional support of scholarly communication are academic institutions, professional associations, scholarly publishers, and libraries. Each of these faces disconcerting change: in their markets, in their mission, in their revenue streams, in their operational strategies, and in the technology they use to facilitate their work. Simultaneously, the concept of information management is used to reinvent the role of librarians. As a result, knowledge workers in these fields face instability on practical levels, and ambi-

---

Czeslaw Jan Grycz is Chair of the Scholarship and Technology Study Project at the University of California, Oakland, CA.

[Haworth co-indexing entry note]: "Technological Change and Its Influence on the Practice and Role of Information Management." Grycz, Czeslaw Jan. Co-published simultaneously in *The Serials Librarian* (The Haworth Press, Inc.) Vol. 25, No. 3/4, 1995, pp. 43-53; and: *A Kaleidoscope of Choices: Reshaping Roles and Opportunities for Serialists* (ed: Beth Holley and Mary Ann Sheble) The Haworth Press, Inc., 1995, pp. 43-53. Multiple copies of this article/chapter may be purchased from The Haworth Document Delivery Center [1-800-3-HAWORTH; 9:00 a.m. - 5:00 p.m. (EST)].

© 1995 by The Haworth Press, Inc. All rights reserved.

guity on philosophic levels. The opening address will attempt to describe the conditions of our dilemma and suggest ways for resolving those conflicts, as a preparation for the sessions to follow.

When Alice met the Caterpillar she inquired: "Please sir, can you tell me which way to go from here?"

"That depends," replied the Caterpillar, "entirely on where it is you want to get to."

In a related vein, Bill Arms of Carnegie-Mellon University reports overhearing the speaker at a conference of academics interested in scholarly publishing. He claims to have heard the speaker calling the group to order with these words:

> Ladies and gentlemen, when I addressed you last year, I told you that we stood at the very edge of a precipice. I am now pleased to report to you that in the intervening year, we have taken a great step forward.

I would like to thank my hosts, Alex Bloss, and his colleagues on the NASIG Program Planning Committee, as well as your President and my friend, Cindy Hepfer, who have invited me to share with you some thoughts on scholarly serials publications, the technological changes that have influenced scholarly communication, and draw some conclusions about the practice and role of information management in the future. We all want to know how to get "there" from "here." In our case as in Alice's, this depends a lot on our understanding of where we might get to if we follow various options. Many in the information management field feel like they may, indeed, be stepping off the edge of precipices as they go forward into an uncertain (and certainly changing) future.

THE HISTORICAL CONTEXT

In my class entitled "Contemporary Issues in Publishing," students are encouraged to trace the development of fairly large historical themes to help them better understand the present. Several such traceries, especially in the development of fields like communications and media, reveal some interesting commonalities. Each is converging on the last quarter of the 20th Century in a way that creates a unique situation in the history of humankind. The convergence suggests a transformation in the making in the way human societies relate to intellectual and information resources.

It is always tempting for human beings to assert that theirs is the quintessential epoch in the history of the world. One must be cautious when any era in human history is labeled unique ... particularly one's own. So before summarizing the most important of these themes, it would be good to identify earlier events that dramatically changed contemporary "knowledge professionals" so that the events of the present can be compared with them.

- The conversion of the scroll to the codex was an important historical occurrence. Codices brought about the need for new storage techniques, ushered in entirely new citation methods, involved new security considerations, and gave wider access to printed literature. Arguably, the librarians and archivists who lived through the transitional period found their jobs considerably changed.
- Urbanization, as a social trend, gave rise to the growth of universities. These became seats of specialized training (with geographically consolidated communities of intellectuals). The communities could also consolidate their books and resources, the better to share them with one another. This led to establishing institutional libraries. The responsibilities that grew from cataloging and retrieving books from disparate sources were a far greater complexity than managing a private library for one individual.
- The invention and impact of the printing press (which spawned a proliferation of printed materials, and gave impetus to the profession of publishing) was also a critical turning point in history. Scholars have associated the popularity of the printing press with wide scale social change and the emergence of democratic forms of decision-making.
- Automated bibliographic management systems created an impact on the jobs of librarians when they were installed in place of physical card catalogs. Making collection information

widely available through OPACs was one result of such automation efforts. Access to collections catalogs permitted new flexible methods of finding information. The audience for library services grew larger as a result, and some suggest that with library automation, librarian's focus shifted from collections management to "patron management."

All of these were significant changes for the knowledge professionals of their time. Now let us consider the trends that have converged on our time.

- Binary digital storage mechanisms have made it possible to capture and record (on the same medium) text, images, color, sound, animation, performance, and active program linkages. A unified and standardized method of communicating written, drawn, uttered, and imagined forms of human thought makes possible a more compelling kind of communication than has ever before been available to teachers, researchers, and scientists. The set of electronic communication standards is like a new electronic "alphabet." This communication capacity built on these building blocks is enormously powerful and is rapidly becoming globally ubiquitous.

How might this "rank" with the changes listed above? Historians credit the ascendancy of the alphabet (and, by extension, of widespread literacy) to the fact that alphabets are uniformly comprised of a very limited set (usually < 30) of abstract symbols (which can be readily mastered at any early age). These symbols can be variably assembled to form a limitless supply of new words. While the skill set can be learned at an early age, the vocabulary extensions can be learned over a lifetime. Similarly, the emergence of digital platform-independent and transportable standards for creating, viewing, and manipulating representations of variable data has been a critical development. It permits software to be developed which can appeal to a broad horizontal market, because the market will have become familiar with the basic operating and transmission standards. As a result one can realize training efficiencies. People can become comfortable with the basics, and develop more sophisticated skills with specialized applications as the need arises.

Like the alphabet, the creation of simple standards (Operating conventions, ASCII, graphical interfaces, exchangeable files) are coupled with tools built around them which can be simple or sophisticated. Together, they provide limitless creative opportunities for those who wish to communicate, educate, or share their ideas with others. The fact that this is such a widespread phenomenon suggests that it will have a proportionally powerful impact.

- A globally distributed electronic network now girds the world. Conduits of rapid broad-band communication synergies with digital data make it possible to economically share information the world over. Contrasted to the cost of delivering physical books, the new technologies suggest an efflorescence of data communication, e-mail growth, and file exchanges. Statistical reports maintained by The Internet Society (and other network providers), corroborate this through growth in data communication and use.

The ability to interact with communities that are larger than one's department, local community, or institutional grouping has, historically, had social and intellectual impact. Current telecommunications capabilities are already beginning to realign disciplinary loyalties, making it possible for "niche" studies to be profitably undertaken. Linking like-minded individuals over a considerable geographic distance strengthens the bonding between them. Conversely, loyalty to a University or institution can be diminished in view of these new bonds. The immediacy and interactivity promised by new technology will be important sociologically as it facilitates new electronic social and professional groupings. These are likely to reshape our institutions of higher education, and political and social boundaries as well. Some have argued that nothing in human history previous to this (except the recent trend for global economic interdependence) will have had a similar wide scale impact.

- Pressure for self-determination and democratic collaboration is another factor mentioned frequently in connection with the Internet "environment." While the dynamic urge for freedom among human beings is not unique, self-determination becomes a greater urgency if there exist transnational electronic communities which develop and reinforce affinity among like-minded individuals. One can therefore imagine an invigorated form of interactive collaboration, tools for creating multiple-author documents, new forms of self-regulating peer-review mechanisms on the net, and a return to a mentor-student relationship. All these developments can occur "on the network," rising from the requirements of the users of the network.

In a print-based communication environment, the responsibilities for keeping up the flow and providing orderliness were given to specialists. Publishers became gatekeepers as well as distributors; editors and their reviewers became the judges as to whether publication was merited; librarians specialized in classification, storage, and retrieval and relied on a whole host of ancillary services such as abstracters, indexers, and catalog service bureaus. The developments on the network challenge all these established print-based services, and challenge them (us) to retain or develop their pertinence in a new electronic environment.

I have just outlined only three historical trends that converge on our time. Given additional time, it would be possible to consider several more trends, those from within the entertainment industry, or from the journalism and newspaper communities. Political change and community action could be spotlighted. Changes in the application of technology to communication, per se, rather than its reception could be analyzed. Regulatory and legal modifications could be studied. Each of these, it can be asserted, would support the contention that we are, indeed, in a unique position in our age. Our feeling of ambivalence is probably because we face an enormous crisis and that the effect of the convergence of all these disparate elements promises (or threatens) to transform our world . . . the world in which we work, define our jobs, and earn a living.

THE THREAT

I often speak in favor of the positive aspects promised by these trends. But I would like to take this opportunity to couch my remarks in slightly more somber ways than I usually do.

I have enjoyed the good fortune to be given the opportunity to be involved in Central and Eastern Europe (CEE). In the countries that make up CEE (Poland, Czech and Slovak Republics, Hungary, Romania, and Bulgaria) my colleagues and I have developed relationships with various types of libraries: national libraries, university and research libraries, public libraries, and many smaller collections being put together by non-government organizations (few of which qualify as "libraries" by any formal definition, but certainly perform the jobs of libraries in a functional sense).

It has been sobering to observe how keen is the widespread belief among these libraries that electronic connectivity is a key, necessary for social change and economic growth. Peoples, who for forty years were subjugated by the former Soviet regime and were isolated from Western information resources, are acutely aware of global networks and the benefits they promise. The demand for connectivity is startling.

I recently participated in a seminar held in the city of Ploiesti. I did not know very much about Ploiesti before becoming involved in this project, so you can imagine my surprise when I was told that our very modest proposal for a workshop on library management and Internet resources attracted over sixty professional and acting librarians from all over Romania! They traveled from as far away as 250-300 miles (not always in very convenient traveling circumstances). Each signed up to learn how Romanian and global electronic networks could be used to access and retrieve information on behalf of their patrons. Discussion in the hallways in between workshop sessions seemed to be equally divided between enthusiastic supporters, and temperate caution about what could be done given the reality of the Romanian circumstances.

In many ways, the response to this Romanian workshop reflects the response of many of those in the forefront of networked information environments. That is to say, the rapidity of network evolution is as disconcerting as it is gratifying. Are we stepping into a bold new future, or . . . over the precipice?

Looked at positively, the Romanian reaction seems predicated on the belief that worthwhile intellectual resources are to be found scattered about the network like so many golden nuggets, and that librarians are obliged to learn how to gather as many nuggets as possible for the benefit of their patrons (or to satisfy their own intellectual curiosity) within chosen specializations. Looked at with a more jaundiced eye, one can legitimately question whether the Internet (as we currently know it) will satisfy their expectations.

The attitude in Romania is consistent with those of libraries in the United States and Canada who are—themselves—rapidly turning from a collections-oriented financial model, to an access-based budgeting model. The forces encouraging such change are similar in both regions of the world, and are influenced by:

- The price of maintaining physical collections;
- The price of print-based publication and its transport;
- The amortization of electronic infrastructures within a community;
- Timeliness (on the one end of a continuum) and the abbreviated shelf life (on the other end) of certain kinds of information;
- Changing patron demands, and
- (Even such mundane things as) real estate values, and alternate uses for library buildings.

THE REALITY?

Is it fair to ask whether libraries in developing countries will be satisfied with that to which they are so eagerly gaining access? This question is not easily answered. Those of us who traverse the net, and use it on a daily basis to augment service to our patrons, recognize its volatility and unreliability.

- The Internet is presently comprised of largely undifferentiated chaos;
- Navigation tools are primitive (notwithstanding their impressive programming);
- Basic access to the network can be difficult to obtain;
- TCP/IP access software can be frustratingly challenging to configure;
- Access to the network is by no means ubiquitously distributed or guaranteed;
- Legitimate security risks hinder the fulfillment of universal or open access;

- The absence of commercial-quality business disciplines and applications makes the Internet an inhospitable place in which to conduct business.

These factors and others like them probably account for the reason my Washington D.C. colleague on the Central and Eastern European Library Project, Barbara Rodes (Library Director of the World Wildlife Fund), repeatedly cautions: "We must not raise expectations beyond the capacity to deliver real, useful information."

In many ways the expectation of the Internet has already been raised beyond its present capacity to deliver satisfaction to librarians and scholarly publishers. It functions best (and has proven its value) as a social milieu (as opposed to a publishing medium, or an online research environment) in which self-policing and creatively-motivated individuals can collaborate and work together.

Its quality as a social milieu is why it holds such attraction for scholars and researchers. We may intuit that the network holds far greater promise for us as professionals, but it is not evident that the network will evolve into the place we want it to be without our active participation in making it come about. One of the greatest challenges facing librarians and information specialists consists in rallying a concerted effort to "civilize" the network in ways that will be attractive to professional knowledge workers, without destroying the collegial informality of what presently exists.

INTEGRATION OF OLD AND NEW WORLDS IN SCHOLARLY COMMUNICATION

A number of policy and economic decisions made over the past several decades have resulted in the fragmentation of the scholarly communication system into the constituent parts I mentioned earlier. Each has developed its own "territory" and defends its prerogatives in a way that conflicts with creative problem-solving.

In the conference that confronts a "kaleidoscope of possibilities" you will be exploring multifaceted options. I would like to conclude these remarks by asking you to consider several of mine.

The existence of resources on the Internet is an undeniably rich resource. It is one that will characterize our society and this age in which we live. However, there are few "signposts" on the Internet to its most important information. One can waste a lot of time "surfing" the net. And when resources are located that seem to match one's queries, there are no quality indicators to provide clues as to whether the information is verified, objective, reviewed, or otherwise comes from a reputable source.

It is in these areas that librarians have an important role to play. Librarians are not only knowledgeable about the intricacies of subjects and disciplines, they are familiar with individual leaders within disciplines. They know a good deal about classification of sub-discipline characteristics, as well as knowing about how disciplines fit into a larger intellectual schematic. Librarians would contribute a great deal to the Internet by applying their skills and suggesting solutions for the orderly classification of new Internet information resources, and by evaluating and ranking of existing ones.

Librarians might also confront the issues of volatility which currently are so disconcerting on the network. One can find a very important repository of information one day, only to find that it has inexplicably disappeared the next. Libraries have always provided—among their other services—an archival role. It is quite likely that they will have to evolve methods of providing that role in an electronic environment as well.

The librarian will have to unify information that is contained on disparate forms. One frequently hears the question "How long will it take to transform our current primarily print-based system to an exclusively electronic one?" If one considers that the sophisticated system of print we enjoy today has developed over a minimum of 500 years, it is likely that it will take a century or so for the electronic conventions to match the sophistication of print. Even if I am unnecessarily conservative in making such a suggestion, the likelihood exists for many years to come, that librarians will have to provide access to print, electronic, video, animation, and all manner of multimedia information.

There has not yet evolved on the Internet a measurable standard by which to judge quality. We all benefit from the existence of such standards in print, even though we may be only subliminally aware that we react differently to a sewn casebound book, or a mass-produced paperback; to the imprint of the University of British Columbia Press, or to one by a commercial trade house. Each of these gives us some recognizable intuition about quality. No similar analogs as yet exist for the electronic world, nor have we had sufficient experience to learn how to interpret the clues that may be contained in headers, tradition, or reputation of various host administrators.

It is too early to tell whether scholarly publishers will be able to maintain the value of their imprint on the network. They will surely have to engage in far more aggressive forms of leadership, service, and involvement in the communities of scholars that already exist on the network than they appear ready or able to contribute. Librarians have a distinct advantage because of their breadth of experience in any given subject specialization to know what is worthwhile and what is not. It may be that one of the critical reshaping roles librarians will need to assert is the granting of an online "imprimatur." Already vestiges of such a review judgement exist in the very selections process by which journal subscriptions are made by individual libraries.

CONCLUSION

Librarians have often tended to observe the environment of the Internet as an external object to be studied and analyzed. I hope these comments have suggested that the Internet is more properly defined as a social milieu (as dynamic as the people inhabiting its space). If it is a milieu, then librarians have a decidedly important contribution to make to it. If they are to do so, however, then they must roll up their sleeves and become active participants in the Internet culture, nudging it and shaping it in a way in which their own skills and contributions are visible and available.

It is only in this way that the expectations laid upon the electronic environment can hope to be fulfilled. Because of the richness of the new digital environment, and its promise to transform communication, it is particularly critical that librarians take up this challenge. By doing so, I might add, the "step forward" mentioned by Bill Arms' friends will inevitably have a softer landing.

The Future of Publishing

Robert Weber

SUMMARY. For three and a half years, Mr. Weber's firm has been facilitating two-day, highly interactive public workshops on Mapping the Future of Publishing and the information industries. In the past year or so, several new issues and themes have emerged that concern both publishers and users of information, including the personalization of information through modularization or "chunking," and the use of encryption-based metering technology to control and charge for information access and use. Publishers also face critical strategic business issues in migrating from print to electronic publications. This paper explains the workshop process and what participants think about these important issues.

Let me again thank October Ivins for extending the invitation for me to be here. When she called, I think she had a little speech prepared about all the reasons why I should come and speak to you. About three sentences into her speech I interrupted and said, "Yes, of course, I'd love to do it"; there was dead silence. I appreciate the opportunity to speak to librarians because even in the electronic age, the library community is one of the few professional communities that has a charter, a handle on the structure of knowledge and information. We are at the wrong end of the information firehose, and the questions I think that all of us are struggling to answer are: (1) how do we navigate and (2) how do we find things both on paper and electronically?

Robert Weber is Principal, Northeast Consulting Resources, Inc., Boston, MA.

[Haworth co-indexing entry note]: "The Future of Publishing." Weber, Robert. Co-published simultaneously in *The Serials Librarian* (The Haworth Press, Inc.) Vol. 25, No. 3/4, 1995, pp. 55-64; and: *A Kaleidoscope of Choices: Reshaping Roles and Opportunities for Serialists* (ed: Beth Holley and Mary Ann Sheble) The Haworth Press, Inc., 1995, pp. 55-64. Multiple copies of this article/chapter may be purchased from The Haworth Document Delivery Center [1-800-3-HAWORTH; 9:00 a.m. - 5:00 p.m. (EST)].

What I would like to do this morning is to share with you ideas that have come from the series of public workshops conducted by Northeast Consulting for the past four years.

The first few workshops were co-sponsored by the Association of American Publishers. After that, Northeast Consulting continued on its own, holding workshops four times each year. Each workshop is designed to accommodate thirty or forty people who work mainly in teams for two days. We provide participants with a series of visions (called endstates) about the future of publishing and allied industries. We also provide a database of approximately 185 hypothetical events that stretch between now and a five-year time horizon. Here is one example of an event: there is a multimedia-capable PC in schools for $400 a seat. Although that is not likely to happen tomorrow, we do want people to think about questions such as: if there were such a multimedia-capable PC at that price point, how might that change education and, furthermore, what are some implications for people in school publishing?

In these workshops we also ask people in teams to build scenarios, to tell stories, and to create fiction and narratives about how the world got from here to some future vision. I am not going to speak about the contents of the workshops per se, but I do want to share with you many of the conclusions that participants have drawn over the last four years. Specifically, what I want to share is how those conclusions have changed over time. I also want to suggest that the issues raised in these workshops have some relevance for your day-to-day efforts.

Let me mention also that when October invited me, she specifically wanted me to convey to you, as somebody doing work with publishers, what is on their minds? What are their hot buttons? What are the things that are keeping them up at night? Therefore, I will be trying to convey the things that we have heard in these workshops that are of concern to publishers and only tangentially touch on library issues.

In 1991, when we did the first workshops, there was a lot of cognitive dissonance. As a matter of fact, one of the people who was involved in the first workshop, and who was instrumental in getting the whole thing going, said to me afterwards, "You guys are out of your minds. The world is not going to look like anything that you suggested and all this networked information is just pie in the sky." Needless to say, I was pleased when two and a half years later the same person grabbed me and said, "You know, almost everything that you talked about seems to be coming true." So, it is not that we have an infallible crystal ball, but rather there is a collective wisdom that emerges out of these processes that keeps track of where things are moving. Let me share with you a couple of stories.

This presentation is really about changes in point of view. You might think about these workshops as the cure for mural-dyslexia. Do you know the definition of mural-dyslexia? That is when you cannot read the handwriting on the wall. It is also about perspective and I have a perspective story. This one goes by very quickly. It is a New York City story.

There was a turtle who was in Central Park in New York and this turtle was mugged by a gang of snails. When taken to the police station and asked by the detectives on *NYPD Blue*, "What happened?" the turtle said, "I don't know. It all happened so quickly." I think that is about like the change in the publishing industry. Things are happening very quickly.

Another brief true story–I was invited by one of the scholarly publishing societies to give a talk to its governing board in 1991, and the president of the society said to me (off-line before I gave my talk) "Now somebody's going to ask you about microform." And I said, "Okay, somebody's going to ask me about microform." Well, I did this whole speech about the future of publishing and how the world might change, and sure enough the first person during the question and answer session was a gentleman near retirement; he put up his hand and very indignantly said, "The things you're telling us are just what they told us about microform and look what happened. Why should we believe you?"

There are lots of pied pipers for technology and I wear that hat on many occasions. But, let me also caution that the problems entailed with new information technologies are extremely difficult. The rate of change will probably not be like anything I am going to talk about this morning. But we will get there eventually.

Back in 1991, there was a lot of disbelief that networked information and a commercialized Internet would happen; and then we saw a change in the collective consciousness. The paradigm shift that occurred was from what I call "Old World" to "New World" publishing. By Old World publishing, I mean that kind of publishing that has gone on for at least 400 years, if not a millennia. It is print-based; it is understandable; it is predictable; and it is the stuff with which you are all more than completely familiar. New world publishing is that which is going to be fast, it is going to be electronic and information-based, and presents a whole host of problems for people in the publishing industry.

In the spring of 1993, participants were far more ready to accept the proposition that New World publishing based on networked information would happen. We stopped getting arguments about it and the workshops settled down to a, "well, if this is what's coming, how shall we respond to it, and more importantly, how can we make money at it?" For the scholarly society folks and the university presses, the question was "How can we continue to recover our costs and not put an undue burden on the universities and the societies with whom we are affiliated?"

One of the trends we began talking about at this time was what I call the "personalization of information." This idea refers to the notion that individuals acquire information in small chunks—articles, chapters, even paragraphs and single images—rather than in larger units, such as books and issues of periodicals. We are not there yet; however, a number of technologies are moving us in that direction, including intelligent filters, Knowbots—Knowledge Robots of the kind envisioned by Vint Cerf and Bob Kahn at the Corporation for National Research Initiatives—concept-based search, and, of course, the World Wide Web and its Graphical User Interfaces such as Mosaic.

During the 1991-1992 period, workshop participants did not believe in networked multimedia. When they thought about multimedia, their vision of it was CD-ROM publishing. But one of the things that is driving Internet usage today, as many of you are aware, is the Mosaic front end to the World Wide Web. The Web enables development of important multimedia applications. These are being adopted not only in universities, but also by many of the large corporations with whom I work as a way of making corporate information available on the Internet.

Another thing that is going to drive Internet usage and that will affect publishing and information access and distribution is the advent of video conferencing on the Internet. I do not know if any of you are familiar with the Cornell product, CU See Me desktop video conferencing application. This is a harbinger of things to come; there will be others in this market soon. One should expect Intel's ProShare desktop video conferencing and screen sharing product to be available for use over the Internet by the end of 1994. But multimedia publishing that incorporates images, video, or sound will come and it will affect scholarly publishing, especially in the areas of the visualization of scientific information.

What we heard this year in April during the seminars in San Francisco and in Boston that is new was the beginning of acceptance of the Internet as a place, a virtual place, a cyberspace place, a place without physical embodiment, for doing electronic commerce. This is of importance to information distributors, publishers and packagers, because there are information shopping malls cropping up all over the Internet. Steve Outing has counted nearly fifty newspapers that are planning to provide (or who are doing so now) newspaper information electronically and a large majority of those will be on the Internet. I find it a little surprising how quickly the transition toward networked information is happening.

What happens to serials in this kind of environment? I think that besides the personalization of information, another trend to expect is what I call answer-based kinds of systems. People want to be able to ask questions of relatively focused scope and to get back that part of one or several articles that contains the information. Later in this decade or early in the next, on-line providers will be able to synthesize that information into something more coherent, something like a real, focused answer to a specific question.

Publishers have a dilemma regarding multimedia, which for many involves the production of CD-ROMs. I have a number of commercial publishing clients who argue that doing multimedia on the Internet is no different than doing multimedia on CD-ROM. I think that is disputable. Publishers have the challenge of becoming competent, of having at the core of their organization the capability to do multimedia publishing involving video and video clips, and not just text and images. Video requires a kind of expertise that, for the most part, most print publishers lack. Of course, to the extent that video becomes further incorporated in scholarly publishing, this provides yet another media requiring cataloging and public access.

Let me say something about the disintermediation wars now underway. The publishing, information repackaging, authoring, and distribution industry is being taken apart and reconstructed. Technology is forcing restructuring so that the "over-the-hill and through-the-woods" from the creators to the users of information is changing. Paul Evan Peters, Executive Director of the Coalition for Networked Information, says that this is really a process of remediation and that publishing will be remediated in some, as yet unknown, fashion. I think he is right. I also think that one of the challenges for people in the library community is: what role will libraries play as distribution channels and as the nature of the publishing business changes? The metaphor that comes to my mind is that the industry is playing musical chairs, and a couple of chairs are being taken away. When the music stops, who is going to have a chair? I think it is important for universities in general and people in the library community to consider this question closely, and I understand that you are already doing so.

Let me come back to an earlier theme. If the personalization of information is a correct forecast, then the important questions include how to charge for chunks of information and for which chunks there should be a charge. Publishers have not yet figured out how to go from a print-based revenue model to an electronic-based revenue model without doing damage to their profitability. Only a few of the most brave are willing to cannibalize their existing businesses, but these tend to be smaller, privately held businesses.

The other issue that publishers have is how to move from a print-centric to a multimedia-centric point of view. One of my favorite quick one-liners is, "The most dangerous thing today in publishing is the CEO of a publishing company with a multimedia demonstration at the annual meeting." Everybody thinks that the company is fully committed to multimedia because they can see it, but what has really happened is that they create a skunk works, or they have outsourced it to some hot, fast multimedia development company South of Market in San Francisco who has done this for them behind the scenes.

The skills that are required to acquire and create multimedia properties in-house have not yet permeated the organizational boundaries of traditional print publishers. And so it appears that the publishing company is doing something important, something significant, and the CEO can get up there and cheer about it. However, for the people who have been in that company for some time dealing with print, their daily lives have not changed in the least. Nothing much has changed about the way they think about the business and the way they interact with authors. They are still acquiring stuff in the same old way in the same old format. Thus, those publishing companies who figure out how to put multimedia at the center of the publishing process will have significant competitive advantages in the marketplace.

I think (and have thought for some time) that rights management is the soft underbelly of electronic publishing and it is going to get more complicated in the next year or two. Numerous publishing houses have no idea what electronic rights they have or do not have. This is especially true for older books that are still in print, some textbooks, and serials where there may be pictures, diagrams, and artwork. In some cases, the electronic rights were not obtained or have different "terms and conditions" attached to them, such as "one time use in the North American market." As you know, cyberspace is global. So what is a publisher to do if years later they cannot find the author or rights holder to get permission for electronic use? This illustrates the kinds of problems engendered by the digital revolution.

Now, let me say something about metering technologies. I had hoped that there would have been at least one, possibly two announcements by this meeting, but they have been put off, perhaps until the end of the year. What to look for is this: digital envelopes. There are encryption-based technologies that will allow publishers to put information in an electronic envelope. Only those people who have agreed to pay for the use of that information will be able to open the envelope and gain access to whatever the publisher has put inside. This metering technology will come to market within the next year. It is quite likely to change some thinking about how information is accessed and distributed. On the one hand there will be those who say that authors and rights-holders need to be fairly compensated for use. This will run squarely up against the tradition in university environments in which people not only feel that information ought to be free, but are often annoyed that it is created within universities, given to publishers and sold back to universities at prices that universities cannot afford. This is an issue that as serialists you have been struggling with for the past decade–the increases in subscription prices. I have little to add on this score; but, metering technology will allow publishers to set different prices for different uses, such as browsing, copying, printing, excerpting, and so on. An open question is acceptance of metering technology by users.

The content providers believe that by owning the rights, they are in the catbird seat, so to speak. But it is also likely that repackagers–people who pull information from different places and put it on the desktop of the person who wants it–end up being most important. There are some well-known examples that suggest future directions. Course packs are a way of doing customized information; customized to what the professor wants. But, if you extend that paradigm to information users generically, it means that the people who publish this or that journal may not be in control. It may be those who pull various pieces together, the repackagers, the document distributors, that have a key advantage in New World publishing.

Besides repackagers, there are the network services providers. Does it matter who runs the network? Probably not. What publishers want is the widest distribution of their information. So there are some attempts by network operators to make special deals with publishers that say "we will be your exclusive distributor," but one wonders how long that kind of paradigm will last. In the end, what this may turn out to be is who owns the customer relationship? To whom does the user, the consumer of information, think of going? In universities, you are the end user, the consumer. One of the future risks to libraries and librarians is that you will not be visible, you will be "out of mind" as a place to get information. So, one of the challenges is how to keep patrons thinking of libraries as rich information sources.

Publishing is not the only industry being restructured at the moment. Some people feel that all this Infobahn, all this Information Superhighway talk is just hype. It was supposed to be here yesterday. TCI and Bell Atlantic were supposed to get together. That is not happening now. Who knows what is happening? The big folks, the AT&Ts and the IBMs are all circling. The smell of money is in the air. Well, that is right, and one of the problems is that when elephants start to dance, the smaller animals better watch out, because elephants have deep pockets. The telecommunications industry, then, is one area to pay attention to since developments there affect publishing and information access and distribution.

The evolution of the Internet is another change in both technology and business that will affect publishers. The Internet is making the transition from what was an experimental, pre-commercial environment that worked okay, but not great, to something that is going to be commercial or industrial strength fairly quickly. In fact, with the exception of funding advanced research projects, the National Science Foundation is getting itself out of the networking business by the end of the decade. As the commercial Internet providers build an industrial strength network, it means that people who have the attention of consumers, who are able to get into that marketplace and create a presence, create brand recognition for the transport system may be able to create brand recognition for information too. In short, network services providers are trying to figure out if they should also become information providers and compete with established brands such as America Online and CompuServe. Where do libraries play in this world? Traditionally, librarians have gone out to Dialog or to Mead Data Central to bring back answers for patrons. One wonders how much longer that will be perceived as a value-added service.

This brings me to a number of other issues. Let me talk about some concerns internal to publishers. Some publishing houses got on the track early, creating PostScript or Standard Generalized Mark-up Language (SGML) databases so they could deal with piece parts. In the school, college, and the scholarly segments of publishing, we will see more of these systems implemented so that the company can manage its intellectual capital in chunks or piece parts. And so database technology will be used so that the publishers themselves can do the kind of mixing and matching that you now see done by repackagers such as the on-line companies, document delivery services, and college stores. Publishers will also be competing directly with powerful new end-user tools for searching, finding, and navigating. These tools allow end users to find things in disparate places and create new composite documents and information bases. Faced with the growing personalization of information, publishers will continue to look for better ways to manage their own intellectual capital and to integrate their information with the next generations of searching, finding, navigation, and metering tools.

Then there is the home. One of the Infobahn hypes is, people will access information in their homes through their televisions. You now have Internet services providers such as Performance Systems International teaming up with Continental Cablevision to provide Internet access through one's cable box. One of the interesting issues concerning information access in the home concerns the interface. Is television the right interface for information access? There is a difference between what people at Intel call the eighteen-inch interface meaning the computer, and the six-foot interface meaning the television. There is a lot of hype nowadays about convergence, that television and computer technology will come together and be integrated both in the home and on the business desktop. My sense is to be careful of this argument. It is unlikely to happen the way people thought a year or two ago. But, it leads to the ultimate question of how, from the home, will children and adults get access to the information that they want, and what role will libraries play? As you know, many organizations are lobbying Congress to ensure that libraries get some funding to provide public access to the Information Superhighway, whatever it turns out to be.

Finally, let me return to an earlier theme, which is the restructuring, the remediation of publishing and allied industries. I think a couple of interesting signs will be who buys Ziff and who buys Mead Data Central. I wonder who might be willing to spend one or two billion dollars each, for either of these companies. Who buys each of them and the selling prices will be very suggestive of where the industry is going in the rest of the decade and perhaps about the role of information on the Infobahn. A related question is what happens to libraries? Will you be disintermediated? Some people believe that physical libraries and human librarians will have no important role in a few years. On even days of the week, I believe this to be true; on odd days of the week, I believe it to be false. But in any event, I did not come here with answers, just with questions and to suggest some things to think about in the coming months.

Reshaping the Serials Vendor Industry

Dan Tonkery

SUMMARY. The vendor industry as we know it must develop new products and services in order to remain in the information delivery chain. The economic pressure on library budgets is forcing changes in the publishing industry and user demands. With the shift to on-demand publishing and other electronic services, subscription vendors must be creative to compete and survive.

Reshaping the serials vendor industry is a very difficult topic, especially at this time. When first assigned the topic, I thought I could avoid the real issues and spend some time leading an aerobic workout. Anything to avoid looking at the future of the subscription industry.

During the earlier presentations this morning, the speakers predicted the end of libraries as we know them and suggested that all professional librarians are going to be put out of business. In my speech I am continuing that trend, and I have the pleasure of predicting the end of subscription agencies. If agents do not change, then agents will go out of business. What a depressing time for our industry. However, I am not ready to close our doors, and I maintain that libraries are still going to have a role in the delivery of information. For both librarians and vendors, reshaping our role is critical to our survival for the long term.

Dan Tonkery is President and CEO of Readmore Inc., New York, NY.

[Haworth co-indexing entry note]: "Reshaping the Serials Vendor Industry." Tonkery, Dan. Co-published simultaneously in *The Serials Librarian* (The Haworth Press, Inc.) Vol. 25, No. 3/4, 1995, pp. 65-72; and: *A Kaleidoscope of Choices: Reshaping Roles and Opportunities for Serialists* (ed: Beth Holley and Mary Ann Sheble) The Haworth Press, Inc., 1995, pp. 65-72. Multiple copies of this article/chapter may be purchased from The Haworth Document Delivery Center [1-800-3-HAWORTH; 9:00 a.m. - 5:00 p.m. (EST)].

I want to spend the next thirty minutes talking about reshaping the serials industry. The world is going to be radically different. While many of us may not believe it, change is coming and it is coming at a faster rate than any of us could have predicted.

Digital technology is changing the way we work and the way we live. The investment in research has already been made by various industries, and we now have the capability to digitize almost everything. We have digital television, digital music, digital newspapers, etc. Anything you can find in print can be digitized and changed into a digital artifact. Management is seeing digital technology as a panacea to save costs. Technology is rewriting the rules of the workplace. Many believe, whether it is right or wrong, that there are substantial savings coming from technology. One can operate with less staff, and there is a case for increased productivity. Management, in both our universities and corporations, is seeking a technology payoff. For the last five years, organizations have been investing heavily in capital equipment and software development. Now organizations are seeking some kind of technology payoff. What that means for most organizations is certainly a reduction in staff. Organizations are downsizing. Companies are rightsizing. The library community is not protected from these trends. We see it everywhere, in corporate libraries, medical libraries, and academic libraries. There is a shift in resources from technical services to public or user services. Much of that shift is justified on the basis that we have new technology and new ways of doing things. Library administrators expect to be able to benefit from these technologies and to operate with less staff. Few libraries that I visit have even fifty percent of the technical services staff remaining.

Technology, whether we like it or not or whether we want to endorse it or not, is here to stay. Libraries are not going back to the manual indexes; we are not going back to paper. When you figure that the cost of computing is dropping thirty percent every twelve months, the cost to upgrade or to take advantage of technology is difficult to ignore. Those of us who invested in technology early and bought personal computers have seen radical drops in prices for computer equipment. Four years ago I spent $5,000 per workstation; two years ago the price of a workstation dropped to $3,000; and, now, we install workstations for just under $2,000. It is significant that the industry that is producing technology is constantly trying to find faster and cheaper systems to sell. Librarians and agents can take advantage of this trend. Certainly, we are reaching a critical mass in the whole market. The availability of low cost hardware with extensive capacity is triggering the coming revolution, which will forever change the way we work and live.

Investing in technology is not new. Subscription agents have not been standing around with their heads in the sand. Agents have adopted technology and have made great use of it. There is greater efficiency in our processing activities, from the ordering stage where we use magnetic tapes, to electronic data interchange (EDI) invoicing and claiming, to the Internet. Agents have invested heavily in technology. Take for example, claiming which is very expensive and time consuming. Much time and energy have been invested in EDI for claiming, and we are looking forward to payoffs from EDI in other transaction processing for subscriptions.

The Serials Industry Systems Advisory Committee (SISAC) and the International Committee on EDI for Serials (ICEDIS) are organizations that are absolutely critical to our community. We need standards in order to be able to obtain the payoffs from technology that software and hardware offer us. Since standards are critical to the success of all of us, we need to continue to invest in developing and supporting new standards.

Agents have accepted technology which has allowed for lower service charges. Agents have been able to keep up with user demands and expectations through technology. In fact, we have been able to offer more services with less people. We have re-engineered our workflows. We have gone from mainframe computers to client server systems and now operate large wide-area networks. We have taken advantage of every opportunity we can to lower our operating costs through technology. I believe that agents in general are making the maximum use of technology, software, telecommunication networks, and computing. Our clients will see the benefits of technology in terms of interfaces and a range of services that each agent offers. Technology has already reshaped the vendor industry by allowing smaller agents to have an equal footing with larger agents. Technology has become the great equalizer in many competitive environments, not only in the library field, but other fields in general. Technology allows agents to offer speed and price flexibility and to provide common services, independent of the size of the agent. Technology has enabled agents to create services based on user expectations. We have been able to meet library needs to this point. Technology has already started to change the role of agents as we begin providing article delivery and other services.

There is a central role for agents in the traditional print world. Everybody can see the value that agents provide. Agents have proven themselves in the print world, but I think the real world is changing. Agents are afraid of the new world, and it is this new world for which we must all be prepared. What is past is past. The future, we hope, is going to be longer than the past; therefore, we need to be in a position to take advantage of it. As the information revolution reaches a critical mass, it cannot be ignored, nor is it going to be stopped. It can only be delayed by the economic and political realities of the information revolution. While there is going to be a transition period, I believe there is an accelerating shift from paper to digital, or computer based simulations. What we have seen in our own industry and certainly from our own organization's data is a continuing decline in subscriptions. For the last three years we have seen a six percent decline in subscription volumes each year in terms of actual units. And, if you think of that in terms of both us and our sister companies, it seems there is approximately a twenty percent reduction of subscriptions for science, technical, and medical (STM) materials in the United States. At some libraries the rate is higher and at others it is lower. However, in general, across our entire customer base, we have seen almost a twenty percent decline in subscriptions over a very short period of time. I think that trend is going to continue and is going to force different patterns of usage which will impact scholarly publication. What is even more frightening is that everyone is cancelling the same high priced titles. Cancellation projects tend to be institutional specific without any coordination with other libraries.

The library of the future is going to be a digital library. The virtual library is going to be without walls, offering universal accessibility, with infinite space but no limits on collections. It is actually going to be a network of knowledge systems. The traditional, print-based agent, traveling on the information highway, stands a chance of becoming lost forever in cyberspace. The role that agents have enjoyed for the last thirty or forty years has been based on a print-based medium. We are going to have to change, and we are going to have to change quickly, in order to take advantage of the new world or even to have a place in the new world. There is going to be a transition stage, and I think we are already in that transition phase as we reach a critical point in the new millennium.

I am hoping, not guaranteeing, that the virtual library may need the virtual agent. The virtual agent may serve as the link between the resources of many traditional publishers. There are publishers with vast resources that can take full advantage of the electronic age, digital technology, and offer a wide variety of services and products. However, there is another large group of publishers that are not going to have the resources. These publishers are not going to want to make the investment, but are going to rely on others to do the work for them. The agent is going to develop or utilize technology to make networks of subject-related electronic digital archives or artifacts. The agent's role may be in assisting in the conversion of digital artifacts, specifically in the science-technology-medicine arena. I predict that many STM journals, with an information usage pattern that has a half-life of less than five years, will end up in only digital form. Creating digital archives in the STM field is not a difficult thing to do. Many publishers already have their information in digital form. Information that currently is not in digital form could easily be transferred into that medium if it were not for copyright. There are many of us, both agents and libraries, that would take entire collections and scan them, convert them, and be able to disseminate them; but, we are not able to do so without violating the intellectual property rights of the publishers.

However, there are large cross-sections of materials in the sciences that will be converted and shared in a virtual library environment. Perhaps a virtual agent may, in fact, be able to take advantage of this opportunity. The agent's role in the future is going to be much more in providing services where we are not seen visually. For example, the agent may operate one of the great optical media warehouses. We may find that the agents of the future are different players than the family-owned companies that exist today. New companies in cable, television, or telecommunication conglomerates may be the agents of the future. We know that the world is changing and the family-owned agents have to change, or we are certainly going to be replaced by a new breed.

Agents may have a role in developing the intellectual property rights payment system. One of the services that agents have always performed, although some of you may not like it, is to collect money to pay publishers. In the next world, I am hoping we will still be in the money collecting business. Currently agents play a major role in the payment process and will continue to provide that service in the future. Intellectual property rights are not going to disappear. We are still going to have to support the authors' and publishers' rights; so, there has to be a mechanism for collecting fees and disseminating the funds to the proper organization. In the future you may see a very expanded agent's pricing files. One might soon see prices in our database by page, paragraph, chapter, work, or by other units, such as access time. If you want to use a particular journal and you only need three minutes of it, agents need to develop databases that identify the cost, and invoice a user at the preferred usage rate. No agent has systems in place that can do that today, but that is the way information is going to be used in the future. The virtual library may not buy subscriptions to print-based products; however, it may buy a site license to access certain materials. Many of the information tools that patrons are going to use, the library is going to buy on a piecemeal basis at the lowest denominator. There will be systems in place on your own campus that will allow you to buy from a central warehouse; information in a package where you pay for only what you use. There will need to be a metering system that can track this type of usage. The economic models for highway usage must be developed now, using input from publishers. Agents need to be creative, and publishers need to be inventive in designing different mechanisms that can be used to model information usage in a virtual library environment. In the future, agents may be the toll collectors. I envision a point of sales system in major universities that is electronically linked to our computers and transmits usage data at the end of the day. As usage occurs, that information is sent to the agent for processing before it is sent to the publishers with the proper payment. So, agents may operate a giant electronic cash register system, taking our few pennies, as we always do, as it is processed.

Our ailing, industrial age libraries, publishers, and agents are in for a transformational opportunity that will result in a revolutionary change in the library paradigm. It is not only the agents that have to worry about survival in this age, but also publishers and libraries. All of us are in this together, and we are all going to have to deal with the technological changes. The virtual library is an opportunity for new lines, new partners, and new ways of operating that have never before been endorsed.

The system of scholarly communication is going to be transformed, as there is a generational shift to the younger researchers. The younger researchers are the Nintendo age and SEGA CD players, who have grown up playing with technology. I have a twelve year old son and I bought him a SEGA CD for Christmas. I thought, this is my time to shine. I did some of the first CD work in this country in developing CD-ROM systems. I was hoping that we could sit down and spend an hour together setting up this system. I went out to get the newspaper and when I came back, he had already installed the system and was using it. I felt like an idiot. He says, "CD-ROM, what's the problem? You just plug it in, and it works!"

There is a change occurring in our resource community; there is a change in attitude; there is a change in usage. In the future, scholarly communication is going to be communicated, not on the basis of peer reviewed journals alone, but also on peer reviewed electronic and scholarly communications devices.

Before I finish, there are a few more comments I want to make. One, the print journal, as we know it, will cease in many of the scientific, technical, and medical areas. I am not saying that all journals are going away, and I am not saying all journals in the STM field are going away. What I predict is that a large group of STM journals will not be here in the next five years if the erosion in the number of subscriptions continues. Also, the trend is that access versus ownership is going to increase. In one article delivery company there is a twenty percent increase per month in the usage of the service. The ownership of journals is something that is being questioned, while on many campuses access is a concept that has been almost universally accepted. Publishers who are waiting for the return of the budgets in the library community need to think again, because it is not going to happen. Those budgets have already been reallocated. People are happy buying electronic information; they are very satisfied with access. That faculty are satisfied with this electronic form is something new. Intellectual property rights are stumbling blocks to the free flow of information, and the concerns must be overcome before the flow of information will continue. We still need a new copyright law or modifications in the existing copyright to make it more amenable for the electronic age. New economic models are required, and they are needed now.

In summary, as the library shifts to the virtual library, the traditional agent will have a transitional role. The agent's role will shift into virtual agents, serving as toll collectors operating optical warehouses. The publisher, library, and agent roles will all be changed in the new, virtual information community. My final task is to predict when the virtual library will arrive in your neighborhood. Will it be the year 2000 or the year 2005 (which will actually be the 20th annual NASIG meeting)? The virtual library is something that is real and is endorsed by many faculty and university administrators. It is coming to your campus in the near future. There are hurdles in terms of economics, in terms of how we can pay or support the cost of building infrastructures at our universities, and how we convert our libraries to take advantage of the virtual library. The age of building large buildings and filling them with print materials is gone forever.

Publishers, libraries, and agents are faced with a rapidly shifting future. Agents will have a future in the new technological age, but they will be supporting a virtual library selling virtual services.

Changing Focus: Tomorrow's Virtual Library

Naomi C. Broering

SUMMARY. If libraries are going to play the information game tomorrow, they must position themselves today and take the necessary steps now to become virtual libraries. To move beyond today's electronic libraries to tomorrow's networked virtual ones, libraries will need to extend well beyond their institutional boundaries. We are witnessing the emergence of a new industry in America: the knowledge industry. It involves communications, computers, software, database developers, publishers, and libraries. Libraries will play a pivotal role in the knowledge industry by developing special information packages and by providing direct access to many different print and non- print formats, bibliographic indexes and abstracts, CD-ROM systems, document delivery, full-text-electronic journals, images, and multimedia products. Libraries will offer customized services that seamlessly bring the world of information to users through the Internet, super networks, and wireless communications. Besides personnel and technological reconfiguration, new strategic partnerships with other libraries, commercial enterprises, software suppliers, publishers, campus computer centers, and user communities of educators and researchers will position libraries to become the high profile knowledge management centers of the future. Descriptions of a virtual medical library illustrate progress some libraries have made in these new directions.

Naomi C. Broering is Director, Biomedical Information Resources Center and Medical Center Librarian, Georgetown University Medical Center, Washington, D.C.

[Haworth co-indexing entry note]: "Changing Focus: Tomorrow's Virtual Library." Broering, Naomi C. Co-published simultaneously in *The Serials Librarian* (The Haworth Press, Inc.) Vol. 25, No. 3/4, 1995, pp. 73-94; and: *A Kaleidoscope of Choices: Reshaping Roles and Opportunities for Serialists* (ed: Beth Holley and Mary Ann Sheble) The Haworth Press, Inc., 1995, pp. 73-94. Multiple copies of this article/chapter may be purchased from The Haworth Document Delivery Center [1-800-3-HAWORTH; 9:00 a.m. - 5:00 p.m. (EST)].

INTRODUCTION

We are already working and living in tomorrow's "virtual world." The library world is changing rapidly, and it now has the technology to create the "virtual library." We must begin to look at the future and prepare ourselves for what networked technology is making possible. The message is clear, it is not elaborate; things are changing! Libraries have been receiving the message to change focus for the last two decades. There is no doubt that libraries have reached the crossroads in the 1990s. We must develop libraries that fit the "world of tomorrow." Critical milestones have been reached, but we are at an important juncture. We are in the midst of developing virtual libraries that will offer a broad range of new electronic based services. It is necessary to participate in development of the information infrastructure because it will impact heavily on libraries. Libraries are an integral part of the information highway. Not only must universities and other institutions upgrade their systems, but they must also automate their libraries with systems that can integrate easily to the institution's systems. Stand alone systems that are incapable of networking cannot meet the needs of a highly networked campus, community, or corporation. Researchers and students need access to literature from the office, school, laboratory, or home. The virtual library is making this happen.

The purpose of this paper is to focus on the emerging virtual library and its role in developing a knowledge network. It will cover the importance of the integrated network environment, provide examples of databases and computer software, highlight educational needs, and explore a vision for the future.

WHAT IS THE VIRTUAL LIBRARY?

There are several definitions of a virtual library. I believe the virtual library provides access to multiple information resources and allows users to manipulate them to meet their individual needs. Gapen refers to the virtual library as the concept of remote access to networked worldwide library and information sources. The library is as a synergy created by bringing together technologically the resources of many, many libraries and information services.[1] Van

Wahlde and Schiller see the virtual library as a vision of the library of the twenty-first century in which computers and telecommunications technologies make possible access to a wide range of information resources.[2] Recently, Raymond Kurzweil, in describing the future of libraries, raised the concept of borrowing virtual books from the virtual library by selecting icons from a circa 2000 notebook computer.[3]

What are the components of a virtual library? There are several essential parts. A virtual library has a library information system that provides direct access to multiple modules, including print and non-print formats, bibliographic indexes and abstracts, CD ROM systems, document delivery, full-text, electronic journals, plus e-mail for direct communication with expert librarians. Even beyond basically making these resources available, the virtual library of tomorrow must guide users to information and offer integration, or at minimum interface with other libraries such as community, research, medical, legal, arts and humanities, plus museums, and a variety of institutional systems.

The library system must connect to a network, preferably the Internet. It is not a stand-alone library, it is an essential part of the campus-wide or institution-wide approach with network capabilities, internally and externally beyond the institution. As in virtual reality, where a person can work the computer from within the system, a virtual library will allow users to manipulate electromagnetic resources within the library and through sophisticated networks such as the Internet and the emerging information super highway. For example, as one user may be satisfied with a quick bibliographic search in a small subset, or in a specialty field, others may want to access a large file of the world's knowledge base.

The virtual library will provide users with choices in a "one-stop shopping" manner. The users will select specific pieces of information in a customized manner. Some of the information they select may be locally available in the institution's databases or may be available internationally.

From the perspective of library services, we are already witnessing several changes. An important change is document delivery. Definitely, the virtual library will have electronic document delivery. Users today order requests in a semi-automated manner. Tomorrow, it will be part of the search process. The Library Information System (LIS) already has document delivery integrated into the bibliographic search system.

The virtual library also will have a collection of books and journal articles available electronically in special full-text databases for viewing or printing on demand. In this scenario the user will search a bibliographic system, retrieve pertinent references, view the abstract, and determine instantly whether the full-text article is of interest. The request will then be made online and the document will be sent either to the person's workstation or fax machine (see Figure 1).

Electronic publishing is critical to the virtual library. Libraries are already experimenting with electronic journals. Several associations are converting their journals to electronic format. The publishers are changing their production methods and also offering users other options such as CD-ROMs.

Another change in the horizon is the image workstation in the virtual library. I envision libraries with well indexed and cataloged images of various types available through the public access computers where you currently look-up books, journals or search data-

FIGURE 1

bases. This means an immense number of resources currently in the library's collection will be digitized so they can be searched, viewed, printed, or even pasted into personal documents with the touch of a few keys and clicks of the mouse. The library will be able to transmit slides, videos, animations, x-ray, and voice systems at the public access computers. In addition, the online catalog will provide access to special collection images such as museum objects, photos, paintings, and illuminated texts will be a "new" mode of textbook.

SIGNIFICANCE

Why develop a "virtual library?" If we are going to play the information game tomorrow, we must position ourselves today and take the necessary steps now. Better access to information means we can educate the public, students, and teachers to make informed decisions. Their jobs will be easier, if they can tap a variety of databases in a coordinated manner. The educational and scholarship process will improve. Important benefits are the low cost and time saving factors of endlessly searching and stumbling around for information. The library will provide services previously unavailable and even unimaginable.

Cataloging will be more intensive and comprehensive. All the slides and images will need thorough indexing. Catalogers have an immense job ahead of them. They will need to properly index and catalog images, they will need to review classification schemes to determine appropriateness and perhaps establish new standards. Catalogers, indexers, and database developers have promising careers and long term job security. There are certainly more images in the world than books that will need indexing.

The virtual library will be more responsive to educational needs. Education is changing so rapidly that it is becoming increasingly difficult for students and scholars to stay abreast of the latest discoveries. The information explosion and the volume of literature produced has literally overwhelmed today's students, researchers, and faculty. For example, the 1906 graduating class at Georgetown University was much smaller than our more recent classes of the 1990s. Even though the students' head sizes have not changed at all over the past 80 years, their need to absorb more information has increased immensely. In 1906, they relied on two volumes of the *Index Medicus* for their literature needs. Today they must consult over five volumes of the *Index Medicus*. We are faced with the dilemma of cramming 600% more information into the same brain circumference. Unfortunately, the student's head size or brain capacity has not kept up with the growth of the medical literature. Obviously, students still absorb knowledge at the same rate and they cannot learn everything or memorize everything. The problem intensifies each year, as information continually builds on the past.

What solutions are there for the overwhelmed and overloaded information-seeker? Newer technologies, such as the computer, can complement the student in finding the right information at the right time for problem solving. The key is to find the right blend. The ideal approach, therefore is to merge the best of both worlds by linking the unlimited memory of computers with the superior intuitive ability of humans. The virtual library then must develop pertinent information packages that complement student needs.

IAIMS KNOWLEDGE NETWORK

Let me use the IAIMS project funded by the National Library of Medicine (NLM) as an example of how Georgetown began to develop a virtual library. IAIMS stands for Integrated Advanced Information Management System. The Georgetown approach was to develop a knowledge network in a modular fashion and implement selected biotechnology and biomedical databases that are universally useful to campus users. The strategy was to use selected areas of institutional emphasis that support a broad array of users. The focus of the knowledge network is to emphasize academic information commonly useful to students and faculty. The purpose is to provide free access to these resources, to provide core support services, to seed components based in various units and departments, and to teach users how to access the knowledge network for their daily work.

In the knowledge network, information resources have been organized into a manageable body of biomedical databases and systems. These databases are categorized as bibliographic, informational, research, and diagnostic systems. The library manages and maintains all the databases except the patient systems which are maintained locally in individual clinical departments. The informational category includes the biotechnology (molecular biology) databases.

The resources that need to be brought together may be different at each library but this example illustrates how the concept can be applied at various settings. The knowledge network shown in Figure 2 includes the following:

1. **Bibliographic Databases** include three types of information: references to the Library's print and non-print materials, abstracts of articles, and full-text articles and books.

- *The Library Information System (LIS)* includes the online catalog of books, journals, and non-print holdings of the Medical Center Library with network access to the Law and Main Campus Libraries.[4]
- *The miniMEDLINE System*™ is a greatly enhanced version of Georgetown's user-friendly subset of the National Library of Medicine's MEDLINE System. The miniMEDLINE database includes over 1,000 journal titles with article abstracts.[5]
- *GRATEFUL MED* is a search system used to access the full MEDLINE® file at the NLM. As reported previously in the literature, users merely push a button to access the GRATEFUL MED software to conduct a search.[6] Once completed they transmit it directly to the NLM without needing to perform the dial-up procedures.[7]
- *ALERTS*™ */CURRENT CONTENTS®* Search System is a database of references to the latest articles being published in the world's scientific journals. This search software functions similarly to miniMEDLINE.[8]
- *BIOETHICSLINE* is developed at Georgetown in collaboration with the NLM. It supports instruction on ethics in medicine which is emphasized on our campus. There is further interest in ethics because of the impact of Biotechnology.[9]
- *Full-Text* articles and books includes external access to vendors or other institutions with online texts such as Johns Hopkins University. There is also a small full-text digitized database of recent journal articles in cancer and genetics under development.[10]

2. ***The Information Databases*** currently available to users are factual systems of a mixed variety.

- *The Physicians Data Query (PDQ)* system has approximately 1,000 cancer treatment protocols approved by the National Cancer Institute and a growing directory of over 10,000 physicians and centers involved in cancer treatment.[11-13]
- *The Micromedex* Drug, Poison, and Emergin Dex Information System implemented in 1987 has recently been greatly expanded.
- A *Drug Interactions* knowledge base of drug-drug and food-drug interactions is currently being tested.
- A *Medical Facts File* of commonly asked questions is a library database. It includes pertinent medical information, normal values, statistical data, publishing information, and authoritative sources that users can check when seeking basic knowledge.[14]

3. ***Diagnostic Information Systems*** to support education include a family of knowledge and expert systems. These diagnostic systems are used in a new medical school course on Data Reasoning and Problem Solving, and during clinical rotations.

- *RECONSIDER*, a diagnostic prompting system, was implemented in 1986 to introduce students to differential diagnosis techniques.[15,16]
- *DXplain* is available locally on the Georgetown network, but it is also accessible via a network gateway to Massachusetts General Hospital where it resides.[17-19]
- *QMR* is a knowledge system developed at the University of Pittsburgh. It is used at over twenty student workstations in the clinical teaching environment.[20]
- *ILIAD*, from the University of Utah, is networked at nine library workstations and at clinical locations.[21-22]

4. ***Search and Biotechnology Databases.*** A family of databases have been implemented to accelerate DNA sequencing that supports research activities in the biotechnology field. The annual faculty publications database developed by the library is used to track faculty research interests and their scholarly contributions.

- *Molecular Biology Databases* are maintained in-house that include the NIH GenBANK and the two systems comprising Protein Identification Registry (PIR) developed by the NBRF at Georgetown. Also there is a special GCG sequencing software system developed at the University of Wisconsin that allows scientists to conduct matching computations.
- *Faculty Publications* are compiled annually, published, and placed in the database. A grants database is being developed by the Sponsored Research Office which will be included with the research databases.

5. **E-mail and the Internet.** The most popular service we provide today is e-mail. Through the Internet our users can send e-mail messages all over the world. Users can also access gophers, use listservs, and send data via file transfer protocols (FTP). We provide automatic access to other institutions through a gateway system.

Outcome data compiled for 1993 indicates how e-mail is heavily used and that the bibliographic databases which were introduced to users in the 1980s are still the most popular. The other databases are newer, more complex to use and also require more user training. A vigorous outreach program to train users is on-going (see Figure 3).

SCHOLAR WORKSTATIONS

Development of scholar workstations is an important virtual library activity. The virtual library must assume responsibility for developing scholar workstations that users can customize to meet their needs. Student, faculty, and researcher workstations at Georgetown vary in power and capabilities depending on the needs of the user. They provide user access points to the systems in the knowledge network. Typically, they store local files, maintain dedicated information and software systems, and have access to the network's databases.

The Student Workstations are of major importance in the educational program of the schools. In 1981, computer use was integrated into on-going courses through a variety of partnerships with the library. Fruition of the student workstation concept occurred five

FIGURE 2

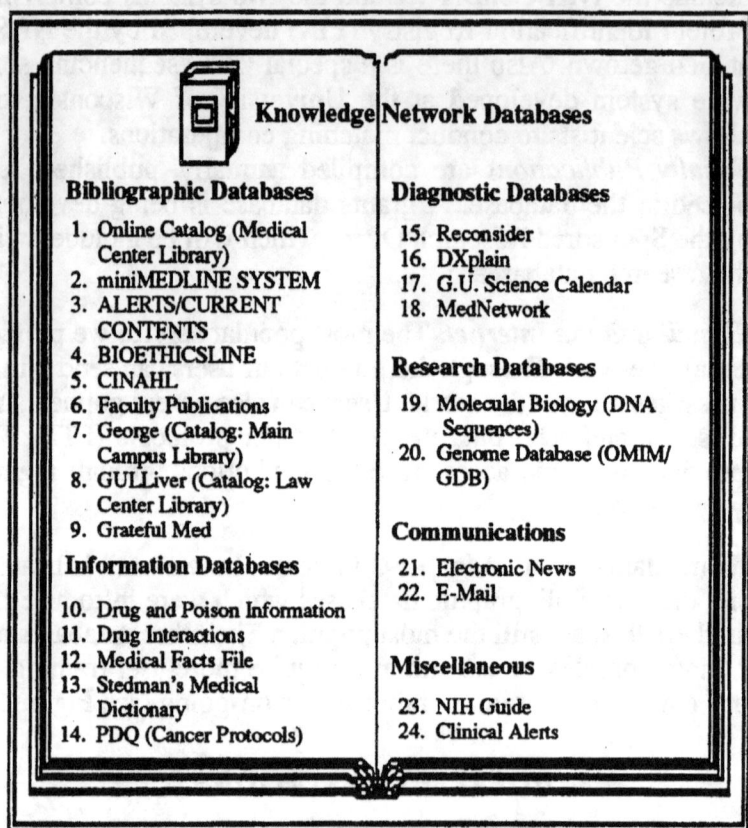

years ago when the MAClinical project was launched. An Informatics Office was established to work jointly with the library. The purpose of the MAClinical project was to place workstations throughout the hospital for student use in preparing history and physicals, and to access the knowledge network. Recently, the MAClinical workstations were extended from nine to thirty computers. There are also eight workstations at affiliated teaching hospitals. Bibliographic searching and e-mail are used the most. We expect document delivery to increase rapidly.

The Researcher Workstation project is designed to provide researchers with integrated DNA sequencing capabilities. It was an experiment to automate the tasks of conducting thousands of sequences in the AIDS research laboratory and for projects in the Biochemistry Department. The workstations, based in the laboratories, integrate database searching with actual lab work-ups. The concept caught on so well that today over ninety researchers at the Cancer Center and in other university departments use the molecular biology databases and sequence matching software. These systems are available free to all network users–saving access time and expenses associated with dial-up to remote systems.

The library offers a three day course on use of the molecular biology systems and the DNA sequence matching software.

The Faculty Workstation was developed to encourage and support use of computers in teaching. We began by developing a project which included over 150 anomalies, an area seldom seen by students during their training experience. We then developed a digital library of microanatomy slides including a syllabus and test questions to help students with self study and assessment.

Our best known faculty project is the Electronic Textbook in Human Physiology. We began with the cardiac cycle and now have

FIGURE 3

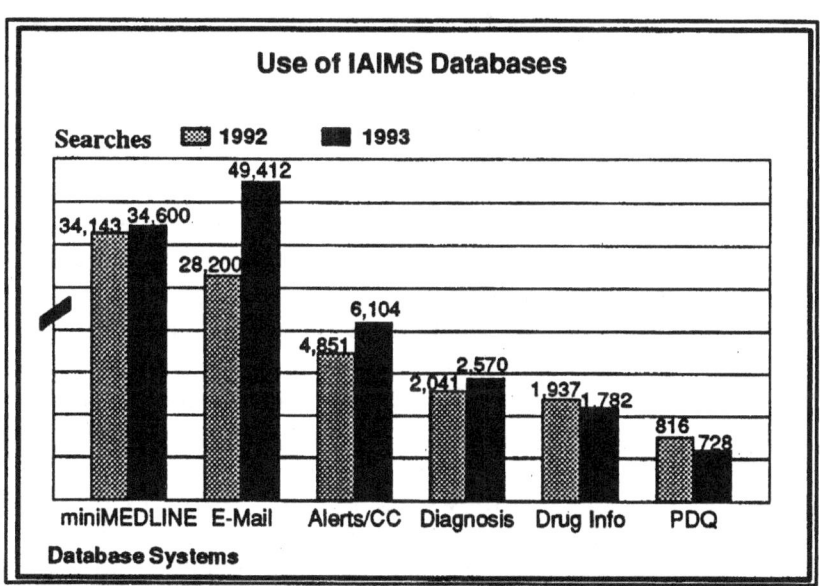

the endocrine, renal, and pulmonary systems. This software includes voice, data, images, and animation.

The Practitioner's Workstation is where clinicians can access and store patient data, clinical investigations, and pertinent clinical trials, and access the databases on the Knowledge Network. To clinicians, the drug, cancer treatment and diagnostic databases are as important as the MEDLINE and e-mail systems.

Obviously for financial reasons, our strategy has been to launch pilot projects and implement a variety of different workstations throughout the medical center and then fully implement the most successful projects. To date, from the perspective of high use and return on investment, we have experienced immense success with the student and researcher workstations.

INTEGRATION: SINGLE MENU ACCESS

In order to compete effectively in today's information environment, system integration is vital. The growing number of information databases and knowledge systems, technological advances and equipment investments, coupled with shrinking budgets, make integration not only a necessity, but the only logical approach to system efficiency. Pivotal to this is having a well developed network system, an easy means to navigate through the system and an interface or integration with the hospital system.

- *BioSYNTHESIS* provides a single access menu for users. It is a key and initial step to system integration which has been achieved with the BioSYNTHESIS retrieval system, developed in 1987. The process included developing initial linkages, interfacing a few trial databases, adding a family of new databases, incorporating multiple database search capability, adding a vocabulary system such as the NLM MESH or Unified Medical Language System, and enhancing the existing LIS to provide users with seamless information transfer. It is a multiphasic program: BioSYNTHESIS provides a single access menu to the knowledge network family of databases which reside on disparate computers; it has an expanded gateway system to additional databases and external systems via

Internet; and under long-term development is a search engine to facilitate complex searching of multiple databases. Of great significance is the simple access menu and automatic log-on to a variety of computers and databases.[23-24]

What can we draw from the Georgetown example that is applicable to other libraries? These figures show how a network can be integrated. Putting the library at the focal point you can see the advantage of being able to link to other resources. The nodes provide direct access for users throughout the campus and externally to other institutions. With the recent convergence of technologies you can see in this illustration the logical relationships between the library, academic computing and educational media. There are opportunities to partner with them to develop special databases and software applications (see Figures 4-5).

The enhanced capabilities available to libraries today mean we can become important players in development of knowledge systems. We can develop information packages on specific topics or disciplines that include a multitude of services and databases. We can design special institutional databases. We can also offer access to locally mounted multiple databases and Internet access to other shared resources.

FIGURE 4

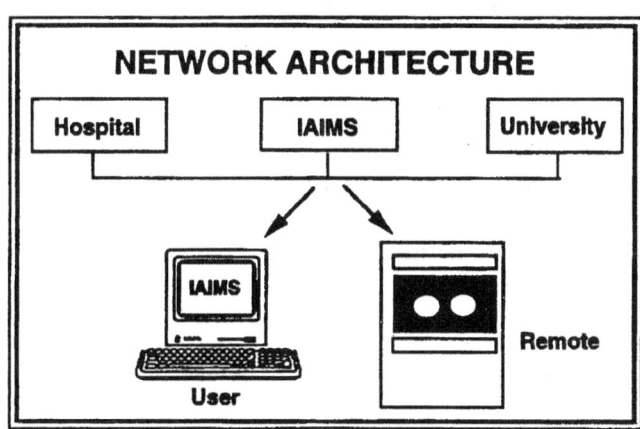

FIGURE 5

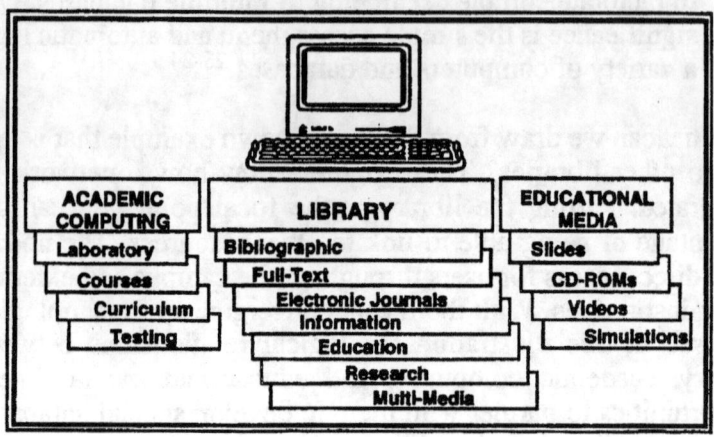

TRAINING AND AN ELECTRONIC EDUCATION CENTER

We have learned that in an environment so rich with resources and computers, it is vital to provide on-going training. Most universities have an academic computing unit responsible for providing technical support, consulting assistance on major hardware and software systems, and training for institutional users. However, many campuses do not provide these services free which often excludes junior faculty, residents, and students who do not have department accounts. It is generally the responsibility of the institution to nurture and maintain strong core support services. These core services generally include the provision and maintenance of computers and networks, the support of educational services, and the variety of programming services devoted to software development for key projects.

If the institution does not provide such a facility, it is a good role for the library. The Electronic Information Center or education center should include computer classrooms, open workstations, technical support for developing software applications, acquisitions and maintenance of hardware, training on use of the workstations, and a collection of software programs.

- *The Teaching Role of the Center.* Users must be taught how to use computers so they can benefit from the numerous available resources. A training program is not only desirable but essential. At Georgetown there is a computer classroom provided in the Biomedical Information Resources Center (BIRC) located in the Library. The BIRC is a 5,000 square foot facility that includes a large Macintosh computer classroom, a smaller IBM PC classroom, a general computer and audiovisual workstation area and two conference rooms with equipment to support special class assignments. There are over eighty computers of a mixed variety: IBM, Apple, Macintosh, and AT&T. Courses are given regularly and evening classes can be arranged for departments. Information access skills, use of computer based education programs, and basic instruction on use of personal computers are provided by the BIRC staff. In addition, training is given on database development, personal information management, and use of factual databases and knowledge systems for problem solving.
- *The Software Collection Program,* begun in 1982, currently includes over 400 titles with multiple copies of popular software. The staff, who also operate the center, work with faculty to encourage educational software development. Emerging from joint ventures with the departments are several pertinent and exciting informatics projects such as the Electronic Textbook in Human Physiology project funded through a Department of Education grant awarded to the Library, the Microanatomy Digital Slide Library supported with in-house resources, the fetal anomalies project funded through our NLM IAIMS grant, a human embryology program, an internal medicine program, and a few others.
- *Electronic Labs, Reading Rooms, Test Sites.* It is important for libraries to implement an education center so they are well positioned for the future. There is a natural progression from the education center to electronic reading rooms, laboratories, testing, and design sites. As more resources become available electronically, libraries will need to provide these facilities and capabilities.

STRATEGIC PLANNING FOR A VIRTUAL LIBRARY

Planning for the future requires a vision of what the library will become. Let me share my thoughts about the changes and issues we should address in developing a strategy that uplifts our libraries. In the first place we must develop a strategic plan that incorporates the mission of our institution. It should address financial resources, the organizational structure, changing technologies, and training needs of our users. It is our responsibility to examine several areas and develop mechanisms for coping with them. The strategic plan should include ways of dealing with the information explosion as a natural for information technology. User services will need to expand as will remote access. We need to examine the pros and cons of collection ownership versus access, and we must be especially knowledgeable about rights of copyright, so intellectual property rights and user rights are not abused or eliminated.

Our strategy should include long term goals for dealing with bibliographic utilities, collection development, computer networks, and information systems networks. A good way to gain experience and to find out what is most beneficial for us is to engage in pilot projects to test the waters. Entering into cooperative endeavors with other libraries to share resources and conduct research studies is another acceptable strategy.

A trend that has already emerged for library systems deals with accepted standards such as Z39.50 and EDI. Also common interfaces and common data exchange format must be developed so our users can navigate easily from one system to another.

To prepare ourselves for tomorrow we must develop electronic virtual libraries. As we look into the future, another paradigm emerges for libraries because the way we do our work will change considerably. We will provide new services:

1. Totally automated libraries will be a necessity in order to communicate and transmit information rapidly.
2. Document delivery systems will be essential. The LIS already has a module where users can search the literature and leave a message that they want the article or book. They can even tell us if they want it faxed, mailed, or if they will pick it up. Fax delivery of articles will become a standard operating procedure.

3. Digital full-text systems will allow us to digitize an article and store it for repeated transmission.
4. Electronic textbooks will become easier to adopt as we begin to conquer the problems of merging illustrations and texts.
5. Full-text databases of journal articles will be implemented in our in-house databases as the cost of computer storage diminishes.
6. CD-ROM systems will switch to magnetic tape for increased storage capabilities.
7. E-mail will be like Xerox™ machines. We will not be able to get along without it.
8. Using concepts from IAIMS such as databases and the institution's in-house network capabilities will place the library's resources on the internal campus or network menu.
9. National networks such as Internet and the emerging National Research and Education Network (NREN) enabled medical libraries to put their catalogs on networks. This will change the old established regional interlibrary loan services. In fact, it will open-up individual borrowing. Imagine lending directly to the user instead of the library.

The virtual library will be a distributed library system with a multitude of libraries that link together. The organization's databases will be available through the library. E-mail will double or triple, hypertext systems will be our new business as will projects in virtual reality, and national networks will connect us to global resources.

ROLE OF THE LIBRARIAN

The librarian will become a key resource for the institution. Instead of merely storing and retrieving information resources the librarian will oversee knowledge management. Finding knowledge, teaching, developing packages for the curriculum, establishing research methodology and supporting scholarship and scholarliness will be our domain. Librarians must examine more closely the cost of book and journal acquisitions versus the cost of providing access to resources. Printing and publishing on demand will be important in the virtual library world.

The fastest growing responsibility is our instructional role. Teaching users computer use, information access skills, navigation of the Internet and the information highway are the most promising pursuits for elevating our image. However, let us not forget our ability to organize images and new formats, and develop new databases. We must begin to develop important databases. Put up gophers, listservs, FTP. Librarians are already experts in using the Internet. Other Internet areas of increasing importance are the ability to put up gophers, listservs, and to handle file transfer protocols.

If we have a new vision with expanded roles, then we must reorganize our library operation. We must deploy staff differently, hire staff with new skills and train our existing staff. We must explore inter-departmental alliances not only with computer services and educational media, but also access multiple disciplinary departments. This is a perfect time to explore corporate partnerships that allow us to develop new products. Partnerships with publishers, vendors and hardware/software and communications firms are but a few examples.

FUTURE TECHNOLOGIES

I believe future technologies will impact libraries immensely. If we are aware of these technologies we can use them in the 90s to help us pioneer even further. In the future there will be:

- High speed computers with very fast CPUs, and computers on every desk.
- Thinking machines, parallel processors, free text searching at high speed.
- Very cheap storage–decreased prices in storage will impact CDs and magnetic tape systems:

    CD will be $1
    CD WORMs $5
    CD RAM $10
    Magnetic Storage costs will drop immensely.

- High quality desk-top workstations with expanded capabilities: TV Examine incorporation of, HDTV, photographs, and printed pages.

- Sound and image in realtime will further accelerate our work. Teleconferencing.
- Pen input devices–Notepad computers.
- Hand held computers–These products have a great chance for success.
- Photo capabilities on CDs are already here. We must incorporate them into our collections:

    Slides on a CD
    Print color from CD

- Multi Media–Already in use in the commercial world will impact homes and libraries.
- World-wide networks and satellite networks with transmission at very high speed will be available.

Rapidly emerging as popular tools are MOSAIC, World Wide Web (WWW), and Wide Area Information Servers (WAIS). There is important work being done to develop knowbot and intelligent agents to help us to retrieve the exact information we need without having to manually search through multiple systems. These breakthroughs will further accelerate and change how libraries provide knowledge resources.

Now that the nation has embarked on creating the information highway, there are new developing capabilities that we need to understand. The proposed information highway will bring together a network infrastructure that facilitates transmission. We are not yet certain of the technologies to be used. However, we are aware that enhancements to the Internet and other capabilities like FDDI, ATM, and cable will play an important role. We will adapt the converging technologies of computers, communication, and software systems. We will use multi media with voice, text, and image. Also, wireless computing networks just like wireless telephones will enter the scene.

Today's highway has three separate tracks: the Internet, telephone, and special networks. We transmit voice, data, and images over these three systems. Tomorrow's highway will combine the three in a transparent manner. We will want to engage in teleconferencing so we will need to install dedicated lines, satellites, and special "black boxes."

Technology is an important part of library business in the future. Changes we can expect are development of:

1. Digital libraries—Most major resources will be online, as will many books, images, and the history of mankind.
2. The book of the future will include electronic books and journals.
3. A new world of publishing with multiple options will emerge. Digital reproduction, color laser printing, scanning at high speed, and on-demand printing will take place.

CONCLUSION

While the groundwork is firmly established, libraries have a tremendously ambitious future and there is much work to be accomplished before implementation nears completion. We are on our way. Computers must thoroughly permeate the institution and research and administrative systems must be completed and integrated. We have a good start, but we believe our work will continue beyond ten years before the "ideal" implementation stage is reached. As for the dream of networking with other institutions on a national system—it is clearly on the horizon. We already network through the Internet and the new information super-highway will accelerate our capability.

There are many difficult questions we need to address:

1. How can we provide all the services users will expect?
2. Are we capable of serving an expanded user base?
3. Who will pay and what are the fees?
4. Can we hire trained staff? Can we afford them and are they available?

Obviously the library is not like it was in the past. It is changing rapidly. In conclusion, bear these two quotes in mind. One is from John Henry Newman who said, "To live is to change and to be perfect is to change often." The other statement was by Charles De Gaulle who said, "Embrace the inevitable."

NOTES

1. D. Kaye Gapen, "The Virtual Library: Knowledge, Society, and the Librarian," In *The Virtual Library: Visions and Realities* ed. by Laverna M. Saunders (Westport, CT: Meckler, 1993), 1-14.

2. B.V. Wahlde and N. Schiller, "Creating the Virtual Library: Strategic Issues," In *The Virtual Library: Visions and Realities* ed. Laverna M. Saunders (Westport, CT: Meckler, 1993), 15-46.

3. R. Kuzweil, "The Futurecast: The Future of Libraries, Part 3: The Virtual Library," *Library Journal* 117, no. 5 (March 15, 1992): 63-64.

4. Naomi C. Broering and B. Cannard, "Building Bridges LIS-IAIMS-BioSYNTHESIS," *Special Libraries* 79, no. 4 (Fall, 1988): 302-313.

5. Naomi C. Broering, "The miniMEDLINE SYSTEM TM: A Library-Based End-User search System," *Bulletin of the Medical Library Association* 73, no. 2 (April, 1985): 138-145.

6. H.M. Schoolman, "The Physician and the Medical Literature: From Index Medicus to MEDLARS to GRATEFUL MED and Beyond," *Archives of Dermatology* 122, no. 8 (August, 1986): 875-876.

7. Naomi C. Broering, J.S. Hylton, R. Guttman, and D. Eskridge, "BioSYNTHESIS: Access to a Knowledge Network of Health Sciences Databases," *Journal of Medical Systems* 75, no. 2 (1991): 139-153.

8. *The Library Information System Developed by the Dahlgren Memorial Library* (Washington, DC: Georgetown University, 1988).

9. T.J. Kahn and C. Orr, "Bioethicsline: An Overview for Searchers," *Medical Reference Services Quarterly* 3, no. 3 (Fall 1984): 1-21.

10. Naomi C. Broering, H.E. Bagdoyan, and J.S Hylton, "A Digital Full-Text Cancer and Genetics System to Enhance Patient Care," presentation, Seventeenth SCAMC Meeting, October 31-Nov. 3, 1993.

11. "PDQ: A New Database on Cancer Therapy," *NLM News* 37, no. 9 (September, 1982): 4.

12. S.M. Hubbard and V.T. DeVita Jr., "PDQ: An Innovation in Information Dissemination Linking Cancer Research and Clinical Practice," *Important Advances in Oncology* (1987): 263-277.

13. S.M. Hubbard, J.E. Henney, and V.T. DeVita Jr., "A Computer Data Bases for Information on Cancer Treatment," *New England Journal of Medicine* 316, no. 6 (February 5, 1987): 315-318.

14. Naomi C. Broering, H.E. Bagdoyan, and J.L. Banks, "Medical Facts File," presentation at the Seventeenth SCAMC Meeting, October 31-November 3, 1993.

15. M.S. Blois et al., "RECONSIDER: A Program for Generating Differential Diagnoses," *Proceeding of the Fifth Annual Symposium on Computer Applications in Medical Care* (New York: IEEE, 1981).

16. M.S. Blois et al., "RECONSIDER: An Experimental Diagnostic Prompting Program: UCSF ACP Computer Workshop 1983," *Medical Information Science* (1988): 7-24.

17. G.O. Barnett, J.I. Cimino, J.A. Hupp, and E.P. Hoffer, "DXplain: An Evolving Diagnostic Decision-Support System," *JAMA* 258, no. 1 (July 3, 1987): 67-74.

18. M.S. Packer et al., "Updating the DXplain Database," *Proceedings of the Twelfth Annal Symposium on Computer Applications in Medical Care* (New York: IEEE, 1988), 96-100.

19. M.S. Packer et al., "Evolution of DXplain: A Decision-Support System," *Proceedings of the Thirteenth Annual Symposium on Computer Applications in Medical Care* (New York: IEEE, 1989), 949-951.

20. R. Miller, F.E. Masarie, and J.D. Myers, "Quick Medical Reference (QMR) for Diagnostic Assistance," *M.D. Computing* 3, no. 5 (1986): 34-48.

21. H.R. Warner et al., "ILIAD As An Expert Consultant to Teach Differential Diagnosis," *Proceedings of the Twelfth Annual Symposium on Computer Applications in Medical Care* (New York: IEEE, 1988), 371-376.

22. R. Cundrick et al., "ILIAD as a Patient Care Simulator to Teach Medical Problem Solving," *Proceedings of the Thirteenth Annual Symposium on Computer Applications in Medical Care* (New York: IEEE, 1989), 902-906.

23. Naomi C. Broering, H. Bagdoyan, J. Hylton, and J. Strickler, "BioSYNTHESIS: Integrating Multiple Databases into a Virtual Database," *Proceedings of the Thirteenth Annual Symposium on Computer Applications in Medical Care* (New York: IEEE, 1989), 360-364.

24. Naomi C. Broering, H.R. Gault, and H. Epstein, "BioSYNTHESIS: Bridging the Information Gap," *Bulletin of the Medical Library Association* 77, no. 1 (January, 1989): 19-25.

PLENARY SESSION II: AN INTROSPECTIVE VIEW OF CHANGE AND CHOICE

Getting Past the Rapids: Individuals and Change

Linda Moore

SUMMARY. Both the nature and depth of the changes we are experiencing today are dramatically different from the changes experienced in the last fifty years or more. Using the metaphor of the North American Voyageur, this imaginative approach will give insights into how we as human beings can end the negative games we play, learn how to respond to change, and how we can approach change in a more positive way.

Good morning! You should be aware that I will wander around a lot as I talk just to keep you all awake on this Saturday morning,

---

This is an edited transcript of a motivational talk by Linda Moore, Chief Executive Officer, TranSKILLS, Hamilton, Ontario. Her presentation is based on concepts developed in her book *Getting Past the Rapids: Voyageur Lessons Learned* (1992), Hamilton, Ontario: TranSKILLS.

[Haworth co-indexing entry note]: "Getting Past the Rapids: Individuals and Change." Moore, Linda. Co-published simultaneously in *The Serials Librarian* (The Haworth Press, Inc.) Vol. 25, No. 3/4, 1995, pp. 95-109; and: *A Kaleidoscope of Choices: Reshaping Roles and Opportunities for Serialists* (ed: Beth Holley and Mary Ann Sheble) The Haworth Press, Inc., 1995, pp. 95-109. Multiple copies of this article/chapter may be purchased from The Haworth Document Delivery Center [1-800-3-HAWORTH; 9:00 a.m. - 5:00 p.m. (EST)].

with the Vancouver sunshine falling. I believe that dealing with individual change is critical to our well-being. Seeing you here this morning confirms that you do too.

I think the important thing I am seeing in life is definite patterns in terms of how human beings handle change. What I find even more fascinating is that the individual, a real person, is the one who actually creates an idea. What is even more fascinating is that when an individual develops a vision or an idea involving change or growth, that vision or thought does not go further until a collective group of individuals has a will and commitment to implement it.

THE VOYAGEUR METAPHOR

What I want to do with this issue of change is find a simple metaphor that explains change without being threatening. It is very hard when you have to look inside yourself and deal with change. I wanted to have something that is somewhat removed but something to which everyone can relate. I think that in many ways, all of us are explorers today. It is a very different landscape and a very different time, but like the North American voyageur, we have an unknown future landscape. I went back to the first explorers of North America and found that they were not Europeans. In my narrow thinking, I had started with the Europeans, but I was ignorant and misguided. I learned a great deal from this and I am not alone. One of the things we are finally starting to appreciate, primarily through our formal and informal education process, is that there were indigenous people (about two hundred and thirty million), who were in North America long before the Europeans. We believe that these people had a heritage going back to an earlier journey which brought them across the Bering Strait more than forty thousand years ago. They were explorers who moved down and through North America, exploring rivers, discovering new vegetation, and learning new ways to survive and thrive.

Another very interesting observation of which many people are unaware is that when the first European explorers and the voyageurs arrived, it was the native women who helped them through the first few winters. In most native tribes and most of the first nation assemblies, the women were the ones who made the moccasins, designed the snowshoes, and prepared the food. They were the ones who made the clothing. They were the ones who took the hunted animals that had been killed, and skinned them, cleaned them, stored the meat, and used the other parts for tools and other household items. Because the women had the ability and the skills to help the European voyageurs survive, the men from the tribes would encourage the women to meet with the Europeans and show them the skills they lacked, so that their particular group would get the first trading opportunities with these new Europeans. Many of our preconceived ideas about voyageurs and explorers need to be reconsidered in light of this growing awareness.

QUALITIES OF A VOYAGEUR

One of the things I find absolutely fascinating is that the people who are the first ones to explore a new place or experience have definite qualities that set them apart from others. These explorers are people who will go down a river not knowing where it is leading, whether that river is inside a computer, a physical journey, or an adventure into their minds. There are definite predispositions of these people.

Moore: Let's think about predispositions of explorers and voyageurs. How would you describe these qualities?
Audience: Risk-taking!
Moore: All right. That's one of them.
Audience: Curiosity!
Moore: What else?
Audience: Courage!
Moore: Lots of it. What else?
Audience: Sense of adventure and fun!
Listening and learning!
Imagination!

Think about some of those attributes in relationship to yourself. Another interesting observation is that the voyageurs created their own maps as they went. There was no map when they started. This is just like you and I experience today.

Most of us here today are over thirty and started off in a relatively traditional setting. In grade 8, we sat in a classroom and were asked, "What are you going to be?" And then we were asked the same question again in grade 9 and grade 10. I am forty-six and I still don't know what I am going to be! I still only see a little bit into the future. For example, I know today I am going to Vancouver Island, but what that journey has in store for me I cannot know until I experience it. So like us, the voyageurs created their maps as they went.

Moore: What else? Anything else?
Audience: Greed!
Moore: Actually, greed was not the key for most of the voyageurs and explorers. The important thing to them was going where no one they knew had gone. The people that backed the voyagers were into making money, and some call that greed. Most of the early explorers and the voyageurs were very poor, and received little remuneration for the risks they took.
Audience: Didn't they go for the adventure too?
Moore: They did . . . they definitely did! What else?
Audience: Faith!
Moore: Absolutely! One of the things that you have to believe is that you're going to survive! And so you have to have a lot of faith.

Let's see if there is anything else we can come up with as qualities of the voyageur. Another very important element is that they had to work with other people. The canoes and the boats that they used could not be handled by one person. Each person not only needed to know how to handle a canoe, but also had to bring other skills as well. You had to make sure you were with others who were excellent at hunting, could speak some of the native languages, knew a little bit of the trail, knew some of the vegetation, could build a fire, and knew how to develop a lean-to. That took a collective effort and this is a fact the early voyageurs knew well. The first boats used required as many as sixteen men, so it was imperative that the collective group supported each other on the journey. And, so it is for all of us in this room today!

Another fact that is very interesting, although rarely recorded, is that there were women explorers in North America! Now through Women Studies programs and newly released journals, the role of these women is being appreciated. Primarily, however, the early explorers were men.

There is no difference today than in earlier times in terms of voyageur skills. All these same qualities we have been discussing are the same skills that make people successful today, and these skills are more important than ever. The qualities and skills that people have, relating to thriving in a changing landscape, offer an opportunity for our on-going evolution. Each of us already has some of these attributes, but not all of them. We have to begin to understand that the way we were trained to behave was done with mastery. We were taught to be loyal, to find a job, and to stay with the same employer. We were taught that it was very important to be quiet and listen, to determine a single career and stick to it, and an entire series of other values.

But all of these skills and all of this learning are not the skills and experience we need today in order to survive and prosper. It is, rather, those qualities of the voyageur that we desperately need to acquire to ensure our well-being. As voyageurs, we have to step back, find the courage within ourselves, and get help from other people who have those skills. Then, we have to develop those skills and qualities in ourselves.

DEALING WITH CHANGE

What are some of the impacts on your day-to-day life that you are facing in terms of stress, change, and similar things?

Audience: Overworked.
Moore: Okay, what else?
Audience: Underpaid.
Moore: Perfect. What else?
Audience: Not enough equipment.
Moore: Now listen to what you are saying and think about it. I don't want to know right now about your work stresses. Talk to me about you! What are the obstructors and the strains on you personally?

Audience:	Uncertainty.
Moore:	Yes, what else?
Audience:	Money.
	The sense of separation.
Moore:	Yes, the idea that we have a separation between personal and professional lives. What else?
Audience	Not enough time.
Moore:	What else?
Audience:	Not enough staff.
	Constant interruptions.
	Too many meetings.
Moore:	Do you see how this is flipping back into work again? You know why we want to do that? Because this is forcing us to consider how we are really feeling about the changes around us.

I'm forty-six years old and the way I was educated and trained did not prepare me for what is going on in the world today. Thank goodness some of my personal life experience has prepared me! But all of this is scary. So, we attempt to keep moving away from the issue to someplace safer, where we do not have to talk about it. And this is one of the most natural of human behaviours.

One of the things that we have to think about in terms of stress is determining how much longer we are going to run away and not face it. How much longer are we going to put up with avoidance? Someone from the audience just said, "Until you retire." I do not think so. It is not a good idea. Your body and your mind and your spirit can only take so much.

RETRENCHMENT

The key is that we all have stress that impacts us everyday and we keep taking it, and taking it. It is what I call "retrenchment." We know that a change is here, or at least that it's coming. But we do not want to pay any attention to it. So, we retrench.

IGNORING CHANGE

When we retrench, we ignore the change by keeping ourselves distracted. How do we distract ourselves so we can ignore the change?

Audience:	We say, 'I have no time right now.'
Moore:	Exactly. We say, 'I'm so busy today. I'm busy at work and I'm busy with my family, so I can't really pay attention to what is changing.' What else?
Audience:	Procrastinate.
Moore:	Yes, we always say we're going to change, but we really have no intention of doing anything. So what we do is, ignore it. How else do we ignore it? How do we distract ourselves?
Audience:	We get the person who has already changed or learned a new skill to do the work for us.
Moore:	Exactly! We say, 'Oh, I don't have time to learn it right now. I can't sit down and learn this. Will you do it for me, please?'

When I sit down at my personal computer at TransSKILLS, I rely on a lady that works with me. Her name is Diana. Diana is very computer literate and has taken the time to learn. She comes into my office daily, and rescues me from myself and my avoidance of change.

Moore:	Is there anything else that we do to distract ourselves?
Audience:	We say the change won't last.

We are masters at this. But eventually you know that change IS happening and it WILL last! We also begin to appreciate that while we ignore changes, we are increasing our chances to adapt. Ignoring a change is the first step all of us take, but eventually, we move to a next step in the process of change.

RESISTING CHANGE

The next thing we do is rebel. We cannot totally ignore a change, so we resist it. And believe me, every single human being goes through this stage. I don't care how much of a voyageur they are, everyone goes through this process. Now, the way we resist is to talk about change. We don't do anything, but we talk about it a lot. As an example, we can talk all we want about the changes that impact your profession throughout this week, but if you go home and do exactly what you did before, and do not begin to consider the impacts on you and become proactive, then no change has occurred in you.

THE GAMES WE PLAY

The other way that we resist change is playing some pretty deadly games with ourselves and other people. I have four of these games from Eric Burne who collaborated with Jackie Schiff to develop "Transactional Analysis." Their approach is a very good articulation of human behaviour.

AIN'T IT AWFUL!

The first thing in the series of these games is, "Ain't It Awful!" Now, about what do you play "Ain't It Awful?" Give me an example.

Audience: Downsizing.
Moore: Wow, ain't it awful?
Audience: Outsourcing!
Moore: Ain't it awful? What else?
Audience: Hiring practices.
Moore: Now, see, we're doing it again! We're talking about work again, not you personally! What other things do you play "Ain't It Awful" about?
Audience: Taxes.
Moore: Yes. We're Canadians, we can talk. We're allowed "Ain't It Awful." What else?
Audience: The National Debt.
Moore: Whoever's, all of them. Okay, what else?
Audience: Teenage daughter.
Moore: Teenage children, period. I kicked mine out, and it's much better now. Much better. All right, what else?
Audience: Not enough vacation time.
Moore: Okay, that gives you a little hint on how we play that game!

YES ... BUT

Now, some brave soul, after all the "Ain't It Awful," has an idea to solve a problem. They say, "I think I have an idea." Then they explain their idea, and then we begin the next game. "Well, yes, that's very good, but it has been tried before. We did it once, and it did not work." Now, we are being somewhat facetious in talking about this, but what percentage of time and energy do you think that these two games absorb?

Audience: Seventy percent.
Eighty percent.
Moore: Around ninety percent.

I recently went to a party and I was going to practice not playing either one of these games at a social event. After about fifteen minutes, I had nobody to talk to! For example, I started talking with someone about the arts. I thought that was a pretty safe topic. "But you know how much they cut back our theatre?" "No, I didn't." And away it went into "Ain't It Awful!" These two games eat up about ninety percent of conversational time, and it happens all the time.

ATTACK/DEFEND

Now, the next game in this process is "Attack/Defend." If I were the one who finally had a suggestion or solution which everyone played, "Yes ... But" with, I would be discouraged. I would be upset because I am trying to come up with ideas and nothing is happening. In defense of myself and my ideas, I would begin to attack others. Part of what we need to do is support each another and not get into these kinds of games. But once you have started this whole attack/defend mode, the situation often dissolves and becomes very destructive.

We do it just as much in our personal life. We like to avoid facing it. Instead, we discuss it as an ailment of our workplace, and/or being the fault of someone else. We never want to think we are part of the game. Well, we are! The discipline it takes not to play is intense. But, if we are conscious of the problem, it helps to reduce wasted energy and increases our ability to cope with change.

COVER YOUR BACKSIDE

Now, the final game we will discuss this morning is "Cover Your Backside." If we continue to play games this is exactly where we end up. So, what we end up doing is creating unbelievable amounts of administration and structures so we can survive the "Attack/Defend" game. What kind of "administratrivia" do you have in your profession?

Audience: Reports nobody reads.
Moore: What else?
Audience: Record keeping policy.

Another example of "Cover Your Backside" in the private sector is expense control. An example is keeping track of how many hours you were away, how many kilometers/miles you went, etc. Ludicrous! Because this is getting to the point where everything details activity rather than accountability. Everything becomes a matter of following the process. You are asked, "Did you fill out the forms?" rather than, "Did you get the job done?"

I have an example from a company where I once worked. The company had a manual inventory control system in all their stores. This is a chain of one hundred retail stores, and every night, each store manager had to write down, by hand, from the ticket stubs everything about the item sold: the size, the colour, and the sales number. The people at the head office were wondering why they did not seem to be getting the sales they had expected. I said, "You have a policy that says, if they do not get their inventory sheet in the mail to you by seven o'clock each night, they go on suspension, or worse! Don't you think that has something to do with it?" So then I said, "Maybe you should automate it, and maybe they should just concentrate on sales!" And they said, "Maybe, maybe." Well, to make a long story short, they implemented the system and it made a difference in the sales. They had become so detail-oriented that they forgot customers, merchandising the stores, and that the outcome must always take priority over the game of "Cover Your Backside."

If you were a voyageur, going down a river, which in metaphor, we are, do you think you would be making supply lists as you paddled through a swiftly moving current? I doubt it! The voyagers did have accountability–accountability to stay alive. Some of them were literate, and some of them some kept journals. But I do not think they wrote their journals as they paddled rapids, but rather at the fireside in the evening.

RETRENCHMENT OR SOLUTIONS

The final step before facing true change is "retrenchment." We go back and look for answers in old solutions that worked before. We see change coming; we cannot ignore it anymore; we have to deal with it. We try to deal with it by using our existing information and solutions. What are some of these solutions? In Canada we form a task force if it is really important. We form a committee if it is not as important.

What else do we do in terms of retrenching or solutions? Canada loves commissions even better than task forces! If you have a task force, you have to write a report. Then you take that report, and you give it to somebody, usually, another committee. No matter how much energy we expend to avoid new solutions and/or change, in the end, we have to change.

CATALYST FOR CHANGE

Eventually, we have to change. The catalyst causing change differs for different people. But a lot of it has to do with the tolerance of the status quo. This is a sad example to use, but it is the most graphic one I know–males or females staying in abusive situations. For some people, a relationship becomes history the moment someone even begins to physically or emotionally abuse them. There is a continuum, extending to people who are almost willing to have their lives placed on the line, and they will stay. Depending on your tolerance for an existing scenario, you will stay or not stay in a situation that is not necessarily positive. Some people like me have a very low tolerance for the status quo if it is not moving them forward. For other people, it is different. Someone from the audience this morning said, "I guess until I retire, I will have put up with this." You are much, much worthier than that. If you are miserable, do not stay in a marriage or relationship, a job, or whatever. You are far too valuable as a human being to do that.

Now, once you find your tolerance level for change, you have to bring back the qualities of the voyageur and say, "What can I do about this? How can I work on this?" What I want to do now is give you a couple of ideas, as voyageurs, how to deal with some of this change.

VOYAGEURING TIPS

As a first step, scout the landscape. There are all kinds of people around who have been through similar changes. I remember that in the early eighties I said that we were probably going through the biggest change since the Industrial Revolution. I arrived at that thought as I read about the pre-Industrial Revolution. The writers and the individuals they described at the time exemplified the patterns I was seeing all around me in 1981! What we want to do first, then, is scout the landscape and discover who is out there, who has also been going through this, and who has been successful.

Next, you need to hang out with voyageurs. You need to hang out with the individuals who are facing change head on. Learn by reading about them, watch them on television, watch videos about their lives, or meet today's voyageurs in person. Do not hang out with people who are going to play negative games.

You also must learn to take it a day at a time. None of this is trite, if you really practice it. We are going through such massive changes at this time and at our age (at least some of us), it is difficult to deal with. What do you think voyageurs did when they were going down a river in a canoe and they heard the waterfall sounds? They did not know what they were about to face but they took it moment by moment and did not worry about the danger until they had to face it. Sometimes, they would send a volunteer to scout ahead to see what was happening. That metaphor is exactly what we have to do here.

Next, you need to know that you are allowed to hit the shore. When you are rafting or canoeing, and you are starting to run into a piece of a river or a lake that you do not know or understand, think of pulling into the shore and scouting the landscape. We need to think about deciding on a course of action. But, how many of us take time to think about ourselves, our lives, our priorities, and how we want to deal with our own lives in a proactive, positive way?

I have a friend who is a technocrat and walks before he thinks. He can do anything that has to do with technology. I let him install the first office network. I let him bring up the Internet first, and when he gets all the bugs ironed out and he knows it is a safe bet, I will get it. I will stay on the shore a little longer. My friend will go right on into anything new. His attitude is, "I know it sounds like rapids, but when we get there, we will figure it out."

Another hint is that we have to learn to "portage." I have a strategic plan and in this plan, I determined that by August, we are to be at a specific place. Now, the fact that the whole world changed in June means that we have a choice to go all the way with the original plan or change mid-stream, which may slow down reaching the goal. But often, the only way forward is to portage around a problem.

One of the hints in portaging is saying, "I am going to do something differently," but not tell anybody you are doing it. Do not say to your supervisor, "Oh, I think I'd like to try this, is that okay?" because your supervisor is probably going to say "No!" Just do it and see if it works. If it does not work, you can just keep quiet about it and you will have learned something.

Another "portage" tip is that you are allowed to jump the canoe. I can not say this strongly enough. If you do not like what you do, the people you work with, the organization you are in, the person you are married to, your children, you can get rid of them, maybe all at the same time! I am not being entirely facetious.

I had a wonderful job. I was a single mom with a wonderful job in a big company. I had plenty of security and opportunity. I was young, aggressive, and miserable. It took so much to quit, but I was not prepared to stay miserable. Quitting was the best decision I ever made in my life, because other wonderful things have happened since. I probably would not have experienced these wonderful things if I had stayed where I was. The problem is, until you jump off the cliff, you do not know if you are going to fly or crash. So we stand on the edge teetering, and we hope either somebody is going to push us off, or we drop off so that we do not have to make the decision for ourselves!

Moore: What kinds of things will cause you to change? How bad does it have to get before you do?
Audience: I could get sick.
Moore: All right, that's one way. Lots of people are doing that these days.
Audience: We lose our jobs.
Moore: Yes! What other reasons will cause us to change?
Audience: Winning the lottery.
Moore: Yes. Winning the lottery, I dream about it all the time.

About five percent of the people that I talk to about all these things change because they see an opportunity. I have been looking the past few days at people to see which of you perceive this as a time of opportunity. Some of you are ready to stay and others see new changes and are ready to jump the canoe.

I will give you an example of an opportunity I see. I am going back to Ontario and hire a part-time serials librarian. I have massive amounts of information that I have been trying to figure out how to organize. Until now, I had never thought of asking somebody from a library with skills in organizing information. I am going to hire this person part-time to start organizing all of our information. I am typical of a small business. What a wonderful new market niche for serials librarians! But, you have to see the opportunity. One way is to come to conferences of your own peers. Another way is by hanging out with people other than librarians. You need to spend time with those outside your comfort zone and area of expertise.

The final piece is to do whatever it takes. I am not talking about being unethical. I am not talking about doing something to be harmful to your soul. I am saying, that whatever it takes, do it. Remember the voyageurs and think about that metaphor. Whatever it took to stay alive in the winter . . . Whatever it took to find a portage . . . Whatever it took to get the canoes through the rapids . . . Whatever it took to understand the people that they met . . . Whatever it took, they did.

We are in exactly the same position today. Not everybody is adventurous enough to go down a river rapids. If you cannot travel the river, you can be a backer. If you believe in somebody who is a voyageur, you can support them. You do not have to go down the same river, but you can back them. You can also be their outfitter. You can be somebody who can use your skills and your expertise, and you can help the voyageur get down the river. For example, I think that any of you can help the small business people who are getting started because they need information desperately. This does not necessarily have to go through a traditional library or a virtual library. You can actually be part of that. You can be an outfitter.

But ultimately, you still must go down the river by yourself. You can have people to support you, but only you can make that decision. What I am trying to tell you today is that there are all kinds of ways to approach change. Not all of them are easy, and not everybody is going to do each one of them well. We all go through the same process but each in our own unique way.

As a voyageur, I have found that unless people share and help each other, nothing happens. When we quit talking about important things, many people get very frantic, because we have disconnected ourselves from each other far too much.

It is important as we go through this change to accept other people's fears, to hold their hand, let them cry on your shoulder, and drag them along. We need to be there for each other. We do not consider discussing soulful issues in a group, but rather only with a very special friend. We feel it is far too intimate. We cannot allow the distance between each other to continue. We need to be intimate right now. We are going through too much change. We have to talk about it in meetings. We have to talk about it when we are together. We have to celebrate the fact that we are making it through another day. It is very important. But, I think it is also an exciting and challenging time. And, I think that it is a time of anticipation. It is a time we need to approach with a lot of respect for each other. I think we have to approach it with enthusiasm, and I think we have to approach it with a light heart and a lot of joy.

[Editor's note: The talk concluded with the reading of a poem by Maya Angelou, "A Rock, A River, A Tree."]

PLENARY SESSION III: CHOOSING CHANGE: NEW PRODUCTS AND NEW SKILLS

Electronic Chemistry Journals: Elemental Concerns

Richard Entlich

SUMMARY. Experimental scholarly electronic journals have existed in a variety of forms for several years. The CORE (Chemistry Online Retrieval Experiment) Project, one of the oldest and largest efforts, is now in its fifth and final year. Cornell University's Mann Library, Bellcore, the American Chemical Society (ACS), Chemical Abstracts Service and OCLC have created a system which will provide networked access to over half a million pages of machine-readable text and graphics from ACS journals. The objectives of this collaboration have been to study the numerous technical, logistical, economic, and sociological issues which face publishers, libraries, and scholars in the shift from paper to electronic dissem-

---

Richard Entlich is Preservation Librarian and Full Text Genre Specialist at the Albert R. Mann Library, Cornell University, Ithaca, NY.

[Haworth co-indexing entry note]: "Electronic Chemistry Journals: Elemental Concerns." Entlich, Richard. Co-published simultaneously in *The Serials Librarian* (The Haworth Press, Inc.) Vol. 25, No. 3/4, 1995, pp. 111-123; and: *A Kaleidoscope of Choices: Reshaping Roles and Opportunities for Serialists* (ed: Beth Holley and Mary Ann Sheble) The Haworth Press, Inc., 1995, pp. 111-123. Multiple copies of this article/chapter may be purchased from The Haworth Document Delivery Center [1-800-3-HAWORTH; 9:00 a.m. - 5:00 p.m. (EST)].

© 1995 by The Haworth Press, Inc. All rights reserved.

ination of scholarly research. The library's focus has been on how to ensure that scholars retain unimpeded physical and intellectual access to journal contents after this transition takes place.

INTRODUCTION

The ancient Greeks believed that all matter was composed of four elements. We now know that this is a slight oversimplification. The modern periodic table of the elements now contains 106 entries. Thus, it may at first seem odd that a Veronica search for "Periodic Table" returns numerous pointers to a set of element descriptions containing only 84 items. Even odder, despite the disclosure of this out-of-date information on a widely read newsgroup in February of 1993,[1] the data still exists on the net and can be accessed from several different gopher servers.

Unfortunately, there is no shortage of outdated and otherwise dubious quality information on the Internet. There are, after all, no gatekeepers to keep it out, and no reliable procedures for determining the accuracy of existing networked information. In fact, the rush to fill network sites with machine-readable texts naturally favors informal material such as discussion group archives and older material which has slipped into the public domain.

Commercial and scholarly society publishers of reliable chemical information have been slow to appear on the Internet due to uncertain economics and technical limitations, even though machine-readable text is available. For example, Chemical Abstracts Service (CAS), a division of the American Chemical Society (ACS), has made the full-text of most ACS journals, and that of several other publishers, available via STN International since 1984.[2] Despite the advantage of full-text searchability, these electronic texts are not adequate substitutes for their print counterparts because they lack important symbols and graphical elements, such as figures, photos, and graphs.

In the late 1980s, ACS entered into an agreement with Cornell University's Mann Library, Bellcore, and OCLC to build an electronic library of previously published ACS journals. The intent was to take approximately 200 journal-years of machine-readable text, combine it with available indexing and abstracting data from CAS, add back the missing graphical components, and make it all available to interested users at Cornell via the Internet. This work was to have been completed by the end of the calendar year 1992.

Eighteen months after the originally proposed completion date, we are still not done, and we have scaled back our original plans. However, despite setbacks, we have completed work on two independently-developed interfaces and expect to have processed more than half a million pages by the time the project comes to a conclusion.

Using the CORE Project for example and context, I would like to discuss our initial goals, some of the obstacles we have encountered, and some of my thoughts on where electronic publishing of scholarly journals might be headed. Many of these issues have implications for librarians, and serialists in particular.

PARTICIPANTS

CORE is a large undertaking, making use of the particular skills and strengths of each of the five collaborators. Here is a rundown of some of the most significant work carried out by each:

- The American Chemical Society

  - Provision of original and processed data (machine-readable text, paper, and microfilm from which to scan page images, plus some scanned images)
  - Development of document structure specification for text

- Bellcore

  - Conversion ACS proprietary text markup to Standard Generalized Markup Language (SGML)
  - Scanning of full-page images and extraction of graphics
  - Interface software design

- Chemical Abstracts Service

  - Provision of indexing and abstracting data

- Cornell University (Mann Library)

- Overall project administration
- Network and systems integration and support
- Management of user studies

- OCLC

  - Database design and implementation
  - Provision of text searching engine
  - Interface software design

The project has also benefited from gifts and loans of hardware, software, and data from a number of commercial organizations.

OBJECTIVES

From the library's perspective, the primary goal of CORE is to create a system with a substantial depth and breadth within a single discipline–a critical mass. It is hoped that such a database will be regarded by users as a key resource, to be consulted routinely. Only in this manner can we evaluate the true impact of such a system on the scholarly communication process. Other goals include:

- The design and implementation of a prototypical computer system, database, and networking infrastructure for the storage and delivery of primary scientific literature in electronic form.
- The development, testing, and refinement of user interfaces for searching and displaying full-text with graphics.
- Investigation of various mechanisms for storage and presentation of text and graphics, and their impact on the performance of servers, networks, and users.
- Investigation and analysis of the impact that availability of primary scholarly literature in electronic form has on the information seeking and usage patterns of researchers.
- The generation of quantitative metrics which support the development of equitable charging mechanisms satisfactory to both publishers and academic institutions.

The passage of five years has not had a uniform impact on the achievement and continuing relevance of these goals. Faster networks and workstations, and cheaper mass storage have somewhat de-emphasized (though certainly not eliminated) concerns about how to manage, maintain, and deliver large amounts of graphical data. On the other hand, there is still much to be done in the area of user interface design and many unanswered questions about the impact of such systems on users. As the body of machine-readable text available from publishers grows, issues surrounding text conversion and presentation have taken on greater significance. Economic issues remain largely unresolved.

DATA

The nature of the data in the CORE Project distinguishes it from many other electronic journal endeavors. We have both richly marked-up machine-readable full-text *and* scanned images of printed pages, containing both text and graphics. These two forms of data have dramatically different properties, with significant implications for the journal delivery systems created from them.

Machine-readable text is compact, with inherently low storage costs, and is also fast to deliver, even over moderate speed networks. The addition of markup enhances searching and the ability to use customized fonts, highlighting, hypertext linking, and a customized layout.

Bitmaps, on the other hand, are bulky, requiring expensive, high-maintenance storage systems and are also slow, necessitating minimum Ethernet-speed networks for acceptable performance. They permit relatively faithful reproduction of a previously published printed page, but display device resolution often exacts compromises which degrade readability. However, when dealing with an existing corpus of print publications, bitmaps may be the only mechanism available to capture graphical elements.

Having data available in both forms, we could develop a hybrid system emphasizing the strengths of each. Unfortunately, preparation of the data for such a system has required an enormous data processing effort, the difficulty of which we seriously underestimated.

The effort to optimize the presentation and functionality of retrospectively processed machine-readable data has resulted in highly fragmented articles. Those who think of serials check-in as an onerous task now may be less than pleased with a system in which the average *article* consists of:

- text from two different sources
- two full-page bitmap files for each page (one at 300 dots/inch and one at 100 dots/inch)
- each figure in a separate file
- thumbnail reductions of the figures in a separate file
- equations in a separate file

A typical six page article with a modest one graphic per page thus consists of nearly two dozen separate components. Modern electronic journals, conceived in machine-readable form from the outset should be able to avoid much, if not all, of this fragmentation. However, retrospective conversion of even very good data (whether from an analog source or from other machine-readable formats not originally intended for distribution to subscribers) can be extraordinarily complex, time-consuming, and expensive.

SYSTEM FEATURES

Given the tremendous effort involved in producing such a system, one may legitimately ask why we did not just scan pages for display and use the text for searching, as has been done in other retrospective journal conversion projects. The answer is that we wanted to see how far we could push the available data and produce a system with enhanced functionality. Some of the features available in CORE's hybrid data interface (called Scepter, developed at OCLC) include:

- graphical abstracts (a scrollable set of thumbnails of all graphics)
- individual pop-up bitmaps of graphics from icons embedded in the text
- hypertext citation links
- searching on symbols and diacritics
- highlighting of query terms within documents
- posting of query term frequency within article subsections

- fine level fielded searching (two dozen indexes)
- display of several hundred special characters and symbols

Many of these features derive from the SGML markup included with the text.[3] Combined with the pop-up graphics, which have been extracted from the full-page bitmaps,[4] Scepter provides access to the complete contents of the original printed page. However, despite the drawbacks of full-page bitmaps, and the redundancy that they represent in this system, Scepter provides access to them as well. One may well be prompted to ask why.

First, the various conversions carried out on the data are not perfect. The bitmapped images more reliably represent the content of the original publication. They are also more comfortable for some users, simply because they are in a familiar format. In addition, they provide a basis for high-quality printed output, which very nearly approximates that of the original publication.

Why is a project like CORE concerned about printed output? Are not such systems suppose to replace print? There is, as yet, no evidence that such a transition is taking place. Numerous electronic journal experiments show that users still prefer print on paper for close reading of articles, even if they will accept screen presentations for searching and browsing.[5] In fact, the different characteristics of computer displays and paper mean that an optimal reading experience for the user requires data presentation which is specifically geared to the characteristics of the display medium. This fact alone should provide producers of *de novo* electronic journals with a great deal of incentive to use a flexible, descriptive markup, like SGML, which promotes reusability of data for multiple purposes.

We are excited about what we have been able to accomplish with CORE, but it should not be looked upon as a model for retrospective conversion of scholarly journals, since our data is so unique. More realistically, most conversions will have only full-page bitmaps available for display and perhaps a machine-readable bibliographic entry for searching. In fact, CORE also provides users with an interface that can display only full-page bitmaps (Pixlook from Bellcore) just so we can compare the efficacy of such a system with that of the hybrid interface.

IMPACT ON LIBRARIES AND USERS

Although we have collected some user data in the form of transaction logs, interviews, and surveys, our major user studies will not occur until late in 1994. We hope that these results will provide insight into the many unanswered questions about the efficacy of electronic publishing and its role in scholarship. However, it is not at all clear that usage data from studies in chemistry will have relevance for users in other disciplines.

It has already been postulated by Teresa Harrison et al. that ". . . adoption of e-journals by scholars will not solely be determined by technical innovations or by economic factors, but by the extent with which a journal's design is consistent with the social practices of the discipline and the extent to which it reflects the discipline's need for information and communication."[6] The nature of e-journal experiments and projects, along with their acceptance by users in the past few years goes a long way towards validating Harrison's statement. An examination of some factors which distinguish scholarly disciplines may be useful in predicting how rapidly electronic journals will make inroads and thus impact the serials practices for a particular library.

The existing level of computer/network use within the discipline. In other words, how central are computers to the daily work of scholars in the field. This impacts both on the degree of comfort users have with computers, and also on the likelihood that they already have easy access to equipment. Broadly speaking, one might predict a split between STM (science, technology, and medicine) versus the humanities/social sciences. However, it would be wise to avoid overgeneralization as there are pockets of computer illiterates in STM, as well as avid computer users in the humanities/social sciences.

Nevertheless, an examination of the literature reveals some fairly predictable trends. Commentators on and proponents of electronic journals in computer-rich fields (e.g., physics and math) rarely if ever mention the need for a computer and network connection (as well as the expertise to use them) as a barrier to the adoption of e-journals.[7] On the other hand, those in the humanities and social sciences, where both funding to purchase equipment and the training to use them are issues, nearly always do.[8] Even the medical community, which may generally be thought of as relatively well-equipped and technically literate, has expressed some doubts.[9]

Strength and/or cohesiveness of existing publishing enterprises. Although non-traditional electronic publishing has had a major influence on scholarly communication in a few small sub-disciplines, [10] most disciplines have too many concerns about the maintenance of quality and credibility associated with existing society or commercial publishers in their disciplines to permit radical changes in publishing practice. Most will wait for existing publishers to take a leadership role. If there is a strong central publisher in the field, change can take place more smoothly than if there are numerous competing publishers, each of which may see some benefit from promulgating its own electronic publishing standards.

The rate of growth of the literature. Pressure towards electronic publishing is heavily fueled by the extent of the serials crisis within a discipline. If rapidly burgeoning rates of publication have led to an explosion in the cost and quantity of titles, and a corresponding cutback in the percentage of the field's output available at any one institution, a move to electronic journals will seem very attractive to users. Again, this is most likely to be the case in STM disciplines.

Citation methodology. Historians and others in the humanities have concerns about the authenticity of electronic documents.[11] The lack of pagination and the ease with which machine-readable texts can be altered are grave flaws from the humanists perspective.[12] Also, humanists require access to intermediate documents, showing corrections and changes, documents which are rarely preserved in electronic archives.[13]

Strength of ties to the past. In many disciplines, materials published more than a few years ago are much less frequently consulted than more recent publications. Thus the prospect of having a cutoff between an all-electronic corpus and a print archive is not all that daunting. However, in fields which consult the old as often, if not more often, than the new, a dichotomous collection is highly undesirable.

Importance of rapid access to new publishing. In other words, how rapidly are new developments coming? Some disciplines developed active preprint distribution systems long before electronic distribution of articles was feasible, because they could not tolerate the delays inherent in traditional publishing. Such disciplines, which have already adjusted to the changes necessitated by the domination of preprints over established journals, are obviously ripe for transition to electronic distribution.

Existence of a standard document format. Electronic publishing is greatly simplified if documents are prepared in a standardized fashion. If authors are already submitting manuscripts to print publications in a standardized format, then there is one less barrier to electronic publication.

Character set utilized. As is evidenced by the overwhelming predominance of ASCII in existing electronic journals, disciplines which can manage with ASCII have an easier time getting published. Not only is author preparation of ASCII manuscripts simpler, but there are few compatibility issues for readers of ASCII documents.

CONCLUSIONS

Despite the likelihood of widely varying timetables for penetration and acceptance of electronic journals, some prognosticators have forecast the imminent demise of paper journals and, consequently, the elimination of any role for traditional publishers or for librarians.

Choosing change puts librarians in a much better position to weather the worst impacts of the publishing revolution. The CORE Project collaboration has brought Mann Library experience and access to expertise which could not have been purchased at any price. It also brought hardware which could have been bought at a price, but not one we could necessarily have afforded. We are quite pleased, for example, that one of the legacies of CORE will be several Unix workstations. Unix workstations are becoming more and more of an essential part of the information delivery infrastructure on the Internet.

Besides embracing technology, we need to recognize the many opportunities for applying traditional skills in the newly emerging infosphere. One productive avenue I have found for identifying such opportunities is simply to follow the emerging literature describing proposed electronic journal systems, or to use the emerging systems and look for the weak points. Some areas where it is clear that too much faith is being placed in technology (or too little thought given to its limitations) are cataloging, classification, and preservation.

For example, there seems to be a fairly widespread notion that full-text indexing (usually via some version of WAIS) provides all the organizational structure necessary for exploring the literature of a discipline. However, as has been pointed out by Myers et al., "Information is not self-organizing, and librarians are the ones trained to organize it."[14] Cataloging on the Internet is an entirely arbitrary affair, with even basic descriptive elements such as titles, being modified at the whim of the gopher or WorldWideWeb administrator.[15] The creation and maintenance of permanent archives has not been given sufficient attention.

Poorly thought out scenarios need to be forcefully challenged by librarians, with clear, cogent, experience-based arguments on why they will not work. We need to develop credible and workable plans for cataloging and classifying networked resources, insuring equitable access to information through negotiation of reasonable site-license agreements, and guaranteeing long-term preservation and access of machine-readable resources.

In order for libraries to step confidently into these roles, librarians need to accelerate both the acquisition of relevant computing equipment and the expertise to use it. Electronic journal advocates who envision a continuing role for libraries have been justifiably critical of the state of readiness of most libraries to take advantage of newly emerging opportunities.[16]

Choosing change means controlling our destinies. The years ahead are likely to be exciting but dangerous ones for serialists. Standing on the sidelines and waiting for change to come may seem safe, but on the information superhighway, it is a sure way to become a casualty.

ACKNOWLEDGMENTS

The CORE project is a collaboration led by Cornell University and includes, in addition to Cornell, Bellcore, the American Chemical Society, Chemical Abstracts Service, and OCLC. Among the people who direct this project and contribute most of the work to it are Jan Olsen, Richard Entlich, and John Udall of the Albert R. Mann Library, Cornell University; Lorrin Garson of the American Chemical Society; Lorraine Normore of Chemical Abstracts Service; Michael Lesk, Dennis Egan, Dan Ketchum, Joel Remde and Carol Lochbaum of Bellcore; and Stu Weibel, Mark Bendig, Jean Godby, and Eric Miller of OCLC. The collaborators are grateful for the support of Digital Equipment Corporation, Sony Corporation of America, Springer-Verlag, Sun Microsystems, Inc., and Thinking Machines, Inc.

NOTES

1. Bill Quimby, "Periodic Table of the Elements," *PACS-L* (26 February 1993).

2. Stu Borman, "Advances in Electronic Publishing Herald Changes for Scientists," *Chemical & Engineering News*, 71, no. 24 (14 June 1993): 10-12, 14-16, 18, 21-24.

3. For a description of the role of SGML in CORE, see Erik Jul, "SGML plays important role in electronic publishing," *OCLC Newsletter*, no. 200 (November/December 1992): 13-15.

4. See Michael Lesk, "The CORE Electronic Chemistry Library," in *Proceedings of the Fourteenth Annual International ACM/SIGIR Conference on Research and Development in Information Retrieval*, Chicago, IL, 13-16 October 1991 (New York: ACM Press, 1991), 93-112, for details on the graphics extraction process.

5. Edward J. Valauskas, "Paper-Based or Digital Text: What's Best?" *Computers in Libraries* 14, no. 1 (January 1994): 44-47.

6. Teresa M. Harrison, Timothy Stephen, and James Winter, "Online Journals: Disciplinary Designs for Electronic Scholarship," *The Public-Access Computer Systems Review* 2, no. 1 (1991): 25-38.

7. Paul Ginsparg, "Computopia, Here we Come," *Physics Today* 45, no. 6 (June 1992): 13, 15, 100; Andrew M. Odlyzko, "Tragic Loss or Good Riddance? The Impending Demise of Traditional Scholarly Journals," *Surfaces* 4, no. 105 (28 February 1994): 1-45.

8. Scott A. Shamp, "Prospects for Electronic Publication in Communication: A Survey of Potential Users," *Communications Quarterly* 40, no. 3 (Summer 1992): 297-304; Matthew B. Gilmore and Donald O. Case, "Historians, Books, Computers, and the Library," *Library Trends* 40, no. 4 (Spring 1992): 667-686; Michael E. Stoller, "Electronic Journals in the Humanities: A Survey and Critique," *Library Trends* 40, no. 4 (Spring 1992): 647-666; James H. Sweetland, "Humanists, Libraries, Electronic Publishing, and the Future," *Library Trends* 40, no. 4 (Spring 1992): 781-803.

9. "Journals in Bits and Bytes: Electronic Medical Journals," *The New England Journal of Medicine* 326, no. 3 (16 January 1992): 195-197.

10. Gary Taubes, "Publication by Electronic Mail Takes Physics by Storm," *Science* 259, no. 5099 (26 February 1993): 1246-1248.

11. Gilmore and Case, 675.

12. Stoller, 655-656.

13. Sweetland, 783-784.

14. Judy E. Myers, Thomas C. Wilson and John H. Lienhard, "Surfing the Sea of Stories: Riding the Information Revolution," *Mechanical Engineering* 114, no. 10 (October 1992): 60-65.

15. For example, Odlyzko (q.v.) can be found in Gopherspace under the following self-styled titles (among others): Andrew Odlyzko: article on electronic mathematics journals Demise of Traditional Publishing (by Andrew Odlyzko) A-Odlyzko.ascii

16. John Franks, "What is an Electronic Journal?" *PACS-L* (21 January 1993); John Franks, "The Impact of Electronic Publication on Scholarly Journals," *Notices of the American Mathematical Society* 40, no. 9 (November 1993): 1200-1202. (Reprinted in *VPIEJ-L* (4 November 1993)).

Adventures in Information Space: Biomedical Discoveries in a Molecular Sequence Milieu

Mark S. Boguski

SUMMARY. Since the mid-1970s, DNA and protein sequence data has led to remarkable discoveries that are revealing the fundamental causes of cancer and genetic disease. By the year 2005, the Human Genome Project will produce a complete blueprint of human biology. Scientists and physicians access these data in GenBank®, a NIH database developed, maintained and distributed by the NCBI. These sequences are linked directly to molecular structure databases and to the biomedical journal literature through bibliographic databases like MEDLINE®. This new knowledge management system functions with the use of e-mail, CD-ROM products, and Internet client-server applications, and blends the world of print publishing with primary source data residing in globally accessible databanks. Current systems require that human beings initiate specific search, analysis, and retrieval requests. However, software robots already maintain and update these data, and "intelligent agents" will soon be available for the automated and targeted dissemination of new research findings. This paper discusses the development of this new working model and speculates about the impact of future technological advances, the effect on how researchers and physicians work, and possible applicability to other research disciplines.

This is a summary of a presentation by Mark S. Boguski, Investigator, National Center for Biotechnology Information, National Library of Medicine, and Acting Director of Bioformatics, National Center for Human Genome Research, National Institutes of Health, Bethesda, MD.

[Haworth co-indexing entry note]: "Adventures in Information Space: Biomedical Discoveries in a Molecular Sequence Milieu." Boguski, Mark S. Co-published simultaneously in *The Serials Librarian* (The Haworth Press, Inc.) Vol. 25, No. 3/4, 1995, pp. 125-131; and: *A Kaleidoscope of Choices: Reshaping Roles and Opportunities for Serialists* (ed: Beth Holley and Mary Ann Sheble) The Haworth Press, Inc., 1995, pp. 125-131. Multiple copies of this article/chapter may be purchased from The Haworth Document Delivery Center [1-800-3-HAWORTH; 9:00 a.m. - 5:00 p.m. (EST)].

© 1995 by The Haworth Press, Inc. All rights reserved.

In the mid-1970s, it became possible to rapidly read the language of life, written in DNA sequences. Since that time, DNA sequences, and other biomedical data, have been growing exponentially (Figure 1) and by early in the next century the Human Genome Project, aided by laboratory robotics, will produce a complete blueprint of human biology in 3 billion letters.[1] Even before then, by 1996-1998, we will have the complete genomic sequences of several "model organisms" including the bacterium *E. coli*, the yeast *S. cerevisiae*, and the nematode *C. elegans* which share a remarkable degree of similarity, at the basic biochemical level, with mammals including mouse and man. Consequently, these data from model organisms will help us interpret human gene sequences. But DNA and protein sequence data have already become the common currency of biomedical research and have led to many remarkable discoveries that are revealing the fundamental causes of cancer and genetic disease.

Scientists and physicians access sequence data in GenBank®, a database located at the U.S. National Library of Medicine. GenBank contains all known genetic sequences and is developed, maintained, and distributed by NCBI–the U.S. National Center for Biotechnology Information.[2] GenBank is part of an international collaboration that includes the DNA Database of Japan and the European Bioinformatics Institute. Researchers who publish articles about DNA or protein sequences also submit their data electronically to GenBank and receive an accession number that uniquely identifies the data. Accession numbers provide keys for readers of the literature to search and retrieve the data electronically. Thus, in genetics and molecular biology, electronic publication has not replaced the printed literature but serves as an essential adjunct to it in the form of public-access databases.

For example, NCBI computers process in excess of 5,000 database queries per day. These queries come in the form of e-mail or direct client-server interactions over the Internet and are usually formulated by the researchers themselves rather than by specialists in information science.[3] Nevertheless, a rapidly-growing subdiscipline of molecular biology and genome research is "bioinformatics," a field that concerns itself with the development and applica-

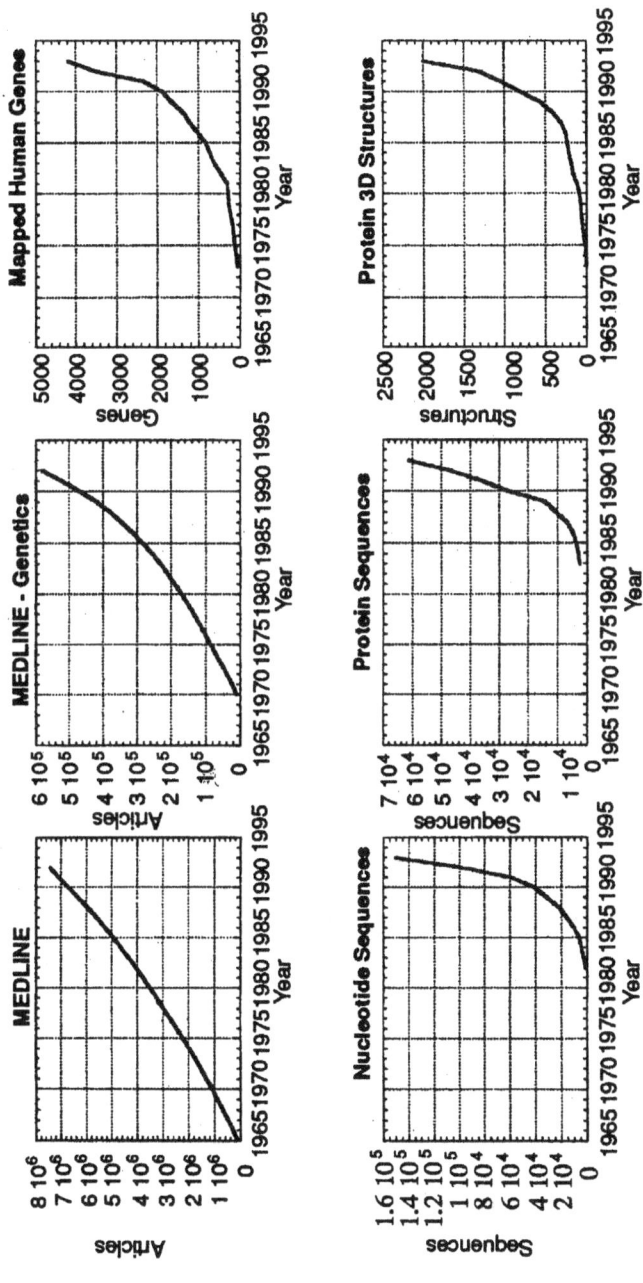

FIGURE 1. Cumulative Growth of Biomedical Research Data. MEDLINE currently contains over 7 million abstracts derived from published articles in approximately 4000 biomedical journals. The genetics subset of MEDLINE contains about 60,000 articles and is growing more rapidly than the literature as a whole. The number of mapped human genes, nucleotide (DNA) sequences, protein sequences and three-dimensional structures is increasing exponentially. In particluar, GenBank is doubling in size every 20 months and currently (Release 83.0) contains more than 191 millions DNA bases in 182,753 individual sequences. For more information consult references 2 and 5. Much of the information in these separate and distinct databases has been integrated in the *Entrez* system (Figure 2).

tion of computational tools to the organization and study of electronic data.[4]

GenBank sequences are linked to the biomedical literature and other sources of information (Figure 2) via a database and software system, *Entrez*, developed by NCBI for integrated information retrieval. *Entrez* employs a "point and click" graphical user interface, runs on Macintosh®, Microsoft Windows®, and Unix® systems, and is available on CD-ROM and as a free Internet service (contact info@ncbi.nlm.nih.gov). In addition to providing explicit links between genes, the proteins they encode, and the literature that describes them (Figure 2), the *Entrez* system also includes "value added" annotation in the form of emergent connections computed from the data itself. *Entrez* includes similarity links among MEDLINE® records, produced by a process known as "neighboring" which is based on the presence and frequency of informative terms in the titles, abstracts, and subject headings. Such statistical text neighboring has applicability to other knowledge domains. *Entrez* also includes computed similarities among sequences, a concept biologists call "homology searching."

Database homology searching is an analytic method that resembles familiar forms of information retrieval in the sense that one uses a string of characters to retrieve matching character strings.[5] But homology searching goes beyond this concept because the process of retrieval itself often creates new information in a very explicit way. Matching sequences may establish connections, often surprising and unanticipated, between diverse biological systems with implications for human disease. One of many examples would be the relationship between a yeast pheromone signaling molecule and cystic fibrosis.[6]

Biologists are interested in not only exact matches but also imperfect matches, which may represent divergent cognate genes in other organisms.[7] The rules for allowable mismatches are based on our knowledge of molecular evolution and a statistical theory that permits us to estimate how likely it is that a particular level of similarity is due to chance.[8]

The basic operation is to take a new gene sequence (also known as the query sequence), compare it sequentially with all known sequences in a database, and rank the database sequences in a "hit

FIGURE 2. *Entrez* Database Integration. A number of diverse databases (Figure 1 and reference 2) make up the interrelated data sets that are available via the *Entrez* retrieval system. In addition to those data sets mentioned in the text, *Entrez* also provides a taxonomic classification of genes and proteins according to the organisms from which they were isolated. By 1995, *Entrez* will also incorporate a molecular modeling database consisting of three-dimensional structures of proteins and nucleic acids. *Entrez* is available on CD-ROM by subscription from the U.S. Government Printing Office or as a free Internet service from NCBI (contact info@ncbi.nlm.nih.gov).

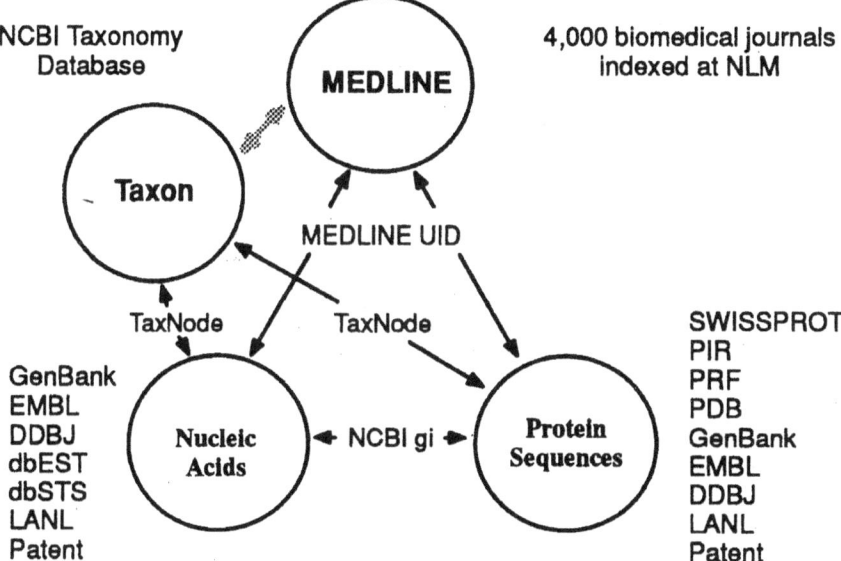

list" with respect to how closely they resemble the query. The results may be positive, negative, or equivocal. One studies the "alignments" between query and database sequences with the goal being to find a resemblance of sufficient magnitude to justify an inference of functional similarity. The implicit hope is that the matching database sequence(s) will have a known function or phenotype that will be able to shed light on the new sequence.

To illustrate one application of database homology searching, I turn to a popular novel and movie. The premise of Michael Crichton's *Jurassic Park* is that molecular biotechnology will permit the resurrection of extinct species from fossilized DNA. In his book, Dr. Crichton presents us with a "dinosaur" DNA sequence that "probably contains instructions to make a single protein—say, a hormone or an enzyme."[9] However, when this data was compared against GenBank (the analysis took only a few seconds), the DNA actually turned out to be a thinly disguised version of a man-made "vector" used to propagate cloned DNA in bacteria.[10] When presented with this finding, Dr. Crichton responded: "I am sorry I was not clever enough to insert a more interesting sequence; frankly, it never crossed my mind that anyone would have the interest to investigate it."[11] He underestimated the curiosity of molecular biologists who perform this kind of analysis every day.

Current electronic information systems in molecular biology require that humans initiate specific search, analysis, and retrieval requests. But soon, new data will be accumulating so rapidly that much of the analysis and annotation process will of necessity be automated. Software technology will also permit the automated and targeted dissemination of new research findings to all potentially interested parties. *Entrez* already includes answers to questions that have yet to be asked and is a forerunner of "intelligent agents" that will be programmed with our interests and tirelessly search information space, automatically notifying us when relevant new data becomes available.[12]

GenBank and NCBI are accessible via the World Wide Web.[13] The Uniform Resource Locator (URL) is:

http://www.ncbi.nlm.nih.gov/

NOTES

1. F. Collins and D. Galas, "A New Five-year Plan for the U.S. Human Genome Project," *Science* 262 (1993): 43-36.

2. D. Bensen, D.J. Lipman, and J. Ostell, "GenBank," *Nucleic Acids Research* 21 (1993): 2963-2965.

3. E. Krol, *The Whole Internet User's Guide & Catalog* 2nd ed. (Sebastopol, Calif: O'Reilly, 1994).

4. Mark A. Boguski, "Bioinformatics," *Current Opinion in Genetics and Development* 4 (1994): 383-388.

5. S.F. Altschul, Mark S. Boguski, W. Gish, and J.C. Wootton, "Issues in Searching Molecular Sequence Databases," *Nature Genetics* 6 (1993): 119-129.

6. S. Tugendreich, D.E. Basset, Jr., V.A. McKusick, Mark S. Boguski, and P.A. Hieter, "Genes Conserved in Yeast and Humans," *Human Molecular Genetics* (in press).

7. Ibid.

8. Altschul et al., "Issues in Searching Molecular Sequence Databases."

9. Michael Crichton, *Jurassic Park* (New York: Knopf, 1990), 103.

10. Mark S. Boguski, "A Molecular Biologist Visits Jurassic Park," *Biotechniques* 12 (1992): 668-669.

11. Michael Crichton, personal communication to author, 1992.

12. Mark Boguski and J. McEntyre, "I Think Therefore I Publish," *Biochemical Sciences* 19 (1993): 71.

13. Krol, *The Whole Internet User's Guide & Catalog*.

Grabbing the Bull by the Tail: Holding on During Change

Marjorie E. Bloss

SUMMARY. In our professional world today, we are experiencing change on three fronts: technological, economic/political, and organizational. Any one of these taken by itself would cause us to modify significantly the ways we do business. As luck would have it, dramatic changes are occurring in all three simultaneously. This paper reviews the nature of these environmental changes. It then examines them in relation to the library profession. Finally, it urges serialists to view change as an opportunity by encouraging them to shape change rather than letting change shape them.

INTRODUCTION

Why call a paper "grabbing the bull by the tail?" My first reason is highly selfish. I thought a catchy title might tempt you to stay through at least part of this presentation, even though I know it *is* Sunday and the beauties of Vancouver call. My second reason is more descriptive, and recognizes that no matter how exciting and stimulating change is, there are days when we feel we are being taken for a precarious and messy ride.

What this paper really is about is control: how to take control of

---

Marjorie E. Bloss is Director of Technical Services, Center for Research Libraries, Chicago, IL.

[Haworth co-indexing entry note]: "Grabbing the Bull by the Tail: Holding on During Change." Bloss, Marjorie E. Co-published simultaneously in *The Serials Librarian* (The Haworth Press, Inc.) Vol. 25, No. 3/4, 1995, pp. 133-145; and: *A Kaleidoscope of Choices: Reshaping Roles and Opportunities for Serialists* (ed: Beth Holley and Mary Ann Sheble) The Haworth Press, Inc., 1995, pp. 133-145. Multiple copies of this article/chapter may be purchased from The Haworth Document Delivery Center [1-800-3-HAWORTH; 9:00 a.m. - 5:00 p.m. (EST)].

our professional situations rather than letting them take control of us. My intent is not to recommend that we become dictatorial control freaks. Rather, my hope is for us to develop beliefs in what we are doing coupled with convictions that we speak from knowledge and with authority. At the same time, we need to be secure enough in these beliefs and convictions so we can remain flexible and open to new ideas; all in all, a pretty tall order. How do we achieve this level of control, especially with changes in our professions occurring so quickly?

A CALL TO ACTION

For anyone in our related professions wishing to live a peaceful, stable professional life, the last ten to fifteen years have been disquieting to say the least. Librarians, publishers, and vendors alike share the feeling that they are all impersonating the Red Queen in *Alice in Wonderland,* who had to run faster and faster simply to stay in one place. As soon as we think we are almost in control of our situations, they change. In fact, this description is optimistic. In reality, our situations are changing even *before* we are almost in control of them–an unnerving circumstance indeed.

Change is happening all around us, at many different levels, and at a furious pace. Change, whether individual or institutional, is messy, emotional, social, political, and cultural or countercultural in nature. These realities need to be factored into the change process from the very beginning.[1] A number of theorists dealing with management issues have frequently used the word "chaos" with "change"–an association that most certainly has negative connotations. Often, we find it difficult not to take change personally, especially if it is our job that is changing or being eliminated altogether, or our work flow that is shifting due to technological changes, or our organization that is undergoing drastic cuts in budget and staff. Too often, we believe we are at the mercy of circumstances over which we have no control.

In order to achieve some control over a situation, we must first analyze and understand it. Therefore, I would like to discuss how change is affecting our environment economically and politically (and I keep these two together because as soon as you talk about money, you are also talking about politics), as well as technologically, and organizationally. Finally, I would like to identify what we might be able to do in order to control our own destinies rather than having them get the upper hand. For those of you who like such things enumerated, I will identify four observations, eight techniques for controlling change, and one obvious truth. Except for this disclaimer, no where in this paper is the word "paradigm" used.

WHERE HAS ALL THE MONEY GONE?

Politics is one of three topics—along with religion and sex—that one is cautioned about discussing in public. I am going to take a chance and discuss it anyway regarding its economic influences on libraries, publishers, and vendors over the past fifteen years. In doing so, I will paint a simplified picture and will use very large brush strokes. While the politics I discuss are those of the United States, I believe the focus on governmental decentralization and a return of many programs to state (or provincial) autonomy has been true for other countries as well.

Ronald Reagan's victory as president of the United States in 1980 was tied to a domestic policy of federalism, a decentralized view of government where many federal programs would revert to state and local control. As president, Reagan identified a number of federally funded programs which, he believed, should be the responsibility of the states. All the budgets Reagan and his successor George Bush submitted to Congress eliminated funding for federal library programs, most notably, Library Services and Construction Act (LSCA) and United States Department of Education Title II programs. Congress obviously disagreed with Reagan's efforts as it restored funding for these programs every time.

Even so, the states were hit hard as the Reagan administration's policies of federalism resulted in more and more domestic programs reverting to local governments. While the programs might have reverted to the states, tax dollars to support them did not necessarily follow, leaving the states with deficits. State and local governments found that the most effective ways to make up the deficits were to raise taxes or cut budgets. Frequently, they did both. These two strategies plus an economic slow-down towards the end of the 1980s had serious repercussions for universities, libraries, publishers, and vendors.

In addition to declining state funds for libraries, the numbers of publications were increasing dramatically as a result of subject specialization and a profusion of newly issued materials from Eastern and Western Europe, and Japan. Furthermore, dramatic escalations in journal prices were occurring for a variety of reasons well known to all of you. For all these reasons, libraries found themselves scaling back their budgets. By extension, publishers and vendors also felt the pinch.

Two other economic issues began to affect colleges and universities during this time. The first had its roots in the economic and political policies of the Reagan administration, specifically, increased limitations on federally funded research. This, too, had a trickle-down effect on librarians, publishers, and vendors as a result of the dollar decline in indirect costs coming into an institution, the amount of research done, and the number of research materials purchased.

The second issue is perhaps initially more social than economic, although the effect on colleges and universities was certainly economic. At the same time state and federal support for higher education and research was shrinking, the number of eligible undergraduates was also declining. This resulted in an eroding financial base for many colleges and universities (public and private alike) that depended heavily on undergraduate enrollment for the major portion of their operating budgets. Understandably, this situation worsened universities' already shrinking budgets.

From all indications, the economy appears to be getting stronger now although it is premature to credit either the end of the Bush administration or the beginning of the Clinton administration for it. As a matter of fact, the Clinton Administration has been no kinder to libraries in funding LCSA or U. S. Department of Education Title II programs than the two previous administrations. This administration, however, claims it is diverting federal library dollars towards the National Information Infrastructure's Information Super Highway, completely ignoring the fact that while building the highway is a worthwhile endeavor, no one is going any where on it without the "cars" of information. Regardless, the financially vigorous days of the Kennedy and Johnson, or even the Nixon administrations are over. So here is Observation Number One: our budgets are not going to increase dramatically, which means we will be expected to continue to do more with less staff and to buy more (or at least provide access to it) with the same dollar amount or less. Even if our coffers did grow at a healthy rate, another component has entered the library budget equation: technology.

WHAT IS THE "NATIONAL UNION CATALOG"?

For those of us who began our library careers before MARC and the national bibliographic utilities (and really, it wasn't that long ago), our experience can be summed up in the statement: "But they never taught me that in library school." I am sure there is a similar analogy for those working in the publishing and vendor fields. Not only have we come a long way since then, we have come a long way in a very short time. During this period, automation has changed our lives in three primary ways: it has increased the efficiency of our work flow; it has made a major impact on the ways in which we communicate; and, it has liberated us from rigid patterns of how we approach information. I would like to examine each of these in some detail.

EFFICIENCY AND STREAMLINING OF INTERNAL FUNCTIONS

In the pre-MARC, pre-national bibliographic utilities world, cataloging was done based on Library of Congress precedent found–if one was lucky–in the *National Union Catalog (NUC)*. I say "if one was lucky," because most *NUC* entries are listed once (by main entry), according to the cataloging code of the day–unless superimposition kicked in. "Superimposition" was the term chosen by the Library of Congress to mean "I know the heading has changed, but there are too many cards in the catalog to erase the old heading and type in the new one, so I will superimpose the old upon the new, and leave things as they are even though I know better." "Shared cataloging" meant using the record found in the *NUC*, either by ordering catalog cards from the Library of Congress, typing the *NUC* cataloging record locally, or even by photocopying those records and pasting them onto three by five cards. These processes were labor-intensive and time-consuming. Furthermore, different departments in the library had to create new files, based on the same information, for different functions–acquisitions, check-in, circulation, and interlibrary loan.

Fred Kilgour, OCLC's founder, was the visionary who put the MARC record to work. He made "shared cataloging" a reality by establishing a consortium of Ohio libraries that were linked by terminal to one central database. The database consisted of bibliographic records in the MARC format that could be used or modified by the other libraries in the consortium. The philosophy behind the database was (and still is) once a library has cataloged a title and entered it into the database, other libraries can simply use that record rather than having to catalog the same title again. The impact on uniformity, consistency and standardization of information was enormous–not only within a single library's catalog but for all others using the same system. Already, we were beginning to experience major changes in our professional relationships. Suddenly, our institution's cataloging records were out there for the world to see. It was a new and sometimes uncomfortable situation. We fluctuated between self-righteousness or defensiveness depending on the record and who contributed it.

We continue to increase and refine our proficiency when using the same bibliographic record for a variety of functions, and our job descriptions and organizational charts reflect it. We now think nothing of keying a record into a system as soon as staff decide to order the title, and adding information to the record as the title moves from acquisitions to check-in to cataloging to circulation and interlibrary loan. Other functions like keying in invoice and check-in data can be done electronically through vendor and library cooperation what with X12 and the work done by the Serials Industry Systems Advisory Committee (SISAC) and the Book Industry Systems Advisory Committee (BISAC). The integrated library system, which existed for many years in theory, is now a reality for many of us.

TECHNOLOGY'S CHANGE ON COMMUNICATIONS

Electronic messaging over the Internet has completely transformed the way we communicate within our own organizations and with the rest of the world. Sending and replying to messages electronically rather than playing infernal games of telephone tag, writing letters, or sending faxes, are only two examples of technology's impact on the ways we communicate. In the same way we experienced the Gulf War while it was happening, we are able to participate immediately in international discussions on a mind-boggling number of topics with an unlimited number of participants, or we can transfer masses of data without benefit of paper.

Technology is also making significant changes in redefining publications, and the changes are affecting the related areas of authorship, copyright, licensing and use agreements, standardization, archiving, and preservation. Projects like Red Sage, Elsevier's Tulip, and Carnegie Mellon's Elixir are rapidly moving us to the day when the majority of scientific and scholarly publications will be issued electronically. Furthermore, technology is having a major impact on document delivery as information is requested and delivered by transferring files or scanning a document that is subsequently forwarded electronically.

LEFT-BRAIN OR RIGHT-BRAIN?

Whether or not we realize it, the way we think and react to information is also changing as a result of automation. Word processing has made us better writers. No longer do we sit with sweaty palms as our work is edited, dreading the words "if you only put the third paragraph on page fifteen on page two, and moved the middle section on page five to page seven, and, oh, by the way, you do not really want to use that word." It was not necessarily the resistance to making changes in content that caused anxiety as much has having to type (on a typewriter) the whole document over and over again.

Technology has expanded the ways in which we combine disparate pieces of information. We are able to augment or winnow down concepts through keyword searching and Boolean operators. We can create management reports from data keyed into a system only once, rather than maintaining separate files of the same information that is organized differently from file to file. While we must input and extract information in a methodical way based on the parameters of the system we are using (left-brain), our minds can wander with considerable freedom when defining our research subjects (right-brain). Observation Number Two is that technology has liberated us from traditional and often rigid ways of approaching information, and subsequently has increased our creativity and imagination.

THE FLATTENING OF THE PYRAMID

Unquestionably, technology has had a profound impact on organizational structures and staffing charts as we continually discover how often our traditional duties and routines overlap. We have begun to see functional relationships differently and are now reorganizing certain activities as a result of integrated information, and streamlining, reconfiguring, or eliminating duties as we previously knew them. A number of libraries have combined pre-order acquisitions with copy cataloging. Others are beginning to recognize the strong link between interlibrary loan and acquisitions. We are witnessing a blurring of functions, often making it difficult to discern where one activity (and subsequently, department) begins and others leave off. At the same time we are redefining positions because of technology, we are also redefining them because of budgetary cutbacks and downsizing. As a result, the traditional organizational pyramid is beginning to look rather squashed.

Until the second half of the 20th century, most organizational structures were described as pyramids. The Chief Operating Officer was at the apex, with senior level staff just below, middle managers below that, and the rest of the staff formed the base of the pyramid or the widest portion. Everyone's position was neatly arranged in an organizational chart that reflected narrowly defined routines with no overlap in duties. Management was viewed as a science and was even called "scientific management" by the leading theorists of the day, Frederick Taylor and Elton Mayo. It was based on production and output, completely ignoring the humanistic needs of the employees. Organizational information was expected to flow from the top down, never from the bottom up or across and employees at all levels were considered expendable.

The shape of our organizational structures is flattening not only because of financial constraints and technological developments, but also because of redefinitions of employee satisfaction. Early management theorists believed that all employees were interested in were their paychecks. More recent theories now believe that having a say in the way one's job is done is part of job satisfaction. The practice of "management by objectives" was the first step in permitting an employee to have a voice in establishing work-related priorities in consultation with the supervisor. Soon thereafter, the concept of job enrichment and enlargement, and the team approach to manufacturing were added. These ideas were first implemented in Japan's automobile industry. They were introduced by Edwards Deming and Joseph Juran with their "quality circles" and "total quality management."[2] The psychology behind these approaches was that employees would become more productive if their duties were broader and if they understood how their jobs fit into the organization as a whole. Employees would gain self-esteem, a sense of personal worth, and a belief that they were working for the corporation as a whole rather than for one small segment of it. In turn, the company's productivity and profits would rise.

Today, the organizational pyramid looks less like a pyramid and more like a bell. Henry Mintzberg, Bronfman Professor of Management at McGill University, identifies five organizational configurations, concluding with one called the "Adhocracy"—a term popularized by Alvin Toffler in his book *Future Shock*.[3] Mintzberg diagrams the Adhocracy "with its parts mingled together in one amorphous mass in the middle."[4] He describes the Adhocracy as a blending of administrative and operating responsibilities into a single effort as they work together in an ever-shifting environment that is both dynamic and complex.[5] These features easily characterize those found in Total Quality Management, or TQM.

TQM is perhaps the next logical extension of the team approach. It recognizes the importance of processes, starts with the needs of the process customer, and works backwards from that point. TQM works within the framework of a company's existing processes, seeking to improve them on a continuing basis.[6] In the same way as the team approach was seen as improving productivity, TQM extends it to problem solving, by empowering staff members at many levels with having a say in the outcomes of their work situations. The United States has joined the TQM game relatively late, only to find that the Japanese have now moved on to another management philosophy. Ironically, the latest Japanese management philosophy espoused by the Japanese is based on zero defects and, as Peter Drucker observed, has a strong resemblance to the "scientific" management theories of the late 1800s.[7] I believe we, ourselves are coming to some of these same conclusions, for in today's lean and mean staffing configurations, we have only so much time for hand-holding and nurturing.

Another management concept that has come to the forefront recently is reengineering. It serves as a balance to some of the theories and practices of TQM. Unlike TQM, reengineering has its basis in complete change and totally starting over again rather than in developing and refining what already exists.[8] "Starting over" can include a complete overhaul of job definitions and the elimination of staff. Understandably, reengineering can be very appealing in light of our diminishing budgets and increased technological capabilities, but very scary to people who have been comfortable with the status quo.

As has been pointed out previously, the flattening of the organizational pyramid is occurring for two primary external reasons. Budget cutbacks are forcing us to eliminate positions either through attrition or by actual layoffs. Simultaneously, technology is causing us to reexamine existing positions and redefine them, usually by enlarging their scopes. I find it an interesting coincidence that management began to extol the virtues of empowerment and the benefits of expanding job responsibilities at the same time as financial support for libraries began to decline and technology integrated a number of previously discrete functions. The timing could not have been better! I cannot help but wonder if TQM and reengineering would receive as much support as they have if these external components were less volatile. It is difficult to assess if these management theories are truly preferable to others, or if they are more a matter of convenience because of present day budgetary and technological considerations.

Even so, we are spending a lot of time and effort involving staff at all levels in shaping their environment, through strategic planning, problem identification, and problem-solving. There is no question that participation in these activities is valuable, but there must be limits. What if staff members are not capable of nor wish to be part of these processes? TQM is based on reasonable people proceeding reasonably. What do you do if they do not? Observation Number Three: There are many management styles and many organizational structures. Examine them all, but choose the ones (or selected portions of ones) that work best for you based on the situations at hand. If a management theory does not work in a particular situation, do something else. Observation Number Four: Use common sense and don't underestimate your "gut" reactions.

AT THE CROSSROADS

We have examined some of the areas where politics, economics, technology, and organizational structures converge and how we, the individuals, are affected. At the onset, I said the real focus of this paper is on how we might gain some control over our professional lives rather than letting them control us. Grabbing the bull by the tail and holding on during change is the first step. The next steps are to climb on the bull's back and control the beast. Here, then, are the eight techniques for controlling change. I would like to underscore that the listing is not conclusive. Feel free to add more.

- Take time to analyze, and draw conclusions about "the big picture." "The big picture" includes the many factors influencing our environment (however defined), and their cause-and-effect relationships.
- We are competing for limited dollars: therefore, we have to play the game the way the game is being played. We must enter the competition ourselves and draw attention to what we do and the fact that we are good at it. This includes applying some business principles, even if they are foreign to the way we operated previously. Two of these principles include: assertively convincing administrators, patrons, users, and customers that our products and skills are worth supporting or buying; and, knowing what our patrons or customers want, to the point

of anticipating their needs before they are aware of them. In a nutshell, we must market and sell our products effectively and aggressively rather than sitting on the sidelines, waiting for them to be noticed.
- Technology is changing our internal organizational structures and relationships through functional integration. It is also modifying the relationships we have with other organizations. Publishers, vendors, and librarians will find themselves working together more closely as their common interests continue to overlap. Not only is this true in our present positions, but we find ourselves crossing over into related professions more easily and more often than ever before as we move from job to job. Consequently, we must gain better understanding of and sympathy with each others' businesses; their concerns, their priorities, and their operations. Your position today may be that of a publisher, but your next job may be as a serial vendor or a librarian.
- In today's environment, we have no room for the "But we have always done it that way," the "Just tell me what to do," or the "Just go with the flow" mind-sets. Be an initiator and problem-solver by anticipating situations before they occur, or certainly before they become problematic.
- We must learn not only to tolerate ambiguity but to shape it into something workable. This is the "when given a lemon, make lemonade" School of Positive Attitude.
- We must try not to take all change personally. There are some things that we cannot control, and it is important to know that. To quote from the movie *Bull Durham*: "Sometimes you win. Sometimes you lose. Sometimes . . . it rains. Think about it!"
- We must take the initiative to insure that our own professional education is ongoing, whether in a formal or informal setting. We continually need to read, think, share ideas with others by using e-mail, participating in meetings, and attending conferences as well as taking formal classes and training.
- Throughout all of this, keep in mind that we are human beings as well as librarians, publishers, and vendors. Remember to laugh–sometimes even at serious things. Have interests outside of your work. Go on vacation. Occasionally, call in well.

In closing, I would like to sum up the ninth NASIG conference with the one obvious truth. If people who work with serials cannot handle change, no one can. Change is second nature to us, for we are always trying to solve the mysteries of title changes, of changes in publishers, places of publication, and receipt patterns. Our daily work requires us to have a natural curiosity, an ability to observe patterns, and to draw reasonable conclusions from them. Tolerate ambiguity? It is the fabric of our lives. The only thing left for us to do is to teach the rest of the world how to work with serials.

NOTES

1. Gerard Egan, *Adding Value: A Systematic Guide to Business-Driven Management and Leadership* (San Francisco: Jossey-Bass, 1993), 141.

2. Peter F. Drucker, *Managing for the Future: The 1990s and Beyond* (New York: Truman Talley, 1993), 106-107.

3. Alvin Toffler, *Future Shock* (New York: Bantam, 1970).

4. Henry Mintzberg, *Structure in Fives: Designing Effective Organizations* (Englewood Cliffs, NJ: Prentice Hall, 1983), 257-261.

5. Ibid, 262.

6. Michael Hammer and James Champy, *Reengineering the Corporation: A Manifesto for Business Revolution* (New York: Harper Business, 1993), 49.

7. Peter F. Drucker, *Managing for the Future*, 182.

8. Michael Hammer and James Champy, *Reengineering the Corporation*, 49.

CONCURRENT SESSIONS: A KALEIDOSCOPE OF CHANGE

CONCURRENT SESSION I: MANAGING ORGANIZATIONAL CHANGE

Managing Organizational Change: The Harvard College Library Experience

Mary Elizabeth Clack

SUMMARY. The author explores the nature of, and myths surrounding organizational change and how the received wisdom about organizational change is being challenged in the current management literature. Drawing upon the experience of the Harvard College Library's planning processes, several strategies are recommended for managing change in organizations today.

INTRODUCTION

Addressing organizational change is a daunting endeavor given the scope and complexity of contemporary organizational structures

---

Mary Elizabeth Clack is Serial Records Librarian/Staff Development Officer, Harvard College Library, Cambridge, MA.

[Haworth co-indexing entry note]: "Managing Organizational Change: The Harvard College Library Experience." Clack, Mary Elizabeth. Co-published simultaneously in *The Serials Librarian* (The Haworth Press, Inc.) Vol. 25, No. 3/4, 1995, pp. 149-161; and: *A Kaleidoscope of Choices: Reshaping Roles and Opportunities for Serialists* (ed: Beth Holley and Mary Ann Sheble) The Haworth Press, Inc., 1995, pp. 149-161. Multiple copies of this article/chapter may be purchased from The Haworth Document Delivery Center [1-800-3-HAWORTH; 9:00 a.m. - 5:00 p.m. (EST)].

© 1995 by The Haworth Press, Inc. All rights reserved.

and processes. We are facing an unprecedented amount of change in organizations today. Our future success will depend upon how well we can manage and anticipate change at all levels of the organization. While the examples and strategies cited in this paper are drawn from my experience with strategic planning as a manager and staff development officer in the Harvard College Library, I think the strategies are applicable to organizational change in many settings.

This presentation will cover the following areas: First, I will describe the nature of organizational change today. Next, I will look at some of the myths on the subject and how two authors are questioning traditional concepts of change and offering some new and creative ways to consider and address it. Then, I will suggest some strategies to employ in coping with a changing environment, using examples from our experience in the College Library, including some thoughts on the role of leadership.

The question is not why or whether we should change, but how to go about it and still retain our optimism and energy, using a constructive approach to what is becoming an increasingly challenging effort. At Harvard we have no "formula" or detailed blueprint for managing change, but we have begun a journey that I hope will be informative and of interest to you.

THE NATURE OF ORGANIZATIONAL CHANGE TODAY

I will begin with some observations about organizational change. First, change is ongoing, constant, and is occurring at an unprecedented rate. It cannot be limited to planned and directed change, tightly controlled by managers. Peter Vaill called the turbulence in our environment "permanent whitewater."[1] But in a talk at last summer's Research Libraries Group (RLG) Symposium on Electronic Access, the keynote speaker, Douglas Van Houweling, said that since one can find a way to navigate whitewater rapids, the image is no longer vivid enough. He prefers the image of flying through smooth air and suddenly hitting a wind shear. It's unpredictable and the "instinctive action is often fatal."[2]

Secondly, change is not an event, but a *process*. William Bridges, in *Managing Transitions*, sees personal and organizational change as three stages: endings, the neutral zone, and beginnings.[3] Endings is the stage in which people identify what is ending, what they might be losing by the change, and what can be preserved to take along to the "new world" in the transition.

This stage is followed by the neutral zone, a period of confusion and ambiguity. This stage is necessary; it can be a time of energy and creativity for some people, and it cannot be abridged before the next stage, beginnings, is reached. If it is shortened or rushed, a true transition has not taken place.

In the beginnings stage, people are prepared and ready to address the new. They can be constructive about the change, if they have enough of a transition period preceding it.

Third, change in organizations is intensely personal, and at the same time, systemic. People going through transition periods will experience change in different ways, depending on their view of the reasons for (and the goal of) the change, their understanding of it, their readiness for it and whether they initiated it (which is often not the case). Transitions are experienced in relation to other things occurring in their lives and reactions of co-workers, managers, and others.

At the organizational level, there is often a ripple effect. A change or series of changes in one part of the system affects other parts, but we often ignore the interrelationships. Jeanie Duck quotes an executive who was talking about handling his job. The executive said that he has the skills to manage complex operational problems. But when it comes to managing change, the same skills and models do not work. He continues:

> It's like the company is undergoing five medical procedures at the same time ... One person is in charge of the root canal job, someone else is setting the broken foot, another person is working on the displaced shoulder, and still another is getting rid of the gall stone. Each operation is a success, but the patient dies of shock.[4]

MYTHS ABOUT CHANGE

Knowing all of the above, people still cling to certain myths about change. There is the myth of planned, linear change processes that can be controlled. How, then, do we account for small, informal, seemingly serendipitous changes that become the catalysts for larger-scale shifts and/or significant changes in direction? And we are often able to see the connections between the two only in retrospect. Another myth is that of the lone, visionary leader who can effectively anticipate and initiate change, working with a small group of advisers.

Last, consider the myth of the stable organization, contained in physical space, with employees who can count on employment in the same function for years at a time. In organizations that are increasingly online or virtual, employees and customers have increased mobility. Employees can be connected to others by fax, modem, or videoconferencing. Customers or users can access services remotely as well.

These simplistic myths do not serve us well. What are the proper perspectives from which to view change? How do we prevent losing the "patient," or our colleagues, along the way? The answer does not lie in thinking of a way "out," but rather by thinking of a way "through" the process.

In doing research for this presentation, I discovered more than a few models for managing change. But they presented a linear and fragmentary view of managing change, predicated on the myths outlined above. They are inadequate to meet our needs today. In search of a fresh perspective, I found the work of two authors more useful. Not surprisingly, they both explore the paradox and contradictions that surface in an uncertain world.

NEW WAYS OF THINKING ABOUT CHANGE

In *Managing the Unknowable,* Ralph Stacey contends that we cannot subscribe to the myth of stability. Managers wish to maintain stability and control: this leads them to employ strategies of repeating past successes or imitating other organizations' effective strategies, while these organizations, if truly innovative, have moved beyond those strategies. A better approach is to accept the future directions of our organizations as unknowable. Stacey calls this state of uncertainty "bounded instability," and defines it as a balance between stability and instability.[5]

How can this condition be described? It concentrates on considering processes from multiple perspectives, allowing for some tension and conflict to arise while doing so. Stacey notes that creative management lies in the "reflective pause between a stimulus and the response to it."[6] Managing the unknowable aspect of change consists of the group allowing strategic directions to *emerge* out of such a process. The paradox, of course, is that one discovers strategic directions through the journey itself. It is a creative process of "making new maps"[7] for unchartered waters–not having a map in advance, but creating one through a process of continual questioning and organizational learning. Stacey sees this as a "paradox of control and freedom" that must be held in balance. In his words:

> This is the fundamental paradox of organization. The structures and behavior appropriate for normal stable management have to coexist with the informality and instability of the extraordinary form of management that is necessary to cope with the unknowable.[8]

Instability is the means for ensuring the vitality and capacity for the renewal needed by organizations.

Margaret Wheatley also addresses questions of change management using ideas from her research on quantum physics, self-organizing systems, and chaos theory. Like Stacey, Wheatley is in search of new perspectives for viewing organizational life today. She questions the Newtonian world view that has had a significant bearing on how we design and manage organizations. The Newtonian view is based on materialism (focusing on things), and reductionism (the assertion that the building blocks of matter can be taken apart and put back together without harm to the whole). This view assumes that by comprehending the workings of each piece of a system, the whole can be understood.[9] This is a predictable and orderly, albeit fragmented, universe.

More recent scientific thinking focuses on a holistic approach to "understanding the system as a system and giving primary value to the relationships that exist among seemingly discrete parts."[10] Connections, relationships, and dynamic processes figure prominently in this systemic view.

Wheatley notes that fluctuations, disorder, and change can play a role in generating new, higher forms of order, and renewed life. Chaos theory teaches that there is a value to unpredictability which can be "held within parameters that are well-ordered and predictable."[11] Wheatley sees current management thinking as encompassing notions of "more fluid, organic structures, even of boundaryless organizations."[12]

Further, "there is a constant weaving of relationships, of energies that merge and change, of constant ripples that occur within a seamless fabric."[13] Embracing contradiction and allowing these interrelationships to emerge and organizational learning to occur provides sources of new ideas, synergy, and renewal.

Wheatley explores the usefulness of field theory as a way to think about organizational life. To explain why things move without direct impact, scientists beginning with Newton have talked about fields. There are gravitational fields, electromagnetic fields, and quantum fields, for example. Wheatley suggests that we should look beyond "small, discrete, visible structures to an invisible world filled with mediums of connections."[14] She recommends that we see culture, values, and vision as fields that should permeate the organization and, like the magnet attracting metal fillings, would influence every person and group in the organization.

Wheatley also believes that we have forgotten the dynamic nature of information, because we think of it as a commodity, as bits and bytes, instead of a force that organizes matter into a structure. To maximize its potential, information should be seen not as a commodity, but as a dynamic process, as in the word, "*in*forma-tion." It is a key source of "structuration," that is, capable of creating structure.[15] In the knowledge-based organization, information is of paramount importance in decision-making. It has to be accurate, but it also has to be the right information. Wheatley asserts that we now spend more energy analyzing and controlling information, when in fact what we should be doing is continually *generating* information for use by groups. All members of the organization derive benefit from new information being created and shared, prompting organizational growth and ensuring vitality and survival.

Participation is another element in this view of information. If all are not allowed access to this dynamic source of energy, only a few people will interpret and use information fully; thus much of its richness and potential is lost. This is a powerful argument for a new way to consider information and participation in the organization. In her words:

> An organization swimming in many interpretations can then discuss, combine, and build on them. The outcome of such a process has to be a much more diverse and richer sense of what is going on and what needs to be done.[16]

STRATEGIES FOR MANAGING CHANGE

These authors have traced an organizational landscape among the shifting sands of change. It is a holistic environment, in which information is widely shared, ideas confer order, and strategies are allowed to emerge. Participation is encouraged and people are guided by shared values as they face the paradox and contradiction inherent in the system. Management is "coping with" rather than controlling.

For the remainder of this presentation, I will address two questions: More generally, what is the best way to manage in the transition? And specifically, what are the best change strategies to employ?

Generally, we need to incorporate paradox in our thinking and stretch our imaginations by holding on to the seemingly contradictory. In the Harvard College Library's Gateway Planning Process, the Task Force on Research Instruction and Reference discussed organizing cultural concepts and questions. As the Task Force explained, they began their work by discussing organizing concepts, stressing the need to achieve a balance between seeming extremes. The group rejected the word "versus" and used instead "vis-à-vis." The report concludes twelve of these pairs of extremes, such as centralization and decentralization, vision and implementation, one-stop service and referral, libraries as collections and libraries as service units, libraries as physical entities and the networked environment, and librarian-directed information gathering and the self-sufficient user.[17]

Secondly, we need to find ways to anticipate change. One of the chapters in our Strategic Plan begins with Wayne Gretsky's maxim, "I skate to where I think the puck will be."[18] Like Gretsky, we have to bring the following skills to bear in coping with change: anticipation, alertness, and flow.

Turning to the second question, more specifically, what are the best strategies to employ while managing transitions in the shaded area?

Strategic planning, with the emphasis on strategic thinking, should become an integral part of the library's work. Mintzberg's central thesis is that a new paradigm for strategic planning is in order. He makes a distinction between the old view of strategic planning as "strategic programming," that is, formal, analytical and detailed, and "strategic thinking," a dynamic process of synthesis, a creative activity.[19] Strategic thinking is better suited to today's rapidly changing environment since it fosters informal learning and creativity at all levels of the organization.

In the College Library's planning process, members of the five task forces[20] were encouraged to push beyond the limits of their current knowledge, go beyond repetition and imitation, and stretch their thinking. To do so, these groups consulted with resource persons in libraries and with specialists outside libraries.

Involve people at all levels of the organization in the process. To include those close to operations in our planning processes, department heads and senior managers were not members of the task forces. This was also the first time that support staff members participated in groups of this sort.

Recognize that the benefits of planning are process as much as product. Our final written plan was not a matrix of recommendations charted in a timeline. It was fairly broad-brush and more like a compass for a journey than a map, although some staff members were expecting a detailed road map. If that had been done, we would have been prey to the myths of stability and control mentioned earlier.

Support an organizational development process, devoting resources to training. Training should focus on both functional training, related to the technical aspects of jobs, and on group dynamics training, which enables staff members to become more effective in sharing information for use by the organization and in participating in decision-making.

An important part of our process was the attention given to staff and organizational development. The Task Force on Staff and Organizational Development was charged with designing the elements of an organizational development strategy in a changing library environment. We began with the vision of the future:

> There will be increasing experimentation and innovation within the Library, particularly with regard to scholarly communication.
>
> More members of the Library's staff will carry multiple responsibilities that cut across lines separating traditional functions. Both technological competence and solid traditional skills will be required. The Library's growing dynamism and broadening concerns will require a major investment in staff development.[21]

In the course of our work, we defined several shifts[22] that had to occur to move the organization in the direction of readiness for change.

- From decentralization to a shared vision of unity amid diversity,
- From specialization and segmentation of tasks to an integrated view of tasks,
- From an emphasis on individual accomplishments to a recognition of the efficacy of collaboration,
- From a reactive environment with sporadic change to a dynamic environment, characterized by innovation and risk-taking,
- From a rigid process culture to one with flexible responses to different situations,
- From a hierarchically governed organization toward one with trust in, and participation of, staff at all levels.

To implement its recommendations, the Task Force recommended the formation of a Steering Committee on Staff and Organizational Development, chaired by me as the Staff Development Officer. Some of the projects we have undertaken since October 1991 include:

- A workshop on organizational change.
- Working with the Harvard Quality Process, the Committee designed a team training program for the newly restructured Cataloging Services Department in Widener Library, covering such topics as effective meeting skills, interactive skills, consensus-building, and a six-step problem-solving process using a library case study.
- An organizational values process which leads me to the next strategy.

Provide a forum for the clarification and discussion of the organization's values and aspirations. Organizational culture plays an important role in shaping people's attitudes, beliefs and behaviors. We designed a process to clarify the organizational values and aspirations of the College Library, and the often unspoken beliefs that drive behavior and performance. It was important that we have a process of discovery, and not a process of indoctrination and inculcation of senior management's values, and that a statement of shared values emerge from the discussions.

"Values: A Process of Discovery" is a College Library-wide exploration of our values and aspirations. We coordinated the process which began in the summer of 1993 with a one-day planning retreat for the Steering Committee. At this meeting, we outlined our objectives:

- to design a useful and meaningful process for an HCL-wide discussion of values,
- to involve as many staff members as possible in the discussions,
- to build support for the process among all levels of staff,
- to carefully record the contents of the discussion,
- to have all library managers and supervisors endorse, promote, and participate in the process.

Because we are aiming for a broader base of support and ideas than our Steering Committee alone represents, several focus groups were conducted with about fifty-five staff members. Participants emphasized the following issues: making the abstract nature of values more concrete and real, discussing the conflict between values and real practice, and focusing on ways to take the process back to the local units and departments, where values are lived.

The Committee designed town meetings on values with consultants from the Association of Research Libraries Office of Management Services. One hundred and thirty-seven staff members attended. The agenda included a discussion of hypothetical values situations, designed to explore how personal values influence decision-making; formulation of "organizational blasphemies";[23] and identification of the organization's core values that will be incorporated in a draft statement of the Library's values. These are statements that seem to run counter to the Library's values, but in fact point to some of the Library's central values. The next step will be to draft such a statement for review by the community.

Last, what is the role of leadership in this changing environment? To manage change effectively, organizations must develop an expanded notion of leadership. Leaders must share the responsibilities of leadership in our increasingly participative organizations.

Max de Pree, former CEO of Herman Miller, distinguishes between two kinds of leaders; the hierarchically ordained and the informally identified, whom he calls "roving leaders":

> In special situations, the hierarchical leader is obliged to identify the roving leaders, then to support and follow him or her, and also to exhibit the grace that enables the roving leader to lead.[24]

To be effective, the formal leader must also follow. This requires flexibility, trust, and openness to influence. To me, this is the most difficult aspect of becoming less hierarchical and creating an environment that is an "enabling one."

CONCLUSION

It is my hope that in delineating some of the challenges presented by change and in offering some strategies to manage it, I have given you some new ways to think about our roles. I believe we can play a part in making our organizations more hospitable to change and our colleagues better equipped to embrace it. If we do, we will be well on our way to creating learning organizations,

> where people continually expand their capacity to create the results they truly desire, where new and expansive patterns of thinking are nurtured, where collective aspiration is set free, and where people are continually learning to learn together.[25]

NOTES

1. Peter B. Vaill, *Managing as a Performing Art* (San Francisco: Jossey-Bass, 1991), 2.

2. Douglas E. Houweling, "Knowledge Services in the Digitized World: Possibilities and Strategies," in Win-Shing S. Chiang and Nancy E. Elkington, eds., *Electronic Access to Information: A New Service Paradigm* (Mountain View, CA: Research Libraries Group, 1994), 15.

3. William Bridges, *Managing Transitions: Making the Most of Change* (Reading, MA: Addison-Wesley, 1991), 5-6.

4. Jeanie Daniel Duck, "Managing Change: The Art of Balancing," *Harvard Business Review* 71:6 (November/December, 1993): 109.

5. Ralph D. Stacey, *Managing the Unknowable: Strategic Boundaries between Order and Chaos* (San Francisco : Jossey-Bass,1992), xii.

6. *Ibid.*, xv.

7. *Ibid.*, 3.

8. *Ibid.*, 8.

9. Margaret Wheatley, *Leadership and the New Science: Learning about Organization from an Orderly Universe* (San Francisco: Bennett-Koehler, 1992), 9.

10. *Ibid.*, 9.

11. *Ibid.*, 11.

12. *Ibid.*, 13.

13. *Ibid.*, 20.

14. *Ibid.*, 49.

15. *Ibid.*, 104.

16. *Ibid.*, 65.

17. *Report: Research Instruction and Reference. Gateway Task Force.* [Cambridge, MA: Harvard College Library Gateway Planning Committee Research Instruction and Reference Task Force, July 1993], 15-19.

18. *Commitment to Renewal: A Strategic Plan for the Harvard College Library.* ([Cambridge: Harvard College Library] February 3, 1992), 7.

19. Henry Mintzberg, "The Fall and Rise of Strategic Planning," *Harvard Business Review* 72 no. 1 (January/February, 1994): 107-108.

20. The five Task Forces were on Collections, Intellectual Access, Reallocation of Space, Services and Staff and Organizational Development.

21. *Commitment to Renewal*, 20.

22. *Final Report: Strategic Planning Committee Task Force on Staff and Organizational Development*. [Cambridge, MA: The Task Force], 5-7.

23. "Organizational blasphemies" are statements that seem to run counter to the Library's values, but in fact point to some of the Library's central values.

24. Max De Pree, *Leadership is an Art* (New York: Dell, 1989), 49.

25. Peter Senge, *The Fifth Discipline: The Art and Practice of Learning Organizations* (New York: Doubleday Currency, 1990), 1.

REFERENCES

Bridges, William. *Managing Transitions: Making the Most of Change*. Reading, MA: Addison-Wesley, 1991.

Commitment to Renewal: A Strategic Plan for the Harvard College Library. Cambridge: Harvard College Library, Feb. 3, 1992.

De Pree, Max. *Leadership is an Art*. New York: Dell, 1989.

Duck, Jeanie Daniel. "Managing Change: The Art of Balancing," *Harvard Business Review* 71, no. 6 (November/December, 1993), pp. 109-118.

Final Report: Strategic Planning Task Force on Staff and Organizational Development. [Cambridge, MA: The Task Force, May 7, 1991].

Houweling, Douglas E., "Knowledge Services in the Digitized World: Possibilities and Strategies," in *Electronic Access to Information: A New Service Paradigm*, edited by Win-Shing S. Chiang and Nancy E. Elkington. Mountain View, CA: Research Libraries Group, 1994.

Stacey, Ralph D. *Managing the Unknowable: Strategic Boundaries Between Order and Chaos*. San Francisco: Jossey-Bass, 1992.

Vaill, Peter B. *Managing as a Performing Art*. San Francisco: Jossey-Bass, 1991.

Wheatley, Margaret. *Leadership and the New Science: Learning about Organization from an Orderly Universe*. San Francisco: Bennett-Koehler, 1992.

Mintzberg, Henry, "The Fall and Rise of Strategic Planning," *Harvard Business Review* 72, no. 1 (January./February, 1994), pp.107-114.

Report: Research Instruction and Reference. Gateway Task Force. [Cambridge, MA: Harvard College Library Gateway Planning Committee Research Instruction and Reference Task Force, July 1993].

CONCURRENT SESSION II: REPORTS FROM THE FRONTIERS OF CHANGE

Wanted: Information Manager: New Roles for Librarians and Vendors

Sharon Cline McKay

SUMMARY. Drawing on her varied experiences in the library and information industry, the author discusses her perceptions of the increasing similarity of skills and functions demanded of vendors and librarians as information managers. The skills and knowledge acquired through library work are exactly what are needed for many positions with library vendors. Librarians are urged to think broadly about what they can do with an MLS degree.

Sharon Cline McKay is Product Manager for Dynix Marquis, Inc., Provo, UT.

[Haworth co-indexing entry note]: "Wanted: Information Manager: New Roles for Librarians and Vendors." McKay, Sharon Cline. Co-published simultaneously in *The Serials Librarian* (The Haworth Press, Inc.) Vol. 25, No. 3/4, 1995, pp. 163-171; and: *A Kaleidoscope of Choices: Reshaping Roles and Opportunities for Serialists* (ed: Beth Holley and Mary Ann Sheble) The Haworth Press, Inc., 1995, pp. 163-171. Multiple copies of this article/chapter may be purchased from The Haworth Document Delivery Center [1-800-3-HAWORTH; 9:00 a.m. - 5:00 p.m. (EST)].

© 1995 by The Haworth Press, Inc. All rights reserved.

INTRODUCTION

I am extremely pleased to be able to share with you some of my personal experiences in working for library vendors, and hope to show how similar the requirements are for the library and vendor environments. Shortly after leaving employment at a library, I was asked to be on a panel discussing "Alternative Careers for Librarians: Other Things You Can Do With a Library Degree." I have always felt that working for a library vendor is a natural application of the MLS, so "alternative" seems an inaccurate term.

Forest Woody Horton, Jr. had this to say:

> ... on the concept of "alternative careers" for librarians. That phrase, and its underlying thrust, implies that working beyond traditional library settings is somehow unusual or exceptional.[1]

The skills and knowledge learned in the course of earning a graduate library and information science degree are the very ones needed in many positions with library vendors. In fact, I will go so far as to say that any vendor serving the needs of libraries and information centers who does not employ any MLS-degreed librarians is deficient in having the necessary resource on staff to fully understand how to maximize that service.

BACKGROUND

To give you a better idea of how I formed my viewpoints, let me give you a brief review of my background. I worked for thirteen years in the General Library (now called the Tom Rivera Library) at the University of California, Riverside (UCR). Initially, I was a student assistant while working on my undergraduate degree. Eventually, I made my way up the ladder in the paraprofessional ranks to be head of Monographs Acquisitions and Processing, two units in the Technical Processing Department. Having dropped out of school, my boss finally forced me to ask myself the question, "What do you want to be when you grow up?" and talked me into going back to school. He pointed out that I needed a library degree to get more promotions. Only one detail stood in my way: I still had not finished the bachelor's degree! With time and patience on my part, with a lot of assistance from my boss and mentor, John Tanno, and with support from others at UCR, I finished my BA degree. When I started library school, I moved from Technical Processing into Reference. This offered me a new challenge, and an opportunity to learn the public service side of libraries.

When I finally finished graduate school at the University of Southern California, I started applying for jobs. In addition to jobs at other university campuses, which would provide a logical transition into the professional ranks of librarianship, I applied for a position at the Cooperative Library Agency for Systems and Services (CLASS) in San Jose, California. This became my first "alternative" job.

After five years at CLASS, I was ready for a new challenge. Unsure about what I wanted to do, I decided to start networking with friends and colleagues to find out if there were any interesting projects in which I could get involved. I found several opportunities, including serving as technology consultant in the creation of the Silicon Valley Information Center (SVIC) at San Jose Public Library. This Center was established to contain historical archives and current information (not indexed elsewhere) on the high tech companies in California's Silicon Valley. We selected the Dynix automated library system. Along with helping to install Dynix and several PC software programs, I trained staff who had never used computers and set up procedures for managing the systems. While doing this project on a part time basis, I also provided bibliographic instruction for master's and bachelor's degree students in St. Mary's College extension programs, taught a few library school courses at San Jose State University Division of Library and Information Science, helped set up an e-mail network for drug and alcohol abuse intervention centers, and in my spare time learned to ride my BMW motorcycle! This was a fun period, during which I learned a great deal about applying my library training and education to non-traditional challenges.

When I had been freelancing for about a year and a half, I was approached by Ben Johnson of EBSCO, who was recruiting for a salesperson for the San Francisco-area office. He succeeded in convincing me that, although I had never held a sales job, I had actually been selling various products and services (and myself) for years without realizing it, through teaching, training, and answering questions about services I provided. I accepted the sales position, covering the territory of Northern California and Hawaii (tough job, but somebody had to do it), selling both subscription services and CD-ROM products. A year and a half later I was promoted to another position, which marked the end of the only sales position I have ever had. (Does that surprise those who think everyone who works for a vendor is in sales?)

Upon being promoted to Director of Library Automation, I moved to Birmingham, Alabama, to work out of EBSCO's international headquarters. What a beautiful place and what wonderful people I discovered! However, my husband was never able to move to Birmingham to join me, so after a two-year period of commuting to California to keep my marriage alive, it was approved for me to return to the west coast. I was already travelling a great deal, so everyone thought I could conduct my responsibilities from anywhere–planes, trains, automobiles, hotels, etc. But, I discovered that Birmingham was now added to my travel itinerary, and the added burden of working 2,000 miles from my boss and peers in the company proved to be too much.

I then left EBSCO to join a small software company near my home, CASPR, Inc. After a year, that job did not prove to be what I had expected, and I started exploring the possibility of working for the company whose software I had installed at SVIC–Dynix. I had known the founders of Dynix since they started the company ten years earlier, and had maintained contact with Paul Sybrowsky, President, and Jim Wilson, Sales Manager, over the years. A chance meeting with Jim at a conference in New York led to an interview and subsequent job offer. My husband was able to move with me to Utah, having established his own consulting business with clients spread across the U.S. and western Europe. My responsibilities as Product Manager include serving as a liaison with our customers, defining and shaping the development of the product, marketing activities, and building relationships with our vendors (hardware, database management software and peripherals).

SURVIVING CHANGE

In surviving the change from a library to a vendor, I have discovered there are both differences and similarities between the two types of employment. Although the similarities outnumber the differences, it is important to be aware of some of each.

Differences

I found the following differences between libraries and vendors. (Disclaimer: Please remember these comments are from my own experience and are not intended to reflect on any particular institution or the library world at large. Your experience may vary.)

Faster Decisions–When I left academe to work for CLASS, I was amazed that I could walk into the Executive Director's office, have a brief conversation, and walk out with a decision I could act on immediately. Similar situations at UCR required that a committee be formed, making sure to involve everyone who could: have input, be useful in making a decision, and have enough clout to make the decision stick, or, be offended if not included, and/or cause trouble for you later.

The Bottom Line–Most vendors are in business to make money. In academe, if a project is not finished by the end of the fiscal year, it can be carried over into the next year. In the vendor environment, there is outcome accountability.

More Travel–Although I have known some librarians who travel more than I do, I have traveled much more with vendors than I did when I worked in a library. On the average, vendors require more travel than libraries. And, it is not always glamorous. Personal time, including many weekends, is often sacrificed. However, this travel can take you to wonderful places, which, if you are lucky, you might find time to enjoy.

Handling Assumptions/Resistance–With some people, I find myself always on the defensive. "No, I am not trying to sell you something." "And why is that bad, anyway, if it is something you need?" Libraries are consumers and vendors are providers of needed goods and services. Not everyone who works for a vendor is a salesperson. And salespeople are not bad–some of them are even librarians! We are fortunate, in our profession, to have so many

MLS-degreed librarians working for library vendors. How many photocopier salespeople have you met who have a library degree?

Similarities

There are several similarities between library and vendor environments. I think that all of us–librarians and vendors–are part of the delivery of information to those who need it. We form the "information chain." We are service-oriented and service-motivated, whether the ultimate goal includes making a profit or not. Individuals in both camps participate in professional associations; in fact, it is part of my job responsibility. And the skills and educational background we obtain in preparation for jobs in libraries or with vendors are often quite similar.

WHY WORK FOR A VENDOR?

If you are now in a library and you have wondered what it would be like to work for a vendor, you might find it exciting to be on the cutting edge of technology. There is a great opportunity to help shape the methods of information provision. I get fired up about having my ear to the ground, learning about the challenges libraries have in serving the information needs of the world, listening to the great ideas everyone has about how to meet those challenges, and brainstorming together to create a synergy of ideas that can be realized in future product development. Being involved in the actual creation and delivery of technological advancements is a heady experience!

Some positions within a vendor's operations allow the individual to be more autonomous than in a library. Organizations can be less hierarchical in a traditional manner and individuals can participate as team players. I am the only person with my job description where I work. It is like being on the staff of a large university library and being the only one working in the Serials Department! After spending thirteen years working in a university library, I have found I like the corporate environment more than the academic, as a personal choice. If you are interested in working for a vendor, you must make that choice for yourself.

WHY WORK IN A LIBRARY/INFORMATION CENTER?

To look at the other side of the coin, one of the things I miss from my library days is being surrounded by librarians. That is why I come to conferences such as NASIG, to convene with my own kind. Although we have quite a few librarians on the staff at Dynix (about 10%), staff and management meetings always include people who will not understand me if I use too much library jargon. We librarians speak our own special language.

Another advantage missing from the vendor scene is the ability to work directly with researchers and others needing information. We vendors are one step removed from that–you are the link. The public services librarian in me always surfaces whenever I see I might be of help, even in department stores and on street corners. Sometimes I think I must have the words "Ask Me" written somewhere on me; I was even asked for directions once in Florence, Italy, by a Spaniard (and I speak neither Italian nor Spanish)! The fact is that vendors often provide new technologies, but they rarely get to see them being used to help people in real life.

MYTHS

As in most things, it is easy to romanticize about something when you think you want to be part of it–it is the "Grass is Greener" syndrome. The first myth is that vendors pay better than libraries. Unfortunately, this profession is plagued by low pay for the amount of education we have. You might get a little more money working for a vendor, but probably less vacation.

The second myth is that travel is glamorous. Anyone who travels for business learns to shrug off the frequent "Have a good time" comments from people in the office. Every time I hear that type of comment, I imagine these non-travelers picturing me flying first class (always), eating in expensive restaurants, touring the sights of big cities, and staying in luxury hotels. This is not a perpetual vacation, folks.

Third myth: Everyone will love you. Nope–some will even be rude, or worse. At a minimum, you will find some people who refuse to let you call on them. On the other hand, you MUST, if not love, at least be nice to everyone, whether you personally like them or not.

Fourth: The hours are short. You will find yourself working long past 5:00 to get a job finished. And, if a customer needs something urgently, you can even work all night and/or weekend. You will frequently have to travel or work over weekends. And, even if you are technically not "on the job" after hours, if you are not at home you cannot do your laundry, play with your cat, help children with homework, relax with a hobby, call your friends, etc.

Fifth: There is no stress. You may be held personally responsible for the success or failure of a project. There are no committees to hide behind—YOU are accountable.

IS WORKING FOR A VENDOR IN YOUR FUTURE?

Now, if I have not totally discouraged you by dispelling those myths, here are a few things to consider if you think you want to work for a vendor: Examine your feelings about vendor representatives you know. Do you wish to be like them? What are your reasons for wanting to work for a vendor? Hang out with a vendor representative and see what a typical day is like. How would you view yourself doing this job?

Talk to people—both ones who represent vendors and ones in libraries. Ask what they think of the idea of you working for a vendor. How would they feel about you selling to or servicing their library? Find someone who left a vendor to work in a library and find out why they switched. Ask everyone if they would do things differently if they could do them over.

Most jobs with vendors are not advertised in *Library Journal,* so do not rely on that type of source for job openings. Do not be shy about asking vendor reps you know about openings at their companies. Some jobs are posted at ALA and other conference job centers, so be sure to check them out. If you cannot attend the major conferences, call companies about a week in advance to see if they are posting job openings and ask for a contact person.

Look for a job that builds on strengths you have already developed. Although it happens, it is probably not wise to seek a job with an automation vendor if you have never used a computer, or to work for a book dealer if you have always been a serials librarian.

Finally, think broadly about what you can do with your expertise. Read Dr. Horton's paper, look beyond the library and information world if you dare, and use your imagination!

NOTE

1. Forest W. Horton. *Extending the librarian's domain: A survey of emerging occupational opportunities for librarians and information professionals,* SLA occasional papers series no. 4 (Washington, DC: Special Libraries Association, 1994).

From Earth to Ether:
One Publisher's Reincarnation

Susan Lewis

SUMMARY. The author discusses the development of a prototype for delivering Johns Hopkins University Press journals in electronic form. The project has been a collaborative process between the university library, the computing center, and the Press. The complexities involved in converting to electronic publishing are discussed. They include: assessing market readiness, shifts in procedures for obtaining rights and permission, determining true publishing costs, pricing strategies, and staffing concerns.

When Alex Bloss called last January and asked me to speak at this conference about how my job had changed with the impact of electronic publishing, I was in the midst of working with a computer programmer to develop "perl scripts" that would automatically convert PostScript files to Internet-deliverable files. This particular process was crucial to developing a prototype for delivering Johns Hopkins University Press journals in electronic form. While the results enabled us to prepare forty-seven articles for electronic publication with a minimum of labor, it differed significantly from the traditional text-preparation procedure normally used by scholarly publishers.

The collaborative aspect of our online journals project did not

---

Susan Lewis is Online Projects Manager, Johns Hopkins University Press, Baltimore, MD.

[Haworth co-indexing entry note]: "From Earth to Ether: One Publisher's Reincarnation." Lewis, Susan. Co-published simultaneously in *The Serials Librarian* (The Haworth Press, Inc.) Vol. 25, No. 3/4, 1995, pp. 173-180; and: *A Kaleidoscope of Choices: Reshaping Roles and Opportunities for Serialists* (ed: Beth Holley and Mary Ann Sheble) The Haworth Press, Inc., 1995, pp. 173-180. Multiple copies of this article/chapter may be purchased from The Haworth Document Delivery Center [1-800-3-HAWORTH; 9:00 a.m. - 5:00 p.m. (EST)].

© 1995 by The Haworth Press, Inc. All rights reserved.

resemble traditional publishing, either. This collaboration involves the university press, the library, and the computing center at the Johns Hopkins University (JHU) in a large-scale effort that will eventually lead to the online publication of over forty of the Press's journals in the humanities and social sciences.

One result of this alliance is a robust prototype consisting of four journal issues, a sophisticated search engine, full-screen illustrations, text and voice annotations, and many additional features. Another is our conviction that electronic journals can not only enhance research and education but be economically priced if certain criteria are met.

The most important result of the JHU experience, however, is the emergence of a new way of doing business for the university press and library subscribers. This involves engaging libraries in a "partnership of interest" with the Press that will enable us to deliver scholarly publications in a way that integrates library involvement and feedback, so we can tailor the form of these publications to serve the actual needs of scholars and readers.

The Project Muse prototype and the trial partnership with the Milton S. Eisenhower Library have enabled us to identify four areas that are key to the success of this larger process. These include marketing, rights and permissions, true costs, and product pricing. The effect of our approach to these issues will also affect staffing and the traditional production process (Figure 1).

MARKET READINESS AND MARKETING

In the context of a partnership, rather than a relationship as suppliers and customers, *marketing* becomes *education*. This is a very different approach, designed to inform and gather feedback, rather than simply announce and persuade, as is done in traditional sales and advertising campaigns. By making education and technical assistance the focus of our marketing efforts, we can actually create a product and a market based on input from those who will use it. This approach is not just mutually beneficial to the partners–it is absolutely essential since libraries must create or have in place an electronic environment that benefits their readers before they can take full advantage of electronically delivered journals.

FIGURE 1

JOHNS HOPKINS UNIVERSITY
PROJECT MUSE

- **MARKETING AND MARKETING READINESS**
- **RIGHTS AND PERMISSIONS**
- **DETERMINING TRUE COSTS**
- **PRICING STRATEGY**
- **STAFFING CONCERNS**

To facilitate the creation of this environment, our initiative will involve assessing library needs so we can provide relevant consultation and information. In other words, educating libraries about the advantages of our approach for their readers will involve working directly with libraries and "focus groups" of users to determine:

- library readiness and experience with full-text databases;
- library hardware and network infrastructure, including "front end" software;
- reader sophistication and usage patterns; and
- online access to reader training materials.

Reader involvement is an important part of the educational process, and the end users of our electronic journals will be encouraged to respond via electronic forms and questionnaires, as they have in the simplified but very useful form developed for the prototype. In one scenario, comments about the local electronic environment are forwarded to the contact person at the local site; comments about the journal content are forwarded to the appropriate editor; and comments about the quality of the electronic product are used by the publisher to improve the product.

RIGHTS AND PERMISSIONS

In the course of conversations between the Press and library at Johns Hopkins, we identified two possible disadvantages of electronic journals from the library's point of view. These are: (1) if the library stops subscribing, it is left without holdings, and (2) if the publisher goes out of business, the digitized materials could be lost to the library.

Because of these concerns, the Press will grant libraries unlimited print copying privileges for their patrons' *personal* use but *not* for course packs or interlibrary loan (ILL). As permitted by fair use and other provisions of the 1976 copyright law, university libraries may provide paper articles for interlibrary loan. They may also send articles electronically for downloading and printing by another library on ILL but not for electronic storage at the borrowing library.

Full subscribers to the Press's electronic journals, in other words, will be able to make unlimited copies for internal use and up to six copies for interlibrary loan. For digitized text, we believe that conversion to media such as film or CD-ROM is entirely appropriate for the purpose of preservation—but not for the purpose of selling print copies or sending electronic copies to file servers located at other universities or other electronic networks, listservs, bulletin boards, etc.

Interestingly, networked document delivery from our database will probably prove to be more economical than interlibrary loan, and may be a profitable replacement for ILL, with mutual benefits to the Press and subscribing libraries. This is another area we are examining closely.

DETERMINING TRUE COSTS

The goal of our collaborative effort is to offer electronic journals and price them, at lower rates than their paper counterparts. But cost-effective pricing is not possible unless electronic publishing is also cost-effective.

To set pricing effectively, we have had to ascertain the economics of electronic publishing, including differences in first-copy and additional copy costs for paper and electronic formats. First-copy costs are those incurred to produce a single copy of the journal, including vetting, editing, and marketing. These costs are constant no matter what format is used. Additional copy costs include manufacturing additional copies, distribution, and storage. These costs are affected by the final form of the journal.

Through data gathered from the Project Muse prototype, as well as our paper-based operation, we have ascertained that additional copy costs are lower for electronic journals than for paper journals. Excluding start-up costs for equipment and labor, we believe we can sell electronic journals for less than paper journals. This projection is based on labor and cost estimates extrapolated from a small prototype and applied to a forty-journal program, and it assumes only a modest number of library subscribers in the first three years. As more subscribers come on board—and as we get better and more efficient in the electronic medium—we expect that greater cost reductions may be possible (Figure 2).

PRICING STRATEGY

Our experience with the prototype revealed that the *ongoing* tasks and equipment necessary for electronic publishing were less expensive than the manufacturing costs for paper journals. The problem, however, involves start-up costs and ongoing costs for the first few years. Unless these costs are covered by grants or special university funding, it is unlikely that in the first three years a paper-based publisher of humanities and social-science journals—even a press with as large a program as the Johns Hopkins University Press—can move to electronic publishing in a way that results in lower prices for libraries.

This leads to a second concern. How can a publisher ascertain a means of licensing, set appropriate fees, and collect payments for the use of electronic materials? Expanding the Project Muse prototype so that it includes all 40 of the JHU Press journals has required a long, hard look at paper pricing and distribution procedures and then comparing them with pricing and distribution for electronic media.

FIGURE 2

JOHNS HOPKINS UNIVERSITY PROJECT MUSE

- INDIVIDUAL RATES FOR ELECTRONIC JOURNALS ARE LOWER THAN RATES FOR PRINTED JOURNALS

- SUBSCRIBERS TO THE ENTIRE DATABASE OF PRESS JOURNALS RECEIVE A DISCOUNT OFF THE COMBINED INDIVIDUAL RATES OF ALL THE TITLES IN THE DATABASE

- CHARTER SUBSCRIBERS RECEIVE ADDITIONAL BENEFITS

Of the two models we considered, site licensing and subscription, we selected the second. Site licensing involves pricing according to each university's full-time enrollment (FTE). It is commonly used by software publishers to distribute a variety of packages on campus. According to librarians and computing-center professionals, these arrangements often seem very comprehensive in the beginning, but they often escalate to an astronomical yearly fee designed to cover possible losses from unlimited access by the university community.

Subscription involves charging a flat rate for an electronic publication–regardless of a university's size–and works the same way as paper-copy subscriptions. For both publishers and libraries, this model is more convenient because it does not require a detailed contractual agreement, offers renewals on an annual rather than a multi-year basis, and is not based on the university's FTE. The disadvantage of the subscription model is that the subscription rate must be set to absorb one-time costs and possible losses in the first five years, especially if the publisher is paper-based and must absorb the costs of moving to electronic media.

The only safe route for the publisher, and one used for a few current experimental efforts, is to project costs and potential subscribers, and then set a price based on conservative estimates. This is usually high, considering the initial investment in equipment and staff, and the uncertainty that enough libraries have the technology in place to accommodate even the most basic requirements in the first few years.

In order to assure that Johns Hopkins electronic journals can be offered for less than paper journals, we developed a financial plan in which grants and special university funding cover one-time costs and revenue losses during the first three years. Over this period of time, the Press will move its paper journals to electronic form at a rate of about twelve journals per year. Although we are still at a preliminary stage in our thinking about subscription arrangements, we hope that they will include the following features:

- Individual journals purchased in electronic form only will be priced lower than paper journals.
- Subscriptions to both print and electronic versions will be lower than the full price of each.
- Subscribers to the entire database of electronic journals (which will move from twelve to forty over three years) will receive a discount off the combined single rates of all titles included in the database.
- Charter subscribers will receive the first year's electronic-journal subscription free, as well as a guaranteed discount for a fixed number of years. There will be no extra charge for any new journal titles added during the current year, and free access reports will be available.

STAFFING CONCERNS

The Press is not changing what it does, but it is changing the way it does it. For marketing, this means engaging in both educational and promotional activities. For rights and permissions, costing, and pricing, it means reexamining the way we do business and crafting a model and financial plan that benefits both the publisher and its library partners.

The shift from paper to electronic media affects us at an even more basic level, adapting our existing staff to a new process and adding new positions with titles like "systems manager" and "technical support." It is in these areas where our partnership with libraries will help us the most. Developing a prototype involves looking to our library and academic computing center for advice, and for descriptions of staff positions essential to the success of an *electronic* venture.

CONCLUSION

According to the April, 1994 issue of *Harper's Index*, the percentage change since 1992 in *New York Times* articles mentioning the "information superhighway" is +2,025. According to the editors of the Digital Information Group's CD-ROM Factbook, CD-ROM revenue will reach about $15 billion in business-to-business-or publisher-to-library-sales by the year 2000. Online revenue will top $20 billion.

University libraries and scholarly publishers need to be part of this revolution by adopting a new way of doing business–a partnership of interest that offers the opportunity to move from space- and resource-consuming paper products to networked, digital text that promises better access to more robust resources with a friendlier environmental impact. The Johns Hopkins experience is just the beginning of this metamorphosis and will certainly not accommodate every contingency at the beginning. We believe, however, that it will serve as a useful model for publishers and libraries to begin developing partnerships with the mutual goal of reinvigorating and redefining the scholarly communication process in the twenty-first century.

Library Cultures in Conflict: Exploring New Roles for Librarians

Johann A. van Reenen

SUMMARY. The author discusses the effect of continuous change and technological advances in the information industry on the role of librarians. Not only are new competencies required, but also new ways of thinking and behaving. Some of these challenge long-held philosophies about librarianship and access to information. A review of services at the University of British Columbia (UBC) brought many of these issues to the front. Librarians seem to react to this challenge to traditional values and attitudes in predictable ways. This is explained in the context of John Enright's ideas on "change and resilience." Lists of future roles, competencies, and strategies derived from the literature and from electronic discussion groups are provided.

INTRODUCTION

We live in the era of knowledge capitalism and this requires new ways of working and thinking. I will explore these roles, and will focus on the attitudes and necessary behaviors to make changes and take risks. The question I would like to pose is: Are librarians ready to work differently? Are they exploring new ways of thinking and new roles for the profession that will lead them to not merely survive, but thrive in the emerging information economy?

Johann van Reenen is Head, University of British Columbia Life Sciences Libraries, Vancouver, British Columbia.

[Haworth co-indexing entry note]: "Library Cultures in Conflict: Exploring New Roles for Librarians." van Reenen, Johann A. Co-published simultaneously in *The Serials Librarian* (The Haworth Press, Inc.) Vol. 25, No. 3/4, 1995, pp. 181-192; and: *A Kaleidoscope of Choices: Reshaping Roles and Opportunities for Serialists* (ed: Beth Holley and Mary Ann Sheble) The Haworth Press, Inc., 1995, pp. 181-192. Multiple copies of this article/chapter may be purchased from The Haworth Document Delivery Center [1-800-3-HAWORTH; 9:00 a.m. - 5:00 p.m. (EST)].

© 1995 by The Haworth Press, Inc. All rights reserved.

I co-chaired two service reviews at the University of British Columbia (UBC). One dealt with the role of librarians at UBC and the other with core users, services, and hours. During the past two and a half years, I have been in a position to ask this question and I have arrived at some initial answers.

At the root of our current challenges are "knowledge abilities": availability, findability, accessibility, understandability, and usability of information to acquire knowledge, or to transform information into useful knowledge. These abilities form a continuum that has always existed at the root of librarianship. We have managed these well in the past, but continuing to do so is becoming more difficult as resources shrink and others do these things as well or better, or at least promise to do so. Change is inevitable.

What are the things that lead or force situations and people to change?

- dissatisfaction with the present,
- a search for excellence,
- running into barriers in achieving excellence, and
- developing practical steps to overcome barriers and reach our vision.

I will explore each of these four "forces," emphasizing barriers to change.

DISSATISFACTION WITH THE PRESENT

One of the greatest causes of dissatisfaction relates to lack of funding. Meeting users' current needs, and anticipating and planning to meet their future needs are equally important. We are, however, funded to do only the first. To do the latter will require creative thinking and the willingness to take risks. The publishing crisis exerts further stress on the system.

We are ageing as a profession and dissatisfaction is a natural consequence. This also leads to an unwillingness to take risks at the mid- to end-career stages, limiting our organizations' ability to change as rapidly as the current situation requires.

Our view of the world and the world's view of us has left many librarians dissatisfied, and the status and image of the profession sometimes leave much to be desired. Roma M. Harris asks, "Has librarianship shunned its service ideals in its struggle to be seen as more than woman's work?"[1] Through research, she has learned that "... the service relationship in librarianship differs from that in many professions. The relationship between client and librarian is much more centered on the client's need than it is on the librarian's role as an expert. I also learned that librarians' work and the services they provide are very much undervalued, both within and outside the profession."[2]

Dissatisfaction and anxiety are also heightened by the wave of electronic developments, which we are trying to assimilate and make useful to our clients. Prentiss Riddle remarked in a recent electronic mail message, "The explosion of the Internet has delivered to our desktops the virtual equivalent of a vast warehouse of unsorted paper. The question which interests me is: how does one convert a mountain of digital pulp into something resembling a library?"[3]

A SEARCH FOR EXCELLENCE

Librarians are known for their dedication and the tremendous efforts they have put into developing access to information for all people. Evidence of this is found in the world's great collections and associated bibliographic tools. We continue to prove this in the new electronic environment, and even the popular press comments on our new roles. An article in *Glamour* reads, "Perhaps more than any other career, technology has transformed the work of the librarian, leaving her with more time to do what she does best: provide information . . . Today's librarian is an information guru who designs systems, evaluates new technologies, and coaches people on how to find the best sources online."[4]

Can we continue to meet these expectations? Are we prepared for the changes required of us? What are the barriers?

RUNNING INTO BARRIERS IN THE SEARCH FOR EXCELLENCE

During my involvement with the service reviews, I observed, as did David Penniman during his term as president of the Council on

Library Resources, that a dichotomy emerged in many of the opinions expressed. The dichotomy can be described as a clash in values and cultures; thus the title of my talk . . . and the first barrier: attitudes toward change. Penniman consulted with numerous stakeholders in the library and information industry.[5] What emerged was placed in the context of John Enright's ideas on "change and resilience."[6] Penniman said that he heard arguments for a culture of resilience versus a culture of solidity (Figure 1).

Libraries need to become learning organizations for both staff and users. The library as a working environment has been so successful in the past that it has stabilized around firmly held positions, such as ownership above all, and cultural values, such as information must always be free to all. In his book, *The Fifth Discipline*, Peter Senge says that "organizational learning disabilities" arise if we view the world in linear rather than holistic ways.[7] This is what happens in most organizations, such as libraries, that have traditionally attracted very detailed and precise personalities. I will mention some of these "organizational learning disabilities" to illustrate this concept:

- I am my position: Most people confuse their jobs with their identities. They focus on their daily tasks to a point where they miss the greater purpose of their organization.
- The enemy is out there: We like to find an external agent to blame when problems arise, but "out there" and "in here" are part of the same system.
- The fixation on events: We tend to dwell on who got fired and recent budget cuts. The events distract us from the long-term patterns of change that lie behind them, and this inhibits us from understanding these patterns and preparing for changes.
- The delusion of learning from experience: We may learn best from experience, but we often never directly experience the consequences of many of our most important decisions.
- Functional specialization and fragmentation: We have taken work, broken it into pieces, and proceeded with the assumption that if everyone worried about their work, the whole world would take care of itself. It is important that these behaviors and situations are acknowledged if we are to overcome the barriers they present.

FIGURE 1. A Culture of Solidarity vs. A Culture of Resilience
* SOME FAVORED PREDICTABILITY AND ELABORATE PLANNING (SOLIDITY); OTHERS VERSATILITY AND IMPROVISATION (RESILIENCE) * SOME VALUED DEGREES AND CERTIFICATION (S); OTHERS VALUED THE SUBSTANCE OF EDUCATION AND TRAINING (R) * SOME SAW POWER ACHIEVED THROUGH HIERARCHY (S); OTHERS SOUGHT TO INFLUENCE VIA NETWORKING (R) * SOME LIVED IN TRADITION AND THE PAST (S); OTHERS LOOKED TO THE PRESENT AND THE FUTURE (R) * SOME FEARED MISTAKES AND AVOIDED FAILURE (S); OTHERS SAW MISTAKES AS A SIGN OF LEARNING (R) * SOME VIEWED CONSISTENT SUCCESS AS A SIGN THAT ALL WAS WELL (S); OTHERS SAW SUCH A TRACK RECORD AS AN INDICATION THAT A CHANCE FOR LEARNING WAS BEING AVOIDED (R)

DEVELOPING PRACTICAL STEPS TO OVERCOME BARRIERS

It has become obvious to me that organizations need to address issues relating to long held beliefs and attitudes. Environmental scans and strategic planning help, particularly with individuals who are of the resilient type, or so-called "early adopters." It is important to provide opportunities for groups to discuss their views about the library of the future in open forums. The resulting conflict is necessary. This process should be limited, and when there is a critical mass of early adopters, the organization should begin operating as if the new paradigm were a reality. My advice to those who work in organizations where this is not happening is to align themselves with others who believe that we need new ways of thinking and working, begin acting in new ways, get the necessary skills, and learn to manage the resulting conflict. A strategic plan for our profession, our libraries, and for our careers should include the extrapolation of future roles and the skills needed to perform these roles, as well as bold strategies to overcome barriers.

Future roles for librarians can be summarized in terms such as information facilitator, provider and integrator, and knowledge server. Other terms include:

- providers of electronic information services,
- change agents,
- institutional publishers of local information,
- electronic consultants,
- simulators of creativity in our organizations through our ability to bring people together on neutral ground, because we are liked, trusted, and are generally seen as non-threatening,
- organizers of knowledge and negotiators of information needs (e.g., SGML has similarities to MARC tagging),
- teachers and coaches,
- faculty liaison, and
- systems designers.

SKILL SETS FOR THE FUTURE

It is clear that we will always need people skills. Collaborating with other disciplines, bringing diverse groups together, and creating problem-solving environments are some of our existing strengths. We can and should capitalize on these.

The types of competencies needed in the electronic information environment are summarized below from an electronic article by John Corbin.[8]

Personal Characteristics

- Service attitude
- Effective interpersonal communication
- Social sensitivity
- Flexibility
- Time consciousness
- Curiosity
- A desire to perform well

Basic Skills

- Information analysis and evaluation skills
- Computer use skills

- Network use and navigation skills
- Word processing skills

General Knowledge

- Nature and creation of information
- Information storage and retrieval
- Information transfer
- Information networks
- Information systems
- Information policy
- Information copyright and related issues
- Information privacy and ethics
- General principles of computing
- Organizational theory
- Information standards
- Information technology trends

Specialized Knowledge

- The clients with whom one works and their information needs
- Clients' discipline(s) and relevant literature
- Specific electronic information service (EIS) being offered and how to use it
- Other EIS that supplement or complement the one being offered
- What resources are available locally
- Where and how to obtain resources not available locally
- Document delivery options
- Evaluation of information received from an EIS
- Evaluation of client satisfaction with an EIS

One then has to ask, "On which skills do I rely now that will not be needed in the future, and which of the above skills do I need to acquire or enhance?"

STRATEGIES (NEW WAYS OF WORKING)

Continuing Education

It is clear that we must work together to obtain additional skills and help each other through changes. There are many ways to do this, including changes to formal education programs in library schools, formal training programs, self education, apprenticeships, learning from each other, and other continuing education events, such as conferences.

Process Simplification

We should help our organizations to improve effectiveness. This requires an understanding of the principles of continuous quality improvement. We should ensure that all technical services processes are directed toward the purpose of public service and access. Public and technical services should not be separated, and we must not fall into the divide-and-conquer trap once again. An example of this is seen in current serials developments (Figure 2).[9] The division of serials processing, information services, and the application of knowledge to produce new knowledge will blur over time and become a continuum, as can be clearly seen in the emergent information model in Figure 2.

Overcoming the "Image Barrier"

It is critical to understand how others see us and how we should act in the larger organization. To crack the "image barrier," librarians need to understand power, influence, and effectiveness (Figure 3).

FIGURE 2. Key Characteristics of Scientific and Technical Information Resource Management Models

INFO. MODEL	UNITS OF ACCESS	BASIC FORMAT FLOW
Classical	Journals	Paper inputs (ip) - Paper access (ac) - Paper outputs (op)
Modernized A	Articles as well as journals	Paper ip - Paper & Network ac - Paper op
Modernized B	Articles as well as journals	Paper ip - Paper & Network ac - Paper & Network op
Modernized C	Articles as well as journals	Paper & Network ip - Paper Netwk ac - Paper & Netwk op
Emergent	Facts as well as articles & journals	Network ip - Network ac - Paper & Network op

FIGURE 3. Equation for Influence
POWER * INFLUENCE * EFFECTIVENESS
HOW YOU REPORT = YOUR POWER BASE
HOW YOUR SERVICES ARE ORGANIZED AND DELIVERED = YOUR EFFECTIVENESS
ALL TOGETHER = YOUR INFLUENCE

We cannot afford to be disdainful of business practices, and we need to address the full range of economic issues associated with libraries and related information services. This inevitably will lead to a deeper understanding of the information industry as a whole, enabling us to answer questions such as:

- What are the unit costs of functions a library performs?
- How and why do these vary across libraries?
- How do these functions fit together to form information services, e.g., document delivery, and what is the overall cost?
- How can we measure benefits of such services?

Administrators and faculty need to be educated to the fact that libraries are being transformed "from labor-intensive craft workshops into capital-intensive high-tech light industry."[10]

Networking is equally important. Scout your organization for individuals or departments looking for someone to delegate their information management functions and offer to do it for them. Get in on top-level company priorities by joining key project teams. Develop strategies for serving the executive corridor. Librarians must manage beyond the library if they wish to survive and thrive.

Capitalize on Current Strengths

We can and should:

- Provide more indepth analyses of information to help users deal with the volume, diversity, and complexity of information.
- Develop navigational tools for information networks such as the Internet.

- Conduct research in how information is used and its usefulness.
- Act as consultants in electronic publishing and copyright issues; become electronic publishers ourselves.
- Act as change agents in the areas of information management, information literacy, and problem based learning; e.g., catalogers in health care libraries can build thesauri for indexing patient records.

Promote Role Models

Examples of excellent practices abound in the literature. I suggest that you read and discuss with your co-workers items such as *Designing Information: New Roles for Librarians*.[11] This work provides case studies and role models worth emulating, and shows that managers reward those librarians who take risks in exploring new ways of working.

CONCLUSION

I began with the observations of David Penniman and would like to end with more of his keen insight:

> What emerged for me was a sense of two cultures battling not only within groups but also within each individual. We all wish at some time to cling to the past, but are forced to live in the present and prepare ourselves and our institutions for the future. We must be committed to learning as a life long challenge. We must work to create learning organizations–i.e., organizations that treat mistakes as a natural part of learning, such organizations (and individuals) don't shut down the 'resilient' instincts within us all.[12]

We cannot resist the metamorphosis happening inside our current cocoon–our old view of librarianship. This cocoon will break, and out will fly an information facilitator and integrator or nothing! It is only natural that this should make us anxious. But look at the other things that we could become, as listed above. We are not the only profession that will be re-inventing itself. We are simply one of the first. To add to our stress, we know that there is no end in sight. As

Rachel Anderson (Director, Arizona Health Sciences Library) said at a conference in 1993: [We are facing a situation of] . . . "perpetual transition," [of being] "not in Oz yet, but not Kansas either."[13]

At another recent conference I heard a wonderful analogy. When asked, "Who has the most important influence on a ship's destiny?" most participants mentioned the captain, the leader. The speaker pointed out that the designers were more important. The best Captain cannot overcome serious design flaws! In charting a course for any of the goals listed above, we need to be designers of excellence. You, as serials librarians, are the designers of future access systems. We count on you. We expect you to move away from the idea of "the more subscriptions the better" to a situation where access and ownership decisions are made based on research that shows how scientists and academics use literature. Mistakes will occur. We should support each other, take what is good, leave the rest, and continue on our way to Oz.

The most important and difficult conclusion I have come to is that I cannot expect to change the organization or the people I work with unless I first change myself, and begin to work and behave differently.

NOTES

1. Roma M. Harris, "Gender, Power, and the Dangerous Pursuit of Professionalism," *American Libraries* (Oct. 1993): 874.

2. Ibid., 874.

3. Prentiss D. Riddle, "Subject Access to Networked Information," e-mail communication from RIDDLE@IS.RICE.EDU (19 April, 1994).

4. "The New Librarian as Info-Surfer," *Glamour* (April 1994): 126.

5. Adapted from: Prentiss D. Penniman, "Solidity vs. Resilience: A Cultural Conflict," *CLR Reports* (Dec. 1991): 1,4.

6. John Enright. "Change and Resilience," in *The Leader-Manager*, edited by John N. Williamson (New York: Wiley, 1986), 59-73.

7. Peter Senge, *The Fifth Discipline* (New York: Doubleday, 1990).

8. John Corbin, "Competencies for Electronic Information Services," *Public-Access Computer Systems Review* 4, no. 6 (1993):5-22. (To retrieve this file, send e-mail message to LISTSERV@UHUPVM1.UH.EDU: GET CORBIN PRV4N6 F=MAIL)

9. Adapted from: Association of American Universities, *Report of the Task Force on a National Strategy for Managing Scientific & Technical Information of the Research Libraries Project* (Washington, D.C.: AAU, April 4, 1994).

10. M. J. Martin, "Academic Libraries as Information Consumers: Implications for Policy Making," *Journal of Academic Librarianship* 17, no. 2 (1991): 97.

11. Linda C. Smith and Prudence W., eds. *Designing Information: New Roles for Librarians* (Champaign, IL: Graduate School of Library and Information Science, University of Illinois, 1993).

12. David Penniman, 4.

13. Rachel Anderson, "Keynote speech" presented at the annual conference of the Medical Library Association, Pacific Northwest Chapter, Portland, Oregon, 1993.

CONCURRENT SESSION III: PROFESSIONAL ADVICE ON HANDLING CHANGE

Understanding Transition: The People Side of Managing Change

Judy Clarke

SUMMARY. As we approach the twenty-first century, our futures will be cast in our ability to embrace continuous change. One of our most critical challenges will be preparing for the needs and expectations of tomorrow. Managing change is not enough. We must emerge with new insights. The future belongs to those who understand the human side of organizational change. The author discusses: understanding why change is so difficult for people; learning the significant difference between change and transition; exploring the process of transition; and recognizing signs of unmanaged transition.

Clearly the message you have heard over and over is that change is inevitable. But even though change is inevitable, we are always

---

This is an edited transcript of a motivational presentation by Judy Clarke, owner of Judy Clarke and Associates, Gresham, OR.

[Haworth co-indexing entry note]: "Understanding Transition: The People Side of Managing Change." Clarke, Judy. Co-published simultaneously in *The Serials Librarian* (The Haworth Press, Inc.) Vol. 25, No. 3/4, 1995, pp. 193-202; and: *A Kaleidoscope of Choices: Reshaping Roles and Opportunities for Serialists* (ed: Beth Holley and Mary Ann Sheble) The Haworth Press, Inc., 1995, pp. 193-202. Multiple copies of this article/chapter may be purchased from The Haworth Document Delivery Center [1-800-3-HAWORTH; 9:00 a.m. - 5:00 p.m. (EST)].

given an opportunity, even in devastating change, to grow, learn, and self-renew. How we do that is separate from the change itself and it is totally dependent upon how we deal with what is called transition. Transition is an internal process that people go through when things in their lives change. I would like to begin by clarifying a very significant difference between change and transition.

Many people have the naive assumption that if you manage the content pieces of what is changing (i.e., staffing, economics, technical pieces), people will simply adjust. Is that your experience? If it is not adjustment, what is it like? It is chaos, depression, confusion, disorientation, and an incredible amount of disruption. So what we are going to look at is the idea of how you manage the internal process that people go through when things in their world change.

Change, as defined here, is something external. Change is when something starts or stops, and takes place at a particular point in time. You can measure it. Change, especially organizational change, focuses on outcome. Change management within your organizational life is often called strategic planning. But transition, unlike change, is an internal process that people go through. It is a psychological reorientation process where people are trying to find new meanings and ways to function in a change situation. We gain a lot of identity from external things, such as relationships, the roles we play, and our responsibilities. When these external things change, people go into a transition which is similar to an identity crisis. So while change is external, transition refers to what goes on inside a person. And transition takes much longer than change. In fact, from the work I have done, I will tell you it takes twice as long as most people anticipate.

People adapt to change at three speeds. First, there is the physical aspect, which is the time it takes for people to comply with the behavioral requirements of a change. Certainly individuals go into a learning curve, learning how to operate new machinery, or new procedural policies. The next piece is the intellectual, which is the time it takes for a person to comprehend why a change is taking place or why it is necessary. Frequently, people will get stuck at the intellectual phase and ask, "Why is this happening? Why are they doing this? Things were going great. This doesn't make sense."

The last part is the emotional piece, which is the time it takes for a person to feel comfortable with a change.

There are other differences between change and transition. With change, especially organizational change, there is a focus on what is going to start or begin. But even positive change requires that we let go of the past. And the process of transition begins with an ending. People must say good-bye and let go of the past before they can emerge practicing the new skills and the new set of attitudes that are required by a change. So even in positive change, people go into a transition that starts with an ending. Now think in terms of unwelcome or negative change, and now think about how difficult endings can be for people. And if it is not their idea or decision to make a change, people tend to hang on for a long time to the ending piece.

So, the process of transition starts with an ending and it finishes with a beginning. Now, the beginning I am talking about is not external. It is internal. And between the ending and the beginning is the neutral zone. Being in the neutral zone is like being between trapezes: You have nothing to hold onto. You have let go of the old, but you are not really comfortable in the new yet. It is basically like hanging out in "limboland" or the wilderness. The process of transition has three phases: the ending, the neutral zone (which is marked by a lot of chaos and confusion), and the new beginning.

Look from the micro to the macro of what happens, especially organizationally, when things change. First, people do not approach transition the same way and they do not move through a transition at the same speed. What this process sets up within our work and home lives is low stability. People are all over the place emotionally. People perceive high levels of inconsistency in the environment, and at no other time is there as much polarity between "us" and "them." Change is stressful and difficult because it requires you to let go, and this leads to a high level of emotional stress. The more you have identified with the past, and if it was not your idea to make the change, the more stressful it is to let go. There is a high, often undirected energy that is played out during this transition process. This emotion usually takes the direction of anger. And anger usually comes out as passive-aggressive behavior. Control becomes a major issue. When a change is introduced and it was not your idea and you do not agree with the decision to implement the change, you tend to feel you lose control of the environment. It is amazing how this anger over loss of control is transferred to relationships with other people. In fact, one of the major ways people attempt to gain control is by withholding communication. They refuse to speak, or be helpful, or provide information.

Past patterns of behavior become highly valued. Conflict increases at a time when people are being asked to work together in teams. With control being such a major issue, people are actually more difficult to get along with and there is more stress. Clearly, managing change is a challenge. And we need to manage change well through understanding the nature of the change, along with the process of transition and the emotions that people go through when their world changes.

I would like to return to talking about the process of transition. Individuals, organizations, and nations go through this process. At the ending point of a transition, people direct their energy toward hanging on. In the neutral zone, people let go. And what do you think is a necessary element when you are in the neutral zone and between trapezes? Faith. The best definition I have for faith is belief without evidence. And those people who are able to really stay up at a time of uncertainty are those who have faith; who believe whatever happens they will be okay, and learn and grow from the experience.

Another way to look at the transition process is that you start with an ending and you go down into the neutral zone before you re-emerge with a new insight that can only be gained from a transition. In fact, Rollo May, a great psychologist once said, "It is in the nothingness that people gain insight." It is when things are no longer as they were and you are no longer able to define who you are in terms of your old roles that transition becomes possible.

To be able to successfully manage a transition, you must grieve for the loss of what was, and deal with the uncertainty and confusion of the in-between time before you are able to accept and be committed to a change. You do not need to agree with a change to get to the point of accepting it. While that may seem obvious, it is very difficult for most people to accept a change with which they do not agree.

I would like to give an example of an unmanaged transition. My friend, Kenny, was a senior executive in a publishing firm in New York. He lost his job three years ago. He has another job now, but it does not provide him with the level of prestige of his former job. Kenny consistently talks about, "I used to be somebody." His identity was wrapped up in something that no longer exists. And so the way he defines himself is based on who he used to be.

One of the major reasons people have difficulty letting go and dealing with endings is because they confuse endings with finality. People forget that the ending stage is the first step towards a new beginning or an opportunity. But some people refuse tenaciously to let go of what was, even though it no longer exists. And they define the past as the "good old days." Sometimes people try to bypass transition entirely. They tend to believe that they can go from the old to the new and never miss a beat. They believe that it is possible to be like an appliance and unplug from this reality and plug in to another, and all operations will continue as usual.

I have a friend who is on her fourth marriage. She has been married to her current husband for about three years and she has yet to unpack her boxes. Her feeling is "no big deal, I can simply leave again." Sometimes people make changes simply to break up boredom and monotony, not realizing the impact that this has on the people around them. Because they bypass their transition, they do not deal with letting go of what was and they are never really committed to where they are going because it would be too difficult and painful to say good-bye. These people make a lot of changes and it never seems to impact them. But what is the downside? What do you miss when you do not go through a transition? You do not learn, you do not grow, and you figure out nothing about where you have been. You have no sense of direction about where you are going.

Sometimes there are so many changes that people simply become lost. People need time to get back on their feet and make a new beginning before dealing with a new set of changes. When people are hit by a sequence of unrelated changes, they become confused about where to begin, what to do, and they ask the same questions over and over again.

Many decision-makers in organizations have what is known as the "phoenix fantasy" about the implications of change for their employees. Even though there is an initial expectation that performance will drop, there is a belief that the organization will rise out of the ashes and be wonderful in a very short period of time. This just does not happen. Instead, there tends to be reality: It takes twice as long as what anyone thought it would take to make the changes work. In these organizations, rather than giving people time to make a new beginning and to get comfortable, another new change is introduced, and then another. I am not saying that we do not have to deal with constant change, but we need to guard against unnecessary change. We also need to guard against piecemealing that continually pulls the rug out from underneath people. If you are a person to introduce change in your organization, it is best to try to package it as much as you can and introduce it at one time. People are very capable of dealing with immense amounts of change, if it makes sense and seems to be necessary.

Occasionally, there will be several people in an organization who are unwilling to make the commitment that is necessary for a change to work. These are people who hold back. Unlike being lost in the wilderness because there are so many changes, this attitude is much more conscious and deliberate. These are people who might as well wear a sweatshirt that says, "Prove it to me that this is going to work." These are individuals who have quit, but they have stayed. They have "retired in place." They do minimal work and hang on to "old baggage." Their attitude is, "Prove it to me that this new method, or this new technology is going to work. We've tried it before and it's never worked!" And these people do not give you a chance to prove that the change will work. It is my belief that these people prefer to be right versus changing their minds and feeling better. Sometimes you can have many people who say, "Prove it to me, this is never going to work," and it doesn't . . . . and they were right. So sometimes, people are much more interested in being right, even if it means failure, than in changing their mind for a change to work.

Sometimes people have to look long and hard at the changes occurring in their organizations and personal lives, and make difficult choices. They need to either make an ending in their current situation and go elsewhere, or get on with things and make the commitment necessary for a change to work. To "quit but stay" has an immense price tag. People's self-esteem and self-confidence are undermined. And having these people in the organization can pull down the rest of the group.

When things change, some people want to ignore it. They want to stay in a state of denial as long as possible. Change is difficult, stressful, and painful. But it is also the only way you grow, renew, and develop.

During my work with organizations, I have noticed that a number of them enable people to stay in a state of denial. Organizational decisionmakers will talk about how "things are going to change around here, you'd better watch out! Things are going to change, get ready, get ready!" But nothing ever changes. Employees are kept in a state of transition and nothing happens. When this occurs, people suffer in resistance. It is not deliberately saying, "I'm going to resist this." There is a suffering that people experience–and it is anger, grief, anxiety, and confusion. This is when people will find reasons that a change will not work.

Sometimes people find it is safer, easier, and they gain a sense of belonging to stay in resistance. I will give you an analogy of what that does. It is a silly analogy, but I think it illustrates my point. When you push an elevator button and the light has come on, how many of you keep pushing the button? Did you know that it takes up to three times as much energy as if you had done nothing and thought about something else? Does the elevator get there more quickly? Of course not, but that is what we do. I am convinced that the child inside all of us believes if we stay upset and unhappy enough about what is changing, we can make things different. But even if we use all of that energy to be upset and push on the elevator button, we can not change the outcome.

So, sometimes people stay stuck and never go on to the exploration phase of transition. In the exploration phase, the question goes from, "Why is this happening? Why are we doing this?" to "How do I move forward from here? How do I make it work?" And when people go through the exploration phase, they eventually end with a sense of resolution and commitment to a change, even if it is a change with which they do not agree.

Most people find that change-related stress comes from worrying about things changing that are outside of their control. Think about it. This is where many people place most of their energy. And this is wasted energy because it diminishes your ability to move forward and deal with important issues. You have to look at what is changing and then differentiate what is within and outside of your control.

We all have strong reactions to transitions, and we either deal with our feelings in what is called a proactive or a reactive way. When people are reactive to change, it means that they are operating from the neck down. They have not engaged their brain. They have become their feelings, and they act on them. What are some examples of behavior that would be considered reactive at work? What do people do? They do minimal work, backstabbing, escapism, cry, yell, slam doors, refuse to talk to anyone. I find refusing to communicate the most hurtful thing you can do to another human being. You can never work out your problems or differences, and you can never grow, if you withhold.

When you are proactive, you engage your brain and act from learned, adult behavior. When you are reactive, you are responding with behavior that you acquired at an early age to deal with threats. When you are proactive, you start with the same emotions but you engage your brain. You make conscious choices about how you will deal with your feelings. And there is another significant difference. When people are reactive, they get stuck. They pick an emotion and they stay there. You know you are being reactive to life when you feel that things are becoming worse over time, and that your situation is not changing. When you are proactive, the intensity of your feelings diminishes with time. Feelings are a natural part of the transition process, but how you manage those feelings, or your transition, is clearly an issue of responsibility. It is your choice of how to deal with them.

There are some things that occur that you cannot control, and the more you focus on this loss of control, the less able you will be to concentrate on the things over which you do have control so that you can move on. Not only does anger take up three times more energy than other emotions, but it is contaminating. People catch it from each other.

What are some of the ideas of what you can do to manage a transition? *Accept and expect that during the time you experience change, you will experience feelings of loss.* When you reach the point in the transition that you accept and expect these feelings, the time it takes to make the transition is shortened.

Build and maintain support. You will need it. Sometimes, this will need to be external and come from the people in your workplace.

Take care of your self physically. Conclusive evidence shows that the more changes that occur in one year, the more likely it is that people will experience a physical illness, and/or an injury from an accident. Usually, people rise to the occasion of a crisis or challenge and do well, but fall flat on their faces within a year. We have only so much adaptive energy and when it is used up, something will happen, if the energy level has not been replenished.

Honoring the past is another tactic to use in surviving transitions. Why is it that we keep reinventing the wheel, thinking we have not been through a particular change? In my seven year old's room, there is a plaque that reads, "The best things you can give your children are roots and wings." I think this is a wonderful description of what all of us need. We need to rely on the stability of our roots, but we also need to be risk takers and fly.

Inventory your assets and strengths. Think about how your assets can assist you in your transition and build on these strengths. Do not focus on your inadequacies.

Create a ritual or ceremony to facilitate the letting go process. It makes the experience real and gives you a chance to express your feelings. It gives you a sense of closure and is a way of legitimizing and honoring the past.

Begin to create a picture of the future and your new beginning. Some people are what we call "awfulizers." They jump into the future, but what do they see there? Something pretty awful. And on the basis of this vision, people prepare and mentally rehearse for the future. There is a saying in my business, "Be careful what you picture; you're likely to get it, whether it is good for you or not." Anytime you face a challenging situation, ask one basic question: Can I handle it? I hope that you can see that you can handle it, and that you can imagine yourself in the situation at your very best.

Control your thinking or self-talk. Most of us are not conscious of how we talk to ourselves. Be certain to pay attention to how you frame what is occurring, and what you imagine as the outcome. As

I said before, we have a tendency to want to be right, versus changing our minds to feel better.

Identify your fears and make plans for confronting them. If you are an awfulizer, identify the worst thing that could happen and make plans to deal with it. This will reduce your anxiety.

Build on your risk-taking behavior. We need to work out ways to take risks. It does amazing things for self-confidence. Find ways of stretching risk-taking behavior–build your wings.

Identify what you want and set priorities. Most people have no idea of what they really want. They wait for others to give them a direction, plan, or roadmap. People spend more time figuring out which car they want to buy and which house they want to live in than trying to understand what is really important to them. And that is something you will discover only through introspection.

Change is inevitable. But you always have a choice about your reaction. You can place energy into a change or take no action. I am advocating taking action on things that you can control. When you focus on things that you can control, you are powerful, energetic, and able to feel committed. On things that you cannot control, let go and do not take any action. This does not mean that you will not have feelings about these changes, but if you let them be there and pass as they will, there is a feeling of relief and release. To place energy into something that cannot be controlled is no more than hanging on. It is like pressing the elevator button, and thinking that the longer you hit on it, the more difference it will make. And all that this tactic gets you is angry and resentful. To take no action on things that can be controlled is giving up. And when you do that, you have moved into the place of being a victim. When people give up, they begin to see themselves as helpless and the situation as hopeless. People who use this tactic to deal with change get stuck. But they do not take responsibility for their situation. They focus on external factors and blame their problems on something or someone else.

There are certain truths under which I operate. One is that change is inevitable, but growth is optional. The other is that we must ultimately take responsibility for ourselves.

CONCURRENT SESSION IV: REAL PEOPLE AND VIRTUAL LIBRARIES

At Ease in Liberspace

Susan A. Cady

SUMMARY. The Lehigh University Libraries has entered the vestibule of virtual reality. The term "liberspace" has been chosen by the Libraries to designate the conceptual space of the virtual library. The author describes the environment and discusses how staff and patrons are functioning within it. Varying perspectives on the interaction between human values and technology are summarized.

Howard Rheingold has written numerous books about the virtual world. Among them are *Virtual Reality*[1] and *The Virtual Community: Homesteading on the Electronic Frontier.*[2] In the latter, he offers a history of the term "cyberspace" in the context of discussing computer-mediated communications (CMC):

Susan A. Cady is Associate Director for Technical Services, Lehigh University Libraries, Bethlehem, PA.

Cyberspace, originally a term from William Gibson's science-fiction novel *Neuromancer,* is the name some people use for the conceptual space where words, human relationships, data, wealth, and power are manifested by people using CMC technology.[3]

The Lehigh University Libraries have chosen to use a similar term of our own invention, "liberspace," to name the conceptual space of the virtual library. I will delineate that environment briefly and then describe how real staff and real users are functioning within it. In closing, I will offer some perspectives about the interactions between human values and technology.

EVOLUTION OF LEHIGH LIBERSPACE

In late summer 1986, Lehigh University in Bethlehem, Pennsylvania completed the installation of a campus-wide network that linked every office, every dorm room and Greek house, and two hundred and fifty public site microcomputers clustered throughout the campus. The two main library facilities, Linderman and Fairchild-Martindale Libraries, served as the public sites for seventy-five of these machines. In addition, every faculty member received a Zenith 8088-based microcomputer for his or her office, and a microcomputer store opened to encourage students to purchase personal computers. The Libraries' online catalog, a GEAC 8000 system, was immediately available over this early digital PBX voice/data network, and, within a few months, the network server offered a full menu of electronic library services.

Today, almost eight years later, the PBX system has been largely replaced by a high speed fiber optic backbone running TCP/IP. Most of the Zenith 8088's have succumbed to 486/33 microcomputers and Unix workstations. Software is delivered via local area networks (LANs). High speed modems accommodate off-campus users and distance education students. Through these technologies and a host of others, remotely available electronic library services and resources have become as ubiquitous at Lehigh as e-mail.

Use of the network has grown steadily over this period. The number of active accounts, defined as users who connected at least once a month, grew from zero in 1986 to about seven thousand in 1991. This represents about ninety-five percent of the university community. Since that time, the active accounts have leveled off, but the daily logins continue to escalate. The 1994 highs are already exceeding 1993 peaks by a substantial number. Numerous equipment and software upgrades have been required as a result, and as soon as new capacity is added, it is immediately consumed. The use and diversity of library services and resources over the network has also gained steadily. One resource, the Dow Jones database, ranks among the top twenty network activities, just behind telneting, reading the sale bulletin board, and e-mail. Among request type library services, the most popular offerings continue to be interlibrary loans, book orders, and photocopy requests. Figure 1 illustrates both the diversity and growth of these services at Lehigh.

The present virtual library consists of

- Fifteen CD-ROM databases (not counting federal document CDs)
- Two locally mounted databases (ERIC and Compendex)
- Sixteen FirstSearch databases, mostly on subscription
- CARL Uncover
- Dow Jones
- Lexis/Nexis
- Luigi, Lehigh's library gopher
- Mosaic/World Wide Web client under construction

Among other things, the Lehigh Library gopher includes many electronic journals and guides to Lehigh's special collections materials.

Using OCLC's SiteSearch product, locally mounted, and remote databases are presented as one integrated list of resources that use the same search interface. Users are unaware of whether they are searching a database housed on a machine at the computer center or in Dublin, Ohio. Coming soon will be a link to Lehigh's serial holdings. It is currently being tested by OCLC and Lehigh. In the near future is a new Z39.50 compliant OPAC, which utilizes a client server architecture and a graphical user interface. This will offer a common interface to SiteSearch and FirstSearch databases, other catalogs, and electronic resources on the Internet.

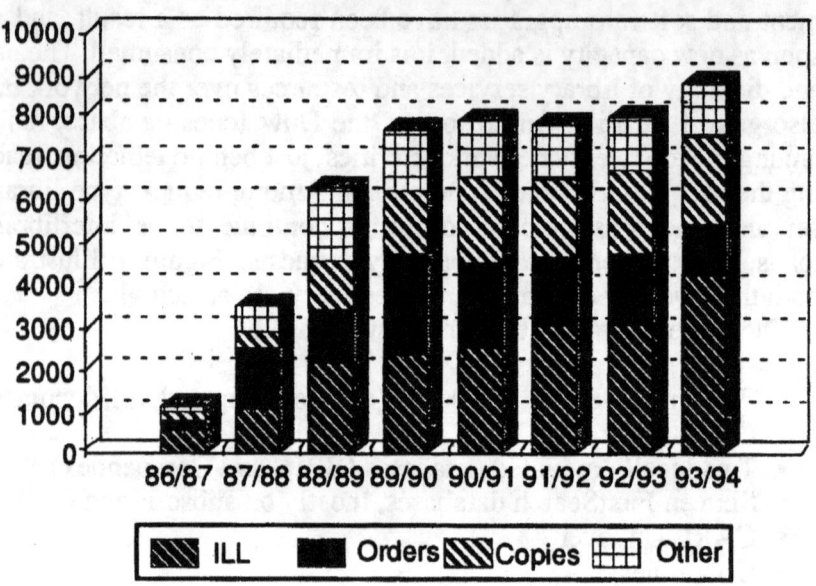

FIGURE 1
Network Transactions
(Request Services)

THE AGILE LIBRARY

Lehigh University, which is well-known for its engineering programs, has a very successful unit on campus known as the Agile Manufacturing Enterprise Center. The Center emphasizes the need to leave old paradigms behind . . . not to behave like a herd of elephants, but like a flock of birds. Lehigh's library is an "agile" organization because of its ability to adjust swiftly to change and offer new initiatives with a small staff. For example, several years ago the Ariel document delivery system developed by the Association of Research Libraries (ARL) was acquired and installed at Lehigh, all within a few months. However, there were few partners for electronic interlibrary loan over the Internet at the time because most larger libraries were waiting for bureaucratic and technical infrastructures to be developed. Agility is part of the campus-wide culture at our institution and certainly has disadvantages, but it is a useful organizational attribute in times of rapid change.

CO-DEPENDENCY

The virtual library makes library services and the people who deliver them very dependent on properly functioning hardware and software. I have chosen to use the term co-dependency because it connotes a sort of neurosis in which two people have an unhealthy relationship. Often it seems that we are locked in the same sort of unhealthy relationship with our equipment and software.

If the network server on campus goes down or degrades to an unacceptable level of performance, users can no longer access major index tools they need for research and assignments. With the cancellation of paper copies in favor of CD-ROM products, the malfunctioning of any of the complicated parts and pieces of our CD-ROM network (CBIS, Novell, the server itself, the cables, the network interface cards, the electricity) means that virtual library patrons are locked out of liberspace as completely as if we closed the physical buildings at random during the day. When the Internet goes down (either the Lehigh connection or a node at a remote location), those resources are as unavailable as a misshelved book. In fall 1993, the Lehigh Libraries staged a "day without technology" widely reported in the library press to demonstrate this new dependency to the campus community.

This adds to the technostress of all jobs. Limited financial resources usually preclude expensive redundant systems. It is unacceptable today for the reference librarian, the circulation clerk, or even the serials staff to rely on someone else (perhaps a theoretical technician) to add paper to printers or to check for a missing file. Depending on an individual's job description, more and more familiarity with operating systems and basic hardware operations is needed. Many librarians entered the profession twenty-five years ago thinking that they would work with books and people, and only occasionally be called on to thread a microfilm reader. They now find themselves having to learn increasingly arcane technical operations just to survive.

STAFF DEVELOPMENT

Obviously, a rapidly changing technical environment requires constant attention to staff development and training at all levels. In today's downsized libraries, it is more difficult than ever to spare staff for teaching and learning. At Lehigh, we make use of many avenues, but among the most cost effective are campus computing center seminars and those offered by PALINET, a regional OCLC network. PALINET, with its long-standing microcomputer support program, offers a wide variety of classes in excellently equipped facilities. Most of these programs are accessible via day trips. The Lehigh Computing Center offers seminars ranging from word processing to encoding documents for the World Wide Web. This summer, the Computing Center will do a reprise of their most relevant sessions for a group composed only of librarians.

It would be helpful to staff and to the virtual library if more employees would upgrade their skills on their own time. The University pays tuition for courses at two local community colleges, but we are talking about real people today. As a supervisor, I walk a fine line between encouraging staff to educate themselves to protect their own future in the workplace, and respecting them for the choices they make in life that do not mesh perfectly with an institutional agenda. Such staff might include a working mother with four small children at home, or an employee who does not drive at all or does not drive at night, or a mail clerk who holds two jobs so he can send his children to college.

ORGANIZATIONAL CHANGES

By the end of 1995, there will be an organizational change at Lehigh University in which the libraries, the computing center, and telecommunications will be merged under one Vice-Provost for Information Services. For this reason, minimal organizational realignments are taking place now in the Libraries. We may soon find our ability to be agile put to the test.

USERS IN LIBERSPACE

Generally the virtual library has been well received by real students and real faculty at Lehigh. The more the resource provides the actual information needed and not just bibliographic citations to it, the more students like it. Give them Dow Jones or Lexis/Nexis rather than indexes to the published literature, even if these resources are consummately inappropriate for their particular quest. A colleague in Philadelphia has a sign on her wall that captures the reasons for this and for the very popularity of the virtual library: "It's about convenience, stupid." Years of experience with distributed electronic resources and services have taught us that while the electronic environment is more convenient for students, it is also more complicated. It does, however, capture their interest quite readily because of its dynamic nature. Locally mounted databases without usage limits allow for the demonstration and use of these resources in large classes. Four hundred and sixty students in two semesters of Engineering I used Compendex, and one hundred twenty-five students in Management I used other resources in formal bibliographic instruction sessions. Students were taught how to log their sessions and send these homework assignments to the librarian as e-mail files for review.

When students need assistance in using the virtual library, or indeed the traditional one, they do not hesitate to ask for help from librarians or each other. Whether they get the right information or not is another question. Faculty do not hesitate to ask for help either, but they are more reluctant to try something new, due to their social standing and their longer affiliation with the print world. In a program launched in spring 1992, librarians went to faculty offices to introduce professors to new electronic resources. We met with about sixty percent of the teaching faculty. At the time, the university was upgrading networking software and librarians often had to install new versions on faculty computers during their visits. When the project was completed, faculty members had their software properly installed to reach these services and had seen at least some of what was relevant to their field. Now more and more awareness of Internet resources has been coming to them through their own professional societies to reinforce our initial efforts.

However, I cannot tell a lie–in the midst of mounting the virtual library, students and faculty on Lehigh's campus are deeply wedded to the library as a place, and to print on paper. As in most universities, Lehigh students still want the library to open more hours and the faculty want more journal subscriptions. Everyone wants the photocopiers to operate more reliably. From the evidence I see, buying stock in companies producing laser printers or plain white paper would be a very good investment. We are in a transitional stage to the virtual library which may come more slowly than we now anticipate. In a recent *New York Times Magazine* article, Nicholas Wade predicted "future non-shock" this way:

> New technology tends to arrive at a snail's pace, for a host of mundane reasons that, if too much dwelt on in advance, would burst the bubble of hope and delusion on which much human progress depends.... Technology does change society, but on a time scale of decades, not years. Looking back, the pace of change can seem almost glacial.
>
> An ironclad conspiracy of interests holds that imminent technological change is about to transform our lives. Investment bankers, stock analysts, publicity agents, journalists, economists, politicians–almost everyone whose business it is to think ahead has an interest in making the future sound exhilarating. It's all good fun, but these many enjoyable wonders needn't be fully believed until seen.[4]

TECHNOLOGY AND HUMAN VALUES

How often has it been said that technology drives change? The same dollar amount buys massive increases in computing power, enabling applications that were impossible to envision a few years ago–image file transfers, global conferencing, powerful client server technologies, new kinds of telecommuting and outsourcing. For example, the United States Post Office recently purchased an empty facility near Lehigh University that will employ about six hundred people who will decipher the destinations for mail. Not one piece of mail will enter the building. Employees working mostly at night will view pieces of mail broadcast over an optical fiber network and remotely direct machines to print barcodes on the envelopes. This facility will be closed in a few years when optical character recognition technologies evolve to the point where machines can read these addresses with acceptable levels of accuracy.

Some historians of technology have shown that the very design of a technology is often heavily influenced by the power structures of the time. One of the major proponents of this view is David Noble whose book, *Forces of Production: A Social History of Industrial Automation*,[5] documents the evolution of numerical control machinery. He contends that technical choices were made to empower management and disenfranchise the skilled worker. Technologies tend not to have relentless internal dynamics which determine exactly how they will be used in society, but there is a period of experimentation and struggle. The radio and telephone are examples of technologies which did not find their niche immediately.

In a recent book review in *College & Research Libraries,* a similar point is made by Joan Ariel:

> As we welcome the potential of powerful new information technologies and the resulting changes in the nature of scholarly research and practice, we must also pay close attention to the power relations embedded in their development, deployment, and use.[6]

The primary focus of the book, *Women, Information Technology and Scholarship,* is on the relationship between gender and information technology ("computer technology in many ways remains one of the last male (read white, educated) bastions"). While one may or may not agree with this feminist interpretation of technology's dynamics, the book underscores the idea that libraries should not yield mindlessly to demands to change in ways that run counter to professional commitments, simply because a new, supposedly value-neutral technology is being introduced. Values are subtly imbedded in technologies, and those who object to their shape may be castigated as Luddites. Another lesson that the history of technology clearly teaches is that predictions about future technologies and exactly how they will affect society are fraught with uncertainty, and that we should be at once skeptical and visionary about the future.

NOTES

1. Howard Rheingold, *Virtual Reality* (London: Secker & Warburg, 1991).
2. Rheingold, *The Virtual Community: Homesteading on the Electronic Frontier* (New York: Addison-Wesley, 1993).

3. *Ibid.*, 5.

4. Nicholas Wade, "Method and Madness: Future Non-Shock," *The New York Times Magazine* (January 16, 1994): 14.

5. David F. Noble, *Forces of Production: A Social History of Industrial Automation* (Baltimore: Johns Hopkins, 1986).

6. Joan Ariel (Review) *Women, Information Technology and Scholarship* edited by Jeanie Taylor, Cheris Kramarae and Maureen Ebben, *College & Research Libraries* 55 (May 1994): 272-274.

The Human Side of the Virtual Library

Marion T. Reid

SUMMARY. Does technology drive change or do human values shape technology? The author discusses this question within the context of the California State University System. The advantages and difficulties of conducting work in remote locations via telecommuting are discussed, with special reference to libraries. The virtual library will promote greater use of information by remote users, but telecommuting is not a substitute for face-to-face interaction.

When talking about libraries of the future, some people say that we do not need to build any more libraries . . . or add any more library additions . . . because we have computers. I think they say this because of their definition of the meaning of "virtual" in the term "virtual library." They believe that "virtual" should be defined as in the first dictionary meaning: "being such in power, force, or effect, although not actually or expressly such." I like the third (rare) definition of "virtual:" "having virtue or inherent power to produce effects."[1] The best definition of "virtual library" I have come across is Pamela Jajko's:

> A virtual library is an entity for knowledge management that effectively incorporates both the traditional library domain

---

Marion T. Reid is Dean of Library Services, California State University San Marcos, San Marcos, CA.

[Haworth co-indexing entry note]: "The Human Side of the Virtual Library." Reid, Marion T. Co-published simultaneously in *The Serials Librarian* (The Haworth Press, Inc.) Vol. 25, No. 3/4, 1995, pp. 213-221; and: *A Kaleidoscope of Choices: Reshaping Roles and Opportunities for Serialists* (ed: Beth Holley and Mary Ann Sheble) The Haworth Press, Inc., 1995, pp. 213-221. Multiple copies of this article/chapter may be purchased from The Haworth Document Delivery Center [1-800-3-HAWORTH; 9:00 a.m. - 5:00 p.m. (EST)].

© 1995 by The Haworth Press, Inc. All rights reserved.

and the use of both telecommunication and computer technology to facilitate the rapid access and use of information by individual users through the apparently seamless integration of knowledge from that library's own resources, from internal, proprietary information of that library's organization and from external, worldwide information sources.[2]

I believe that there *will* be more library buildings ... and books. Currently, only 2 to 5 percent of scholarly information can be found in electronic form. Even by 2001 that figure will rise to only 10 percent at most. Jajko's definition provides for the reality of the library as *both* the traditional place books are stored and where librarians assist patrons in finding information, *and* access through computers and connectivity to electronic information stored somewhere else.

DIMENSIONS OF THE VIRTUAL LIBRARY

The graphic in Figure 1 illustrates a model which facilitates this commentary on the human dimensional aspects of the virtual library. It provides for both onsite and remote staff helping users, who may be onsite or remote, find information that is physically located within the library and/or elsewhere. Mathematically, this model permits the eight combinations of staff, user, and information shown in Figure 2. By "remote" I mean not physically located within the library building. It implies both close by, but not in the same physical structure, and distant.

Note in Figure 2 that the first four combinations are the traditional ones, although the third and fourth may not at first appear so. Regarding the third: librarians traditionally have responded to remote users asking reference questions by phone or via post. Regarding the fourth: reference librarians--especially those in public libraries--have built their own files of local information as a result of phone patrons' queries about what may be found in the community. Combinations five through eight have fewer real models. In fact, it is difficult to imagine having these four combinations without relying on sophisticated computing and telecommunications support. Note also that the more unfamiliar dimensions (com-

FIGURE 1. Virtual Library Dimensions

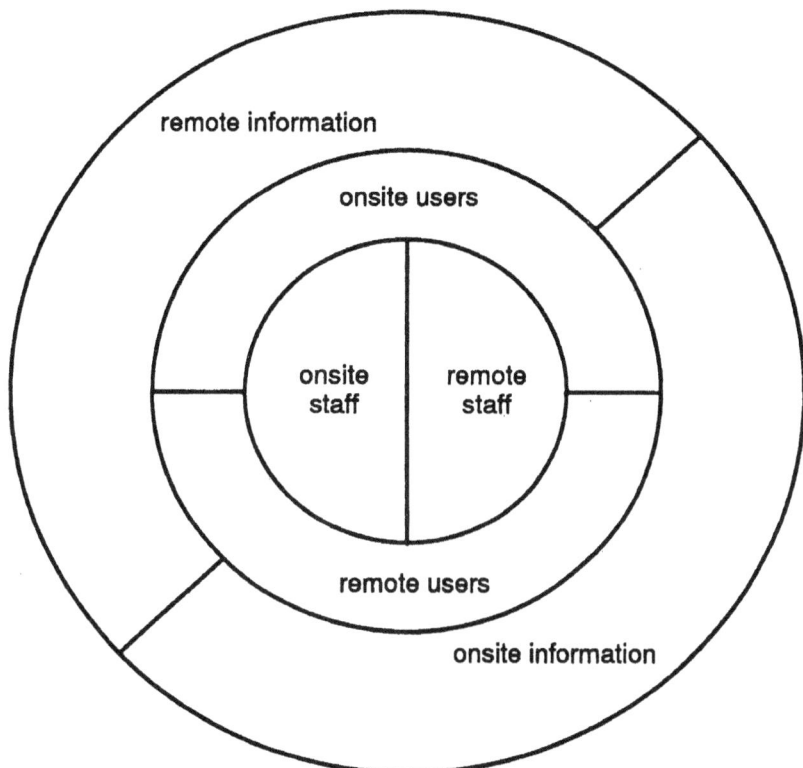

binations two through eight) all require the staff persons and the users they are assisting to be in different places. Actual communication in these instances can be through many methods, including phone, FAX, postal service, and computer. Most of my remarks assume computer connectivity between staff members and users.

CHARACTERISTICS OF USERS AND STAFF

What will our users be like in 2001? Susan Komives has created a compelling profile of the traditional college freshman entering higher education institutions in 1992.[3] By extending this model, one can imagine that the first traditional freshmen who enter college in the twenty-first century (individuals born in 1982 and entering college in 2001) will:

- be very direct; say what they want;
- seek instant gratification;
- have grown up with no national spiritual/ideological leadership;
- be consumer oriented and technologically oriented;
- on one hand, feel special; but on the other hand, really believe that they must assert themselves in order to receive attention; and
- want everything (families, jobs, homes, technology) **now**.

Think about having a lot of these kids as your patrons. Kathleen de la Peña McCook states,

> During the ten-year period from 1981-82 to 1991-92, the overall percentage of ethnic minorities receiving master's degrees from programs accredited by the American Library Association edged up a minuscule 1.2 percent. That is, of 100 new entrants to the profession, 91.5 percent are white today, compared to 92.7 percent in 1982.[4]

Of the five billion people in the world today, one billion are white. Today, the twenty-five largest cities in the U.S. have public school systems in which the majority of students is not white. As a group, librarians in the United States today do not multiculturally

FIGURE 2. DIMENSIONS OF THE VIRTUAL LIBRARY

relationships: staff/ user/ information

1. onsite staff/ onsite user/ onsite information
2. onsite staff/ onsite user/ remote information
3. onsite staff/ remote user/ onsite information
4. onsite staff/ remote user/ remote information
5. remote staff/ onsite user/ onsite information
6. remote staff/ onsite user/ remote information
7. remote staff/ remote user/ onsite information
8. remote staff/ remote user/ remote information

reflect the people we serve. Even if the figures de la Peña McCook cites change significantly in the next seven years, this will still be true.

Certainly, in 2001 libraries will not be staffed solely by librarians who received their M.L.S. degrees in 1991-92, serving only that segment of the population born in 1982. Librarians and library staff represent several generations . . . each with different generational values. Today we serve users from multiple generations . . . each with different generational values. In the 21st century this will still be true. The difference is that to our staffs, we are no longer the fresh, new faces with great ideas to help the users. We are moving into the 'older generations' end of the spectrum and may have different opinions about younger users as well as younger staff.

COMMUNICATING WITH SOMEONE YOU CANNOT SEE

For a moment, return to Figure 2. Six of these eight combinations require the staff member and the user to be in different places. Think about that. How can you relate to someone you do not see? With users, your contact tends to be more transient. With other staff, contact is necessary on an ongoing basis. How can you get something done when you are not physically near the people with whom you are working? Three examples help address these questions.

Example 1. Mary Peterson tells the wonderful story of how Bob Werman, who through his Internet connection daily reported gripping, first-hand commentary on the Gulf War, and Gerald Phillips, a retired professor in Pennsylvania, developed an online friendship. Eventually, they met and primarily as a result of their prolific, ongoing electronic collaboration, have already coauthored two books: *Notes from a Sealed Room* and *Cardiyakking: A Heart to Heart Talk about Heart Disease*.[5] These are people who found each other through the Internet and began conversing.

Example 2. At 4:31 a.m. on January 17th, 1994, Southern California experienced a massive earthquake. You all know pieces of the story: massive destruction; some loss of life; portions of major freeways destroyed. Many people could no longer easily commute from home to work and back. Pacific Bell offered start-up support for those in the affected area to telecommute while the roads were being rebuilt. In many cases, the roads were replaced before jobs were reshaped and the necessary computers and connections were installed to support telecommuting. However, there are some human aspects of this situation which are applicable to our questions.

Since the earthquake, Lorraine Newlon, Director of Admissions and Records at California State University (CSU) Northridge, has had fourteen of her eighty-two member staff work in their homes for the majority of their work week.[6] The CSU Northridge campus was devastated. No building on that campus, which serves 17,000 students, could be used for the spring semester. To survive spring semester, CSUN operated out of more than 440 portable buildings and several large tents. At first, the Admissions and Records staff were assigned sixty-five workstations in a tent. Two months later, they moved into a small room equipped with folding tables, folding chairs, and twenty-five PC's. Since there is such limited space on campus, the fourteen evaluators–those least dependent on constant computer access–were asked to work at home at first four days a week and then three days a week. They came to campus for data entry and to see students.

At this writing, the arrangement is four months old. Although it is too soon to evaluate, those involved have made several discoveries:

- They have had to duplicate some resource materials for all fourteen evaluators to use off-site.
- Now that they have offices at home, some evaluators find it hard to start work; others find it difficult to keep from working.
- Some continue to work their traditional hours; others revel in being able to adjust their work schedules to their personal tastes.
- Some feel isolated; others like their isolation.
- Some are disappointed that their homes are no longer a refuge from work.
- Those with family members routinely at home have had difficulty finding quiet times for work.
- Other staff are envious of the evaluators' arrangements to work at home.

- The initial concern about whether staff working at home would really invest eight hours a day in work has vanished. Output is higher than it was when the evaluators were working on campus.

Although the Northridge experience was the result of a natural disaster, CSUN evaluators may continue to work at home on a part-time basis. Requests have been forwarded for PC's and modems for them to use at home so they can telecommute.

Example 3. The California State University System has twenty campuses. The twenty-first campus–CSU Monterey Bay–is planning to open in fall 1995. As part of the planning process, twelve work groups are due to submit reports on various aspects of campus design by June 30th. I am a member of the Information Processing Work Group. I was drawn into this effort by responding to an e-mail message, becoming part of a reflector list and applying.

The chair initiated our discussions via e-mail. We each introduced ourselves and selected from the list of twenty questions the chair suggested we answer to create the report. The chair tried to have us discuss issues and arrive at some consensus before meeting. Nothing happened. We did not coalesce until we came together on May 6th in Monterey. Our meeting began at 10 a.m. We began to work together as a team within an hour. Although we had not felt comfortable enough in the e-mail environment to make group decisions, we had enough e-mail acquaintance to bond almost immediately once we were in the same room. We met for a total of twelve hours over a two-day period and had three meals together. We are now working almost exclusively by e-mail and I believe that we will finish the project on time.

QUESTIONS ABOUT TELECOMMUTING

There are many questions about telecommuting relationships when you do not know who is at the other end. It is very difficult for a group to work together solely via computer. Human contact is still deemed important. Can you imagine doing your work without daily personal contact with the people with whom you work?

From the perspective of the user, questions include the following:

- Will in-house users feel they are competing with remote users?
- To what extent will we in the library be responsible for the remote user's hookup? Will our staff need to take time to help remote users get connected to our system?
- How much remote user demand will there be? How much of our time will it take? How can we devote already scarce staff to cover remote users and continue to serve those inhouse?
- How do we get inhouse materials to remote users? How do we get them *back?*

Questions about telecommuting staff include the following:

- What kind of work can be done in a remote location?
- Who gets to work in a remote location? Some jobs lend themselves to remote work better than others.
- Does anyone, who wants to work in a remote location, get to . . . or does being able to work in a remote setting depend upon one's job tasks?
- What personal effects will there be for remote staff members? Will their biological clocks cause them to work at hours other than traditional office hours? Does it matter? How hard will it be for them to adapt a portion of their homes to an office environment? Will their exercise patterns change? Will their food intake change? How many more times a day will they walk to the refrigerator?
- What is the institutional obligation for equipment? tools? connectivity? phone charges for long-distance connections? ergonomics of the home office? transporting things? liability?
- What is the extent of the telecommuter's latitude to make decisions independently?
- In a telecommuting environment . . . when staff members work at remote locations on a regular basis for 20 percent or more of the workweek, managerially, how do you interview/evaluate candidates for/decide to hire someone for that kind of job? How do you orient them? . . . enculturate them? . . . incorporate them as part of the work group? They must know, buy into and support the institution's mission. How can you ensure that they will if they are working off-site? How do you train these

people? . . . incorporate them into the organizational structure? Does the reward system change? Should it?

A virtual library–with staff who are telecommuting a portion of their worklife on a regular basis–will require managers and staff who are willing to supervise and/or work in different environments. They must be willing to develop, establish, and define new work habits, processes, norms, and means of communication. The work of telecommuters must be measurable and it should be measured on an ongoing basis.

Some people say that the virtual staff member will work solely in isolation. I believe that the virtual staff member will be working in the library building at least part of the time with other staff.

What are the human aspects of the virtual library? We need to be able to relate to the person we cannot see. In the telecommuting age, we still have the need to know people as people, not just as words on a flickering screen. In the future, if you and I are working for the same single institution, unless one of us is away somewhere on the starship Enterprise, you and I will be working together at the same location at least part of the time.

NOTES

1. These definitions are from *The American College Dictionary* (New York: Random House, 1965), 1360.

2. Pamela Jajko, "Planning the Virtual Library," *Medical Reference Quarterly*, 12, no. 4 (Winter 1993): 52.

3. Susan R. Komives, "Back to the Future: Class of 1996," *NASPA Journal* 31, no. 1 (Fall 1993): 64-71.

4. Kathleen de la Peña McCook, "Diversity Deferred: Where Are the Minority Librarians?" *Library Journal* 117 no. 1 (November 1, 1993): 36.

5. Mary Peterson, "Life on the Internet: Portrait of a Collaboration," *The North American Review* 278 no. 6 (November-December, 1993): 10-11.

6. Lorraine Newlon provided the information in this example in a May 27, 1994 telephone conversation with the author.

CONCURRENT SESSION V: FROM CUTTER HANDMAIDS TO CYBERSPACE GUIDES: THE FUTURE OF CATALOGERS

Tools for a New Age: An Overview

Regina R. Reynolds

SUMMARY. How will the serials cataloger of the future meet the need to catalog an ever-increasing volume of materials in an ever-evolving number of formats? The author provides a tour of the potential tools on the technological horizon, including: expert systems, Standard Generalized Markup Language (SGML), imaging technology, relational database techniques, and hypertext-like links between and among local and remote files.

Sufficiently advanced technology is indistinguishable from magic.
Arthur C. Clarke[1]

Regina R. Reynolds is Head of the National Serials Data Program, Library of Congress, Washington, DC.

[Haworth co-indexing entry note]: "Tools for a New Age: An Overview." Reynolds, Regina R. Co-published simultaneously in *The Serials Librarian* (The Haworth Press, Inc.) Vol. 25, No. 3/4, 1995, pp. 223-233; and: *A Kaleidoscope of Choices: Reshaping Roles and Opportunities for Serialists* (ed: Beth Holley and Mary Ann Sheble) The Haworth Press, Inc., 1995, pp. 223-233. Multiple copies of this article/chapter may be purchased from The Haworth Document Delivery Center [1-800-3-HAWORTH; 9:00 a.m. - 5:00 p.m. (EST)].

The time: YOUR future. The place: a large research library. A woman sits in a semi-reclining chair. A magazine is suspended on a worksurface in front of her. She wears a wrap-around headset and the tip of her right index finger glows red. You watch as she runs her glowing finger over parts of the magazine and then touches some squares on the worksurface. Finally, her fingers play in the air, almost like a harpist's.

In the lower level of this same library, lights blink on the console of an unattended computer. It works silently, but its work encompasses—literally—volumes.

* * *

What is going on here? Just a day in the life of a future cataloging department. The woman is a serial cataloger, and, as you can tell, I am betting there will still be ink on paper magazines out there–like the one in front of her–well into the future. The cataloger is wearing a virtual reality headset and a combination sensor/scanner glove which she uses to capture cataloging data. Then, an artificial intelligence program describes the serial according to AACR4, supplies MARC III tagging, and presents a record for her approval. Finally, the cataloger uses virtual reality technology to weave shapes and colors of subject and classification data into the most fitting visual pattern for her serial.

The unattended computer is receiving electronic data which has been encoded in a library cataloging subset of Standard Generalized Markup Language (SGML) from various WorldNet feeds, performing automated cataloging, and feeding the cataloging back to the WorldNet.

Obviously, the scenes I have just described are fantasy, but the premise of my talk today is that some of this technology is already reality and that the future will hold even more exciting possibilities. So, to catalogers buried under a sea of arrearages, I want to say, "Help is on the way!"

My talk today will be a layman's tour of technologies that hold promise for assisting catalogers. Since my time is limited, the tour will be done at warp speed and even then I will only be able to touch on a small number of the myriad projects currently underway which have the potential to expedite and even transform cataloging.

Among the projects I mention are several from the Library of Congress (LC) since I have had a chance to see many of them first-hand.

SGML

SGML is an acronym for Standard Generalized Markup Language, a technological standard that holds much promise for the future management of textual information. Later in this panel, Daniel Pitti will provide an in-depth technical presentation on SGML; but, since I refer to this standard many times, I want to give a brief, non-technical explanation. Catalogers can think of SGML as a MARC format for textual data. SGML employs tags which use letters and phrases within angled brackets to identify structural divisions of text such as the title page, chapters, paragraphs, etc.; elements within the text, such as the copyright statement; and typographical elements.

An example of an SGML project which involves catalogers is the Electronic Text Center and On-Line Archive of Electronic Texts at the University of Virginia. This project has already put online more than 10,000 SGML-encoded texts, including the entire *Oxford English Dictionary* and several versions of Shakespeare's works. Volunteer catalogers from the University of Virginia Library are being trained to encode the texts. When the encoded texts are sent to a special section of the catalog department for traditional cataloging, the cataloging work is performed more quickly and easily because of the encoding that has already been done.

ARTIFICIAL INTELLIGENCE

How about a computer that could be taught to catalog, generalize from examples, and learn from its mistakes without using any programs? Artificial intelligence, specifically neural networks, might be able to do this some day. Artificial intelligence (AI) is a broad term used to describe machines acting in a way that used to be thought of as the exclusive province of humans. The most common type of AI, especially in library applications, is the expert system, a rule-based deductive program which Paul Weiss will discuss in much greater depth in the next presentation.

Neural networks work by means of their information structure rather than programs, more like the functioning of the human brain. They are still in their infancy but some information scientists feel they hold promise for cataloging because of their capability of learning, of being able to generalize, and their ability to perform partial as well as exact matches.[2]

Instead of a computer that does the whole job, how about one that just gives us a little advice? Zorana Ercegovac of the Information Center at University of California at Los Angeles has developed Mapper,[3] an experimental expert system for map cataloging, that guides a cataloger through the map cataloging process. A cataloger-friendly feature of this prototype is that it provides the cataloger with a button marked "advice" and if the cataloger does not understand the advice, she can click another button marked "explain advice!"

Electronic cataloging in publication (CIP) at LC does not give advice–at least not yet–and is not really advanced enough to be called an expert system, but it is in experimental use right now to produce CIP records for manuscripts received in electronic form. A recent demonstration gave me a little taste of the future which I found quite exciting. Electronic CIP works this way: a publisher sends, via file transfer protocol (FTP), an electronic version of a manuscript which has at least minimal SGML or HTML (hypertext markup language) encoding. Using an OS/2 editor, the cataloger calls up the title page of the manuscript, adds some basic ISBD punctuation, then highlights each cataloging element and clicks on appropriate menu choices. Another menu gives standardized notes that can be added to the cataloging record. After all the data has been highlighted, the program formats and tags it into a provisional descriptive record ready for "clean-up" by the cataloger. The program can also accept scanned title pages as data. At LC, scanning is also being used to enrich existing catalog records for selected business publications with table of contents information.

What is better than assistance in bibliographic record creation? It is assistance in authority record creation! LC just did an informal survey of automated authority projects and turned up about a dozen. I recently talked to Gary Strawn, authorities librarian at Northwestern University, about his project. Using the NOTIS system the program first inspects a bibliographic record and extracts names or fields which are under authority control. These can be personal and corporate names, uniform titles, geographic or topical subjects, or even series. The program next searches all of these names or fields against the authority file and lists any potential authority records which are needed. Finally, the program creates provisional authority records based on the bibliographic data already supplied and adds a 670 (source data found) and a few basic kinds of references. Strawn is currently working on automating the provision of more difficult references.

Finally, how about sending out a scout onto the Internet to find and convert records from other library catalogs around the world for use in your own catalog? LC serial catalogers have begun to investigate this possibility and have found several online catalogs with records of potential use. After appropriate agreements were made with the libraries in question, a cataloger could telnet to the foreign catalog, find usable records and then use a conversion program to allow the record to be imported into the catalog. A future step in this direction would be the development of information-seeking or "knowbot" programs which could be programmed to seek out the most likely Internet source catalogs, find appropriate records, and perform the rest of the conversion and loading steps.

DOCUMENTATION IN MACHINE-READABLE FORM

And while we are fantasizing, how about a solution for the problem of the many linear feet of documentation catalogers need and all the filing that is required to keep them up-to-date! A cartoon I found while preparing for this talk illustrated the solution by showing a Saint Bernard dog with a computer around its neck rescuing someone buried in an avalanche of manuals and papers.

There are many cataloger's workstation projects underway, including projects by OCLC, all three national libraries, and many university libraries around the country. OCLC is working on a MAC-based subject cataloging workstation and together with the Dewey office at LC has come out with Electronic Dewey. LC is putting the classification schedules into machine-readable form and is also working on linking LCSH and the classification schedules electronically.

LC's Cataloging Distribution Service is planning to release *Catalogers Desktop* in the summer of 1994. This is a CD-ROM product which includes the *Library of Congress Rule Interpretations*, subject cataloging and classification manuals, and MARC formats and codes–all in a hypertext format. Catalogers can also add their own annotations which are kept from update to update, and add their own hypertext links. The second edition of *Catalogers Desktop* will include the *CONSER Editing Guide* and the *CONSER Cataloging Manual*.

The long-awaited machine-readable AACR2 is also in the works. The usability of the electronic AACR2 is greatly enhanced by the fact that the entire text is being encoded in SGML.

GOPHER BUILDING, WEB WEAVING, AND CYBERSPACE GUIDING

Even with the best of new tools, some types of information may just be too vast to catalog individually, such as what we now find on the Internet. Although SGML and use of special headers by publishers may make some Internet documents, in effect, "self-cataloging," catalogers' skills at organizing and providing access to information will be needed in the future more than ever.

Catalogers have the potential to become future cyberspace guides, descendants of the current gopher builders and web weavers. Although future Internet retrieval systems will no doubt become more automated and more sophisticated, it will take skills at identifying, describing, organizing, and linking information, such skills as those possessed by serial catalogers in particular, to do the work behind gophers and the descendants of gophers.

Marilyn Geller, a serials cataloger at MIT, described her contributions to building MIT's gopher system, MITosis, in an Autocat posting.[4] She noted that her cataloging knowledge and experience helped her organize menus, set up linking information, determine filing structures, and work with subject heading construction. In another Autocat posting,[5] Karl Fattig, a catalog librarian involved in a gopher project at the University of Nebraska-Lincoln, indicated that his university has a "tidier" and more reliable gopher because catalogers have created a "catalog record" for each link using a combination of slightly modified LC subject headings and natural language.

HYPERTEXT

Hypertext systems, with their direct links (often called "hot buttons") between related information, are yet another area where serial catalogers' linking skills will come in handy. And, since hypertext is heavily used in the growing World Wide Web, there is lots of hypertext linking to be done. The chief advantage of hypertext is that it can provide users with a much more intuitive way to search a catalog than via linear Boolean logic. In fact, many diagrams of hypertext systems show the links going around in circles, much like the typical library user!

Alexandra Dimitroff and Dietmar Wolfram of the School of Library and Information Science at the University of Milwaukee, have developed a prototype system called HyperLynx.[6] The prototype uses a subset of the NTIS database consisting of about 3000 records on library and information science. System users enter the database by browsing an index but once in a particular record they can move about the file by clicking on hotwords (author or subject access points) in the record.

LINKED CATALOGS/DATABASES

How about searching a periodical index and an OPAC at the same time? It is being done right now at many places, including NOTIS libraries, Minitex, and at the University of Florida library system. These libraries have set up "hooks to holdings" which means they have linked their catalog to various indexes, usually by means of the ISSN, which is the common element in both systems. The Florida project was developed by the Florida Center for Library Automation.

In a telephone conversation, Maggie Hogue of the Florida Center for Library Automation described how the center loaded non-MARC citation database records in a format that gives maximum access to the indexable terms in that database, while staying as close as possible to the MARC format. The citation information is put into field 773 and the ISSN is in the MARC ISSN field 022. The 022 is indexed in the standard number index of the citation database and serves as the link to the user's home database.

Thus, a patron at the University of Florida can choose an index, search a term, and get back a citation. He then can check to see which libraries in the system have the cited periodical, and also see a display which will show whether the issue he needs is held by the library and at which location or locations it is held. The user is even presented with specific information as to where in a particular collection the issue he requires is located.

Widespread use of such systems has the potential to free catalogers from making analytics for items covered by indexes which are linked to a library's catalog. For example, at LC we are no longer able to analyze many working papers series. If these series are covered by an index, we are hoping to make the index searchable as part of the catalog and thus lead a user from the citation to the bibliographic record.

An even more exciting scenario is what I like to think of as the "megacatalog" of tomorrow, components of which are already in place today. For example, in addition to being linked to indexes, OPACs will also be linked to encyclopedias, community directories, standard reference works, as well as the entire Internet!

IMAGING TECHNOLOGY

Why should catalogers have to painstakingly keyboard data from a title page, taking valuable time and allowing for the introduction of keyboarding errors? Why not just scan in an image?

Images are already being used in databases by galleries and museums such as the Smithsonian, and by medical libraries. Images were also captured on disk as part of the Library of Congress American Memory project. An idea for using images of title pages as substitutes for transcription was proposed in 1991 by Linda Bartley, Julia Blixrud, and Maureen Landry of LC's serial record division. While this idea has not been pursued further, it presents a novel use for imaging technology.

The proposal is called LiOnCat or Library Online Catalog. This catalog would have a relational database structure with discrete components including a database which contains images of those pages of a publication that constitute cataloging sources. Thus, the cataloger would be relieved of the need to transcribe information that was not going to be used for access, and could instead enter access points only once: in their authoritative form. Another advantage of such a system for serial catalogers would be that whenever a question arose about a potential title change, the cataloger could simply call up the image of the chief source of the first issue and compare it to the issue in hand.

VIRTUAL REALITY

Virtual reality (VR) is one of the most exciting and futuristic of new technologies. It has gotten a lot of publicity in science fiction, is already in limited production as an entertainment medium, and is even being speculated about as the ultimate in safe sex! Virtual reality creates in the user the sensation of being in an altogether different environment. This is most often done by having a user wear a wrap-around headset and a glove which serves as an input device, or a bodysuit which both serves as an input and output device.

Despite its popular image, some information professionals, such as Gregory Newby of the University of Illinois at Urbana-Champaign, see virtual reality as more than "just another pretty interface."[7] Newby sees VR as being able to finally realize that dream of Vannevar Bush's from 1945: the Memex machine, a machine that acts as an extension of a user's own memory. Newby sees many advantages to VR as an interface for databases. Users will be able to interact with systems more naturally and intuitively. VR can present information visually, using shapes, colors, and virtual landmarks. All of these visual landmarks will keep users from the very real experience of being lost in cyberspace!

Newby has done a pilot project using a large projection screen monitor and a DataGlove instead of a mouse. His system resembles The Matrix as portrayed in William Gibson's *Neuromancer* (a science fiction work that has inspired much VR and VR fiction), or in the TV show "TekWar," where cyberspace is represented visually as a place. In Newby's project, users can see relations among data visually, and even reach out and "grab" useful documents.

Another fictional example of how VR could influence catalogs and catalogers of the future is from Michael Crichton's newest novel, *Disclosure*. The novel takes place in a computer company and during one of the climactic scenes, two characters use an experimental virtual reality system to search the company files. They walk on a treadmill and see marble floors, panelled walls, drawers, and shelves. The scene looks like an old-fashioned library! The characters can even open drawers and pull out documents which hang in space as they read them.

So, this trip to the future has taken us back to a future that has an uncanny resemblance to the past! Maybe a virtual reality card catalog would satisfy Nicholson Baker who mourned the loss of cards in his recent *New Yorker* article.[8] The possibilities are fascinating. But where does all of this technology leave the cataloger of the future? In wonderful places, I believe.

First, catalogers will have a lot more choices and opportunities because future cataloging will not be nearly so monolithic as it is today. Various degrees of cataloging will be applied to various categories of publications. And, there will be a continuum of automation from fully automated processing to "hand-crafted" cataloging very similar to what we have today.

Second, cataloging will change, perhaps not as I have described it, but I believe it will change for the better. Technology will influence the rules, probably making them more logical and predictable, so as to become suitable as a knowledge base for expert systems. But the rules will also spur on technological solutions to implementing them, such as neural network development.

Most importantly, however, technology will remain just a tool and catalogers' expertise will be needed more than ever–not only to use the tools but to help build the tools. This will have the best chance of happening if catalogers are proactive with regard to technology, and make themselves known as the information organizers that they have always been rather than the describers and transcribers they are sometimes seen to be.

Finally, for catalogers who fear being replaced by a machine, I offer an image adapted from a computer cartoon: the image is that of two scientists standing in front of an exploding computer. One of the scientists is angrily admonishing his bewildered-looking colleague with the words, "You WOULD have to go and ask it to catalog all the IEEE proceedings!"

As you think about this image, keep in mind that a tool is only as good as the intelligence which designed it and the intelligence which uses it. Good catalogers–especially those who can catalog serials–will never become obsolete!

NOTES

1. Arthur C. Clarke, *Lost Worlds 2001* (London: Sidgwick & Jackson, 1972).

2. Tamas E. Doxzkocs, "Neural Networks in Libraries," *Information Technology, It's for Everyone: Proceedings of the LITA Third National Conference* (Chicago: American Library Association, 1992), 81-83.

3. Zorana Ercegovac, "Design, Implementation, and Evaluation of an Experimental Cataloging Advisor–Mapper," *Bulletin (Special Libraries Association Geography & Map Division)*, 163 (March 1991), 2-28.

4. Marilyn Geller, "Gopher Work and the Future of Cataloging," Autocat posting, Apr. 23, 1994.

5. Karl Fattig, "Re: Gopher Work?" Autocat posting, Apr. 23, 1994.

6. Alexandra Dimitroff and Dietmar Wolfram, "Design Issues in a Hypertext-Based Information System for Bibliographic Retrieval," *ASIS '93: Proceedings of the 56th Annual ASIS Meeting* (Medford, NJ: Learned Information, Inc.), 1993, 191-195.

7. Gregory B. Newby, "Virtual Reality: Tomorrow's Information System, or Just Another Pretty Interface?" *ASIS '93: Proceedings of the 56th ASIS Annual Meeting* (Medford, NJ: Learned Information, Inc.), 1993, 199-203.

8. Nicholson Baker, "Discards," *The New Yorker* (Apr. 4, 1994): 64-86.

Getting the Expert into the System: Expert Systems and Cataloging

Paul J. Weiss

SUMMARY. The author provides an overview of the potential value expert systems have for serials cataloging. Criteria for determining the suitability of a project for use with an expert system are provided and four technical services examples are discussed.

What is an expert system? The term itself is mushy and overused. As with many other "hot" terms, it is often applied inappropriately. There are as many definitions as there are people working in the area. One rather vague definition is a computer system that emulates human intelligence. Another definition is a computer system that automates a task that now requires human expertise. By that definition, what we consider an expert system today would not be one tomorrow. A third is a computer system that models human thought processes. That is a fairly theoretical definition, and cannot be used easily or quickly to judge whether or not a particular system is an expert system. Related to that definition is the statement that if a person is sitting at a computer, interactively typing in and seeing and responding to words on the screen, and that person cannot tell whether a computer or a human is on the other side of the interaction, that system is an expert system. Some writers have tried to

---

Paul J. Weiss is Systems Librarian, Office of the Chief, Technical Services Division, National Library of Medicine, Bethesda, MD.

[Haworth co-indexing entry note]: "Getting the Expert into the System: Expert Sytems and Cataloging." Weiss, Paul J. Co-published simultaneously in *The Serials Librarian* (The Haworth Press, Inc.) Vol. 25, No. 3/4, 1995, pp. 235-241; and: *A Kaleidoscope of Choices: Reshaping Roles and Opportunities for Serialists* (ed: Beth Holley and Mary Ann Sheble) The Haworth Press, Inc., 1995, pp. 235-241. Multiple copies of this article/chapter may be purchased from The Haworth Document Delivery Center [1-800-3-HAWORTH; 9:00 a.m. - 5:00 p.m. (EST)].

© 1995 by The Haworth Press, Inc. All rights reserved.

elucidate what an expert system is by describing its features, including an explanation of the system's questions and results, and machine learning.

There are several advantages to utilizing an expert system. Some are standard for most computer applications. An expert system can eliminate such common human problems as fatigue, boredom, and forgetfulness, and it can free human time for more complex tasks. Some of its advantages are special to expert systems. They spread expertise across space and time, both on the micro and macro levels. That is, an expert system can be used in other parts of a single office, or in places around the world, and can operate twenty-four hours a day, and last well past the human expert's stay at that institution. An expert system can also increase consistency and save money. Advantages of developing an expert system, beyond its implementation, include gaining familiarity with a new technology, and the necessary rethinking of the process being automated. This rethinking can be the most valuable aspect, highlighting contradictions and inconsistencies, as it was in my project to develop an expert system to assist the cataloger in personal name authority work at the National Library of Medicine (NLM).

PROJECT SUITABILITY CRITERIA

When selecting a project, it is important to gauge the suitability of potential areas on which to work. Three aspects to consider are the task to be automated, the domain or subject area of the task, and support.

Task

- The task should require expertise. Otherwise, a normal computer program would be sufficient. One rule of thumb is that experienced people perform the work more quickly and/or accurately than novices.
- More than just simple, linear if-then algorithms should be needed to accomplish the task. Judgement, heuristics (or rules of thumb), and meta-rules (or rules about the rules) are likely used. Uncertainty is involved in the decision-making process.

- The task should be appropriately complex. Human experts perform the task in a few minutes to a few hours.
- The development process tends to proceed more quickly and easily if the task is well-researched and well-documented.
- Absolute perfection is not required. It is often easy to develop a prototype expert system that is accurate 80-90% of the time. That last 10-20% is often where the more difficult (or impossible) development work lies.
- The need for the task is stable; it will need to be performed into the foreseeable future.

Domain

- The domain should be narrow, well-bounded, and self-contained. Common sense is not extensively utilized in the domain.
- Like the task, the domain should be stable. It is unlikely that many new variables or facts will emerge in the near to mid future.

Support

- The necessary resources need to be available. Developing an expert system takes time, staff, and money. Whether present in the same individual or not, staff should have expertise in the task and the domain, as well as in system technology. Money will generally need to be spent on relatively expensive software and hardware.
- The staff should be willing to work on the project. Even more so than other types of projects, it is very difficult for staff to develop an expert system without interest and motivation.
- Support from both management and users is crucial. If management does not support the project, it is unlikely that sufficient resources will be allocated or that the system will ever be implemented. If potential users of the expert system do not support the project, acceptance testing will be severely undermined. This is especially easy to do with an expert system, since it is often automating a task for which only the human experts can evaluate the results.

FOUR TECHNICAL SERVICES EXAMPLES

These examples are given roughly in the order of increasing suitability as expert systems projects. As the support criteria are unique to each institution, they are not discussed in these general examples.

AACR2

Using AACR2 certainly requires expertise. Veteran catalogers tend to output higher quality work than new catalogers. It involves far more than simple algorithms. However, using AACR2 is generally not that complex. While some items and sections of the rules are complex, most parts of catalog records are derived in seconds. The process of using AACR2 is not well researched or documented. We know very little about how catalogers actually use the code.

Although absolute perfection is not required in a catalog record, catalogers tend to emphasize the accuracy of some elements more than others, especially authority-controlled access points. A general cultural shift in cataloging would be necessary to change attitudes about what comprises quality in a record. It is safe to assume that the need to use AACR2 or its successor will continue for many years.

AACR2 as a whole is certainly not a narrow domain; it includes rules for a wide variety of items and data elements. Even rules for one area may be fairly broad in scope. AACR2 is most definitely not self-contained as its use is supplemented by national, utility and local rule interpretations, and other policies. Nor is it well-bounded, as it assumes a good deal of real-world knowledge and common sense. As one researcher in the field put it, "Like most professional handbooks, it is written for those who already know."[1]

AACR2 is irregularly updated by the Joint Steering Committee, but the changes are relatively infrequent and are generally not major shifts in practice.

Classification

As with AACR2, classification does utilize expertise and more than just algorithms come into play, since experts do it better and faster. Complexity varies because some parts of the various schemes are more complex than others. The level of knowledge or familiarity of a subject affects the complexity for each human classifier as well. The process of assigning a classification number is also not well understood or documented. Absolute perfection is not required, perhaps even less so than with AACR2. The need for classification will continue, at least for open-stacks libraries.

The classification schemes themselves can be fairly broad (LCC, DDC, UDC) or narrow (many locally-developed schemes) or in between (NLM Classification). They are more chunkable than AACR2, that is, their parts are usually more independent of one another. More research needs to be done on the process of classification before we can say how self-contained it is, but there does seem to be less consultation of other tools when classifying than when performing descriptive cataloging. Most classification schemes are modified on a regular basis, but most of the changes are not structural. This does depend on the scheme and the subject area. For example, LCC classification ranges for materials on the environment and on computer science have been modified frequently.

Duplicate Record Detection and Merging

This task does require some expertise. Long-time familiarity with bibliographic data improves one's ability to decide if two records are duplicates. It does entail more than just algorithms; there is a lot of uncertainty involved. The level of complexity in the task depends on the level of accuracy desired. A seventy percent accuracy level is easily achieved with simple algorithms; to reach ninety-eight percent accuracy would require much more complexity. Since this task, to a greater extent than the other examples, has already been automated, it is a better understood and documented process. Although it may not be possible to identify all duplicates, it is important not to incorrectly match two records that are not duplicates. As databases become larger, the need for this task will continue to increase in importance.

The domain is well-bounded; generally it is only the data in the records that are used (at least at the present time). It is narrow in the sense that, especially for any one type of material, the records contain much of the same kind of data, but not in the sense that the knowledge about bibliographic data that may be applied can be quite vast. The domain is fairly stable, although the USMARC formats are under continuous revision, and there are exceptions, such as format integration.

Shelflisting

As with the other examples, this task is performed more quickly and accurately by experts than by beginners. Partly because of differing practices over the years, judgement is involved, as when two existing items are not in correct order in the shelflist. With the exception of the shelflist, this task is usually not complex. Shelflisting has traditionally been better documented than other cataloging-related tasks, although much of this documentation is local. Absolute perfection is not required, and in most large libraries that have been around for a while, there is no illusion that it has been achieved in the past. As with classification, the need for shelflisting will continue.

The domain here is narrower than the domains in the other examples; for most materials there are only a few pieces of information that enter into the process. It is also self-contained. Generally no sources other than the shelflist, the item in hand, and a short procedures document are necessary. Shelflisting rules have been rather stable in most libraries.

WHAT YOU CAN DO

So now that you have at least a very basic understanding of what an expert system is, what it can do for you, and how to evaluate potential projects, what can you do now? I see four areas in which catalogers can get involved.

Help determine the suitability of projects. When others in your institution, a professor in a nearby library school, or colleagues across the country embark on a project to develop an expert system, you can help them weed through various ideas on which to work. This is especially valuable when the people working on the project in the early stages are more familiar with expert systems than with bibliographic data and processes. You are the ones who know (although sometimes only implicitly) what really happens in various technical services tasks.

Test prototype expert systems. When colleagues develop a prototype, participate in its testing. Give honest feedback, both on content and the interface. Make sure the accuracy level is acceptable and that the system can handle errors in an appropriate manner.

Develop an expert system. As I stated above, this can be a lengthy process, but the results can be worthwhile. Make certain that the necessary support is available and select your project carefully. Share your results, positive or negative!

Rethink technical services processes. It is necessary in all professions to step back and evaluate not just what you are doing, but also how and why you are doing it. As computer technology evolves, along with user understanding and expectations, it is imperative that we ensure that cataloging keeps pace. We need to optimize cataloging, not necessarily "simplify" it.

NOTE

1. Roland Hjerppe, "Project HYPERCATalog: Visions and Preliminary Conceptions of an Extended and Enhanced Catalog" (Report LiU-LIBLAB-R-1985:3, Linkoping University, Department of Computer and Information Science, Linkoping, Sweden, 1985).

Standard Generalized Markup Language and the Transformation of Cataloging

Daniel V. Pitti

SUMMARY. Standardized General Markup Language (SGML) provides a syntax and a meta-language for defining the logical structure of documents, and conventions for naming the components of documents. The author discusses how widespread adoption of SGML might transform what and how we catalog. If adopted by all components of the information industry, SGML would provide an opportunity to build an integrated information environment in which the catalog would provide a clearly marked path to both traditional and electronic information formats.

Last fall, I attended the Association of Research Libraries/ Association of American University Presses (ARL/AAUP) third seminar on electronic publishing on the network. Speaker after speaker–some teachers, some publishers, some librarians–expressed doubt and uncertainty about where "it" was all leading. The publishers, especially, seemed to be anxious, although here and there a trace of excitement was evident. From the increasingly familiar litany of issues, concerns, and problems mentioned by many of the speakers–copyright, cost recovery, access, various forms of control, peer review, preservation, authenticity–one theme clearly emerged:

Daniel V. Pitti is Advanced Technologies Projects Librarian, University of California, Berkeley, CA.

[Haworth co-indexing entry note]: "Standard Generalized Markup Language and the Transformation of Cataloging." Pitti, Daniel V. Co-published simultaneously in *The Serials Librarian* (The Haworth Press, Inc.) Vol. 25, No. 3/4, 1995, pp. 243-253; and: *A Kaleidoscope of Choices: Reshaping Roles and Opportunities for Serialists* (ed: Beth Holley and Mary Ann Sheble) The Haworth Press, Inc., 1995, pp. 243-253. Multiple copies of this article/chapter may be purchased from The Haworth Document Delivery Center [1-800-3-HAWORTH; 9:00 a.m. - 5:00 p.m. (EST)].

© 1995 by The Haworth Press, Inc. All rights reserved.

whatever else happens on the Internet, the expertise of the professional cataloger will be essential to ensure that people will be able to find and retrieve the information they seek. In fact, most of the speakers really said "librarians," but I, rather we, know what they really meant. The cataloger's experience-honed ability to distill, organize, interrelate, and integrate information is badly needed on the network. To build shamelessly on a bad metaphor, I like to think of today's professional catalogers as tomorrow's information superhighway patrol persons. If there is to be more than data carnage on the information superhighway, mangled bits and bytes strewn among delinquent digital images and unruly, riotous texts, we need the civilizing touch of the preeminent law and order librarian, the cataloger. The day is rapidly approaching, when serial catalogers will be able to fix their steely, pitiless glares on the publisher, who, in a sick abuse of illicitly obtained inside knowledge of AACR2 Rule 21.2, changes the electronic journal title issue by issue in some intellectually trivial but bibliographically significant way, and say to him, "Make my day!"

Another topic that arose again and again at the ARL/AAUP seminar was SGML, or Standard Generalized Markup Language (ISO 8879). If widely adopted, and it appears to be heading in that direction, SGML will help tomorrow's catalogers civilize the network. One speaker at the seminar noted that at the first seminar in 1991, SGML was barely mentioned, and only a few people had any idea what it was. The situation has changed significantly in the last two years. Today I want to explain why most of you have at least heard of SGML, and I want to say a word or two about how it might have an impact on your work.

INTRODUCTION TO STANDARD GENERALIZED MARKUP LANGUAGE

While Standard Generalized Markup Language is both standard (ISO 8879) and generalized, it is not really a markup language as such. SGML does not provide an off-the-shelf markup language that one can simply take home and apply to a letter, a novel, an article, a software manual, or a catalog record. What it really is, in fact, is a markup language meta-standard, or in simpler words, a standard for constructing markup languages. SGML provides a syntax and a meta-language for defining and expressing the logical structure of documents, and conventions for naming the components or elements of documents. One can think of SGML as a set of formal rules for defining specific markup languages for individual kinds of documents. Using these formal rules, a community sharing a particular kind of document can get together and create a markup language specific to that document type. These specific markup languages written in compliance with formal SGML requirements, are called Document Type Definitions, or, DTDs. For example, the Association of American Publishers with OCLC has developed a set of three DTDs: one for books, one for journals, and one for journal articles. A consortium of software developers and producers is developing a DTD for computer manuals. I am working on a DTD for library, museum, and archival finding aids. A colleague of mine at Berkeley has developed a USMARC DTD for use in a prototype bibliographic catalog employing advanced retrieval technology. Document Type Definitions shared and followed by a community are themselves standards. The Association of American Publishers DTD is registered as ANSI/NISO Z39.59-1988, and after substantial revision, has been approved just this year as an international standard, ISO 12083. If I design the finding aid DTD well, I hope to have it serve as the basis for a standard in the library and archival world. Hence, as you can see, SGML is very general and abstract. It exists formally over and above individual markup languages. It is also a standard, which is to say, a formal set of conventions in the public domain, not owned by and thus not dependent on any hardware or software producer. That SGML is a standard offers its users reasonable assurance that the information we create will not become obsolete because of hardware and software developments. This is not true of proprietary data formats.

    The formality and generality of SGML have very important implications. Because SGML syntax and rules are formal and precise, it is possible to write software that can be easily adjusted to work with any compliant Document Type Definition. Typically, SGML software has a toolkit that allows the user to adapt its functionality to their Document Type Definition. As a result, the market driving SGML software development is in principle everyone. This is very different from the MARC software market, which consists primarily of libraries and a few archives and museums. Libraries, archives, and museums are a very small, cash poor community. And while I do not want to insult the MARC oriented software developers–they do the best they can with limited resources–the products available reflect the limited resources. On the other hand, the SGML market includes virtually everyone. The Department of Defense now requires contractors to supply technical information using four standards. SGML is one of the four. This requirement is called the CALS initiative. SGML is now being used by several software producers, airline, automobile, and tractor manufacturers; the Department of Energy and other government agencies; a wide variety of print and electronic publishers; and the Text Encoding Initiative, an international project to provide encoding standards to support linguistic research and the study of literature. To give you an idea of how broad and varied are the potential users of SGML, let me cite just a few of the affiliations of the people who have subscribed to a listserv devoted to SGML related activities in northern California: the Research Libraries Group, Lockheed Space and Missile, Silicon Graphics, Berkeley Department of East Asian Languages, the Institute of Forestry Genetics, Lawrence Berkeley Laboratory, UC Berkeley Library, Dialog Information Services, Berkeley Department of Slavic Languages and Literatures, and many, many more. The list of SGML related software developers reflects confidence in the potential of this market: WordPerfect, Microsoft, Xerox, Frame, Electronic Book Technologies, Avalanche, ArborText, SoftQuad, AutoGraphics, Open Text, Information Dimensions Inc., Exoterica, Object Design, and a host of others. Firms such as WordPerfect and Microsoft are not interested in little markets. Products on the market or under development include Z39.50 compliant client/server databases and object oriented databases; a wide variety of authoring applications; conversion software; and electronic multimedia and paper based publishing tools. In order to understand why SGML has generated such broad interest from both users and developers, let us now turn to discussing the nature of markup and what kind of markup SGML promotes.

In an article now considered by many to be a classic presentation of document markup theory, James Coombs, Allen Renear, and

Steven DeRose distinguished five kinds of markup, three of which I would like to discuss briefly today: procedural, descriptive, and referential.[1] In the last few years, through the use of word processing systems, we have become familiar with procedural markup. Procedural markup consists of processing instructions to the computer. It tells the computer what to do with specified components of the text. For example, in the WordPerfect copy of the paper I am reading, there are embedded commands to center the title on the first page horizontally, and, since the title is long, there are several hard returns segmenting it. Most procedural markup is further characterized by being paper directed, that is, it tells the printer how to put the text on paper. If you want to do anything else with the text, the markup is not of much help. If you want to search for the initialism "SGML" in the machine-readable version of this paper, but only where it occurs in a section title, the procedural markup provides no assistance. Nor does it help if you want to display the text on a computer screen, since paper presentation and monitor presentation are quite different. And finally, procedural markup is characterized by a further limitation: to date all procedural markup has been proprietary. This means, for example, that the documents created on WordPerfect cannot be processed flawlessly on Microsoft Word and vice-versa. Each word processing software package uses its own markup. In this environment, the future of the document is tied to the future of the software.

A second type of markup mentioned by Coombs, Renear, and DeRose is descriptive markup. With descriptive markup, we arrive at the form of markup recommended by SGML. Descriptive markup identifies the logical components of documents. While procedural markup specifies a particular procedure to be applied to a document component, descriptive markup indicates what the component is. Examples are chapter, chapter title, section, paragraph, author, publisher, and cataloging-in-publication data. None of these gives any indication of what procedures are to be applied to these components. But, if you know the elements in a document, then you can have processors to do whatever you want to them. Descriptive markup liberates the document for multiple uses. It is possible, for example, to use one and the same source document to produce printed, electronic, Braille, and voiced synthesized versions, and, for good measure, to produce HTML/Mosaic and gopher versions. Of course the down side of this liberty is that it can be abused, but that is another matter. The fact that descriptive markup can be used in so many different ways is one of its important characteristics. It escapes the single use trap of procedural markup.

It is useful to distinguish two kinds of descriptive markup: structural and nominal. Descriptive structural markup identifies document components and their logical relationship. Structural elements are components that you usually want to present visually in some distinct manner. Examples are chapter titles, paragraphs, block quotes, and the like. Descriptive nominal markup, as you might expect, identifies named entities, both concrete and abstract. Examples are corporate names, personal names, topical subjects, genres, and geographic names. While you may want to visually present these names online or on paper in some particular manner, you usually want to index them in particular ways, to use them to provide access to the source or subject matter of the document. When the data that is being marked up is meta-data or cataloging, then nominal markup frequently identifies data components used to control and provide access to other information.

Referential markup, the last type of markup identified by Coombs, Renear, and DeRose, as its name suggests, refers to information that is not present. It is, so-to-speak, markup in the third person. There are different kinds and ways that one might use referential markup, but I would like to focus on the kind of referential markup that enables something about which most of you have heard, and perhaps with which many of you have some experience, namely, hypertext and hypermedia. In addition to supporting text, SGML also provides provisions for using text to refer to other text, and to refer to other kinds of digital information derived from the full array of native formats: photographs (color as well as black and white); sound motion pictures; drawings; paintings; audio recordings; three dimensional objects of all kinds, shapes, and sizes; maps; manuscripts; typescripts; printed pages; mathematical data; financial data; diagrams; musical notation; choreographic notation; and anything else open to digital capture and being digitally rendered in some useful form. It is possible not only to refer to or point at this other digital information from within SGML based documents, but also to control the notation information needed to launch the devices necessary for rendering the various objects into humanly intelligible forms. It is thus possible to use electronic text to control and manage extra-SGML information objects of all kinds, as well as to provide access to and navigation through them. Let us now turn our attention to a brief discussion of SGML and cataloging.

SGML AND CATALOGING

Cataloging is an activity in which we use information to help us create information about still other information. In the first category are descriptive cataloging rules, rule interpretations, subject cataloging rules, the beloved Conser manual, and much, much more. In the second category are authority and catalog records. Published and unpublished items comprise the third category. Thus, we have cataloging, the catalog, and the cataloged. Currently, to the extent that all three kinds of information are in electronic form, they exist in a framented information environment, based primarily on proprietary markup and proprietary software. The main exception is the MARC based catalog. But, as we have seen, MARC is used by a limited community, more or less in isolation from other information formats and information processing systems. Into this fragmented world enters SGML, which, if widely adopted, offers the prospect of a fully integrated, interoperable information environment.

As we have seen, SGML is a general standard capable of embracing a wide variety of text documents, and of using that text to provide access to and control of a multitude of online information formats. Hence, SGML can serve as the basis of a comprehensive, integrated, multimedia, text-based information environment. In essence, it would be possible to use SGML as the general underlying standard for the information that we use to catalog, the catalog records we create, and the electronic texts we catalog; and further yet, we could use the text in any of these domains to provide entry to and control of extra-textual digital objects.

There are already developments underway or being contemplated that point to an SGML based integrated information environment. John Duke at Virginia Commonwealth University has been encoding the Anglo-American Cataloging Rules, Second Edition (AACR2), using the Association of American Publishers Document Type Definition. While the Library of Congress has made no official announcements, I have been informally told that they are contemplating using SGML to mark up various cataloging tools. If, for example, they were to mark up the *LC Rule Interpretations* and the MARC formats, then it would be possible to create hypertext links between the AACR2 rules, *Rule Interpretations,* and MARC formats, in effect, creating a virtual cataloging tool that integrates what is now inconveniently dispersed. With respect to the catalog, Professor Ray Larson at the University of California, Berkeley School of Library and Information Science, is creating the second generation of his prototype catalog Cheshire. In its second incarnation, Cheshire will be a Z39.50 compliant, SGML based client/server database. Professor Larson and his graduate assistants have created a USMARC Document Type Definition into which to map the catalog records. Cheshire is a catalog that employs probabalistic retrieval software to support natural language subject searching. With the collaboration and assistance of a wide variety of experts from numerous libraries, archives, and museums, the Berkeley Finding Aid Project is developing a Document Type Definition for finding aids. Finding aids are documents used in libraries, archives, and museums to provide access to and control of unpublished collections of primary source materials. In the hierarchical structure of collection-level information access and navigation, finding aids reside between collection-level catalog records and primary source materials. Catalog records lead to finding aids, and finding aids lead to primary source materials. The Berkeley Finding Aid Project envisions a future in which information seekers follow clearly marked paths through library catalogs to finding aids and from finding aids to cultural treasures in a multitude of computer and traditional formats . . . and back. To complete the circle, we need to look at developments in electronic publishing.

There are many activities in the area of electronic publishing and text encoding. The Text Encoding Initiative (TEI) is an international project to develop a suite of Document Type Definitions for texts used in linguistic, literary, and historical studies. The TEI guidelines, numbering some 1300 pages, were published in May 1994. Also in May, the Center for Electronic Text in the Humanities at Princeton and Rutgers Universities sponsored a workshop on documenting electronic texts, with a focus on the TEI header and the MARC record. The TEI header is that portion of a TEI compliant text that functions as the chief source of information. The workshop brought together scholars, publishers, computer scientists, and librarians. Those gathered were in general agreement that the TEI header and MARC records should be symetrical with respect to content designation. In essence, a TEI compliant text would come self-described. The description would migrate into a MARC record. A cataloger would then integrate this description into the target catalog by performing the authority work, subject analysis, and classification. The cataloger supplied information could then be mapped back into the TEI header for use by other libraries, if so desired. In the area of electronic journals, OCLC, an early supporter of SGML and a co-developer of the Association of American Publishers suite of Document Type Definitions, has been a pioneer in SGML based networked publishing. OCLC currently publishes the *Online Journal of Current Clinical Trials, Electronic Letters Online* (a publication of the Institute of Electrical Engineers in Great Britain), and *Online Journal of Knowledge Synthesis for Nursing*. These journals are available to subscribers over the Internet using Guidon, client software developed by OCLC. OCLC, in collaboration with the American Chemical Society, Bellcore and Cornell University, is also involved in an electronic journal experiment called CORE. This experiment is focusing on a large number of journals in the chemistry subject area, and involves both page images as well as structured SGML based text. OCLC is also talking to a number of publishers about networked, electronic publishing of journals. Internationally, more and more publishers are beginning to use SGML and contemplate network publishing. In my own neighborhood, the University of California Office of the Continuing Education of the Bar, and the University of California Press are both in the process of acquiring the expertise to convert their publishing activities to SGML based operations.

Clearly, there is now an opportunity to build an integrated information environment in which the catalog provides marked paths leading to both traditional and electronic information formats. That a civilized environment will emerge from the current Internet development frenzy is far from certain. With the exception of the Text Encoding Initiative, no one else in publishing, to the best of my knowledge, has approached the library community about ensuring compatibility between the encoding of the chief source of information and the MARC format. And in addition to the publishers, there are a host of other commercial and private information producers that are overwhelming the Internet with a chaotic assortment of the good, the bad, and the ugly. SGML, I believe, as a general standard that allows us to structure text and to interrelate many different kinds of information, offers us an opportunity to make the Internet a coherent, standard based, information whole, an orderly information universe. I believe that librarians, and in particular, catalogers, have a professional obligation to actively assert themselves in the creation of this information universe. If librarians sit back and wait to be asked, the disparate and all too shortsighted forces developing the Internet will not think to ask them to participate in the planning and development until it is too late.

At the beginning of my presentation, I indulged in building on a bad metaphor, the so-called information superhighway. A moment ago I used quite a different metaphor, one that I think is far superior, namely, the information universe. At once we elevate the discussion from the earth-bound arena of transportation to the unbounded heavens above. In this view of things, it will be the responsibility of catalogers to ensure that order emerges from chaos. Since this activity is clearly divine, the full assumption of it will allow catalogers, at last, to take their rightful place in relation to the information mortals.

NOTE

1. James H. Coombs, Allen H. Renear, and Steven J. DeRose, "Markup Systems and the Future of Scholarly Text Processing," *Communications of the ACM* 30, no. 11 (November 1987): 933-947.

SUGGESTED FURTHER READING ON SGML

Eric Van Herwijnen, *Practical SGML* 2nd ed. (Dordrecht; Boston: Kluwer Academic, 1994).
Eric Van Herwijnen, *SGML Tutorial* (Providence: Electronic Book Technologies, 1993). (Note: An interactive tutorial for Windows 3.1 and Mac.)
Available from:
Electronic Book Technologies, Inc.
1 Richmond Square
Providence, RI 02906
Charles Goldfarb, *The SGML Handbook* (Oxford: Clarendon Press, c1990).
Anonymous FTP site: sgml1.ex.ac.uk
James H. Coombs, Allen H. Renear, and Steven J. DeRose, "Markup Systems and the Future of Scholarly Text Processing," *Communications of the ACM* 30 no. 11 (November 1987): 933-947.

NASIG WORKSHOPS

Rethinking the Workforce and Workplace: Alternative Ways of Getting the Job Done

Hien Nguyen
Kevin McShane
Bill Willmering

Workshop Leaders

Fred Hamilton

Recorder

SUMMARY. Faced with diminishing staffs and budgets, and the difficulty of recruiting skilled serialists, librarians are exploring alternative methods for getting the job done. Several members of the National Library of Medicine staff describe their experiences with Flexiplace, a program that allows employees to do most of their

---

Fred Hamilton is Head of Cataloging, Prescott Memorial Library, Louisiana Tech University, Ruston, LA.

[Haworth co-indexing entry note]: "Rethinking the Workforce and Workplace: Alternative Ways of Getting the Job Done." Hamilton, Fred. Co-published simultaneously in *The Serials Librarian* (The Haworth Press, Inc.) Vol. 25, No. 3/4, 1995, pp. 255-259; and: *A Kaleidoscope of Choices: Reshaping Roles and Opportunities for Serialists* (ed: Beth Holley and Mary Ann Sheble) The Haworth Press, Inc., 1995, pp. 255-259. Multiple copies of this article/chapter may be purchased from The Haworth Document Delivery Center [1-800-3-HAWORTH; 9:00 a.m. - 5:00 p.m. (EST)].

© 1995 by The Haworth Press, Inc. All rights reserved.

work from home with small purchase orders or contracts for services. Flexiplace is described, and the successes and limitations of working with contracts for special language cataloging, binding preparation, check-in, and other tasks are discussed.

Three librarians from the National Library of Medicine, Hien Nguyen, serials cataloger, Kevin McShane, head of Serials Cataloging Unit, and Bill Willmering, head of Serial Records Section, presented this workshop on "Rethinking the Workforce and Workplace." The many things that can be done through small purchase orders and contracts, and the ability to work in places far removed from the office through electronic communication has caused these National Library of Medicine (NLM) staff members to reconsider the boundaries of their workforce and workplace. The finished product is what counts and it makes little difference whether work is completed by in-house employees in the library, in-house employees at remote locations, or independent contractors.

McShane began the workshop by explaining that the National Library of Medicine is a United States federal agency at the National Institutes of Health (NIH). He also gave a brief overview of contracting at NLM, and described Flexiplace, a federal work program. A contract is an agreement between people and agencies to do a particular job. At NLM, many contracts are small purchase orders, often with a single individual. Flexiplace is a U.S. government program that allows federal employees to work at home. The U.S. Office of Personnel Management has estimated that by the year 2000, twenty per cent of federal workers will be working from their homes.

Nguyen described her experience as a Flexiplace employee. She usually works at home three days a week and goes to the office two days to work. She also goes to her office to pick up and return completed projects. McShane followed Nguyen's presentation with a discussion about supervising a Flexiplace worker.

Flexiplace at NIH began as a pilot program in 1991. At the beginning of the project, NIH gave seminars for Flexiplace workers and their supervisors. The seminars were followed by monthly meetings to discuss the progress of the program. McShane discussed some of the guidelines for Flexiplace participation. For example, working at home is not a substitute for day care. Workers with children at home must have day care, just as they would if working away from their home.

Nguyen gave some possible advantages and disadvantages of Flexiplace work for the employer and employee. Advantages for the employer are: (1) increased productivity; (2) retention of experienced workers; (3) attracting new employees; and (4) accommodation of employees with disabilities. For employees, possible advantages include: (1) being able to adjust time to coincide with optimum effectiveness; (2) decreased stress associated with commuting; and (3) money and time saved in traveling to and from work. It also is advantageous for the community, as it can decrease traffic congestion and pollution.

Possible disadvantages for the organization are: (1) additional expense, i.e., more company supplies, computers, modems, etc.; (2) additional work for computer staff; (3) difficulty in maintaining staff communication; and (4) decreased ability to perform "rush" tasks. Possible disadvantages for the employee include: (1) lack of social and professional interaction; (2) the perception that it might hinder career growth, i.e., possibly not being noticed or considered for advancement; and (3) possible distraction by family and friends. In some places, there is still some resistance to Flexiplace because it challenges traditional ways of supervising and the traditional role of the supervisor.

McShane noted that Flexiplace tends to increase worker productivity. This observation was confirmed in his discussions with other supervisors of Flexiplace employees.

NLM loans most of the materials needed by Flexiplace workers, including personal computers and manuals. Other agencies set different policies on equipment loans and schedules.

As with any job, Flexiplace works best with employees who are reliable. Self-discipline and self-motivation are key requirements for working at home. Jobs that have quantifiable standards are easiest to supervise. At present, fifteen of NLM's approximately five hundred and fifty employees participate in Flexiplace. Many of these employees work as indexers for *Index Medicus*. More Flexiplace positions are anticipated. Flexiplace works well for information workers such as catalogers and indexers. At NIH, computer and systems staff have found that many of their duties can be performed from home. McShane believes that many supervisory duties could be done better from home, if supervisors accept that their presence at the office is not indispensable. People should think in terms of what can be done from home, at least for a day or a few days a week.

McShane brought up the topic of supervising work done by contract catalogers, working on- or off-site. In many ways, this is similar to supervising the work of Flexiplace employees. Like the Library of Congress, the National Library of Medicine acquires material from all over the world in all languages. However, NLM has a much smaller staff than the Library of Congress. NLM must rely on contracts or purchase orders with outside people and agencies. NLM staff are given training to learn how to write and administer contracts. Some NLM contracts are with commercial companies, but others have been with individuals. For example, NLM has contracted for foreign language cataloging with retired catalogers from the Library of Congress, with university libraries, and with individual librarians working at other institutions in other states. NLM also contracts for services of former employees to do certain tasks on a one time basis. There are many tasks that can be done by contract help, including retrospective conversion projects, database searching, and writing procedure manuals. Contracts or purchase orders for services should be customized to suit the needs of an institution.

Bill Willmering stated that contracting has been around for a long time and a lot of people have had negative experiences with it. The National Library of Medicine has contracted a number of services, including binding preparation and "off-site check-in." These contracts began in the mid 1970s, when the library went through a long personnel freeze.

NLM's experience with these contracts demonstrated the necessity of a detailed, specific statement of work. The binding preparation contract required the contractor to follow a very specific set of instructions in preparing the issues for binding. In the off-site check-in contract, each contractor received materials at their local offices. Contractors processed the materials, attached call numbers and security devices, packed the materials, and produced printouts of materials shipped. However, contractors were given great flexibility in how they accomplished these tasks. Over time, problems surfaced because there were few specific requirements in the contract. A lack of bibliographic expertise, communication problems, data transfer from external systems to the NLM system, and shifts in publisher's dispatch sites are examples of some of the problems encountered.

Willmering presented some guidelines that he had found useful in preparing contracts. First, it is important to have a good "Statement of Work." Be clear and concise in stating expectations for the contractor. Quality control is an essential element. Have the authority to enforce your "Statement of Work" specifications, and be careful not to overlook the obvious. It is important to maintain standards.

Contracting is an art. There was some discussion about the best way to present a contract. One of the greatest difficulties is knowing how much responsibility to place on the contractor. If you put too much responsibility on yourself, you negate the value of a contract. It is important that the "Statement of Work" be inclusive.

There are several points to consider about contracts. When determining how often the contract should be re-negotiated, consider past performance. A sealed bid may be a requirement. As a federal agency, the National Library of Medicine is required to consider giving small businessmen special consideration.

Willmering stated that contracting may not be the cheapest way to get a job done, and it does not always save time or steps. But sometimes it is the only way to get a job done.

Approximately 120 people attended the two workshop sessions. Most members of the audience were librarians. The presentations were followed by a question and answer period.

The New World Order:
Serials Management
of Electronic Resources
and Document Delivery

Jeri Van Goethem
Sharon Wiles-Young

Workshop Leaders

Marla Edelman

Recorder

SUMMARY. As libraries shift from journal subscriptions to a bewildering array of electronic options, serials management takes on a new meaning. The processes of budgeting, acquiring, controlling, and implementing networked CD-ROM sources, remote sources, and document delivery sources are discussed. These processes and future challenges are described from the experiences of Lehigh University and Duke University.

This workshop was presented by Jeri Van Goethem, head of the Acquisitions/Serials Department at Duke University Libraries, and Sharon Wiles-Young, serials manager at Lehigh University Libraries. Van Goethem began her presentation by saying that during

---

Marla Edelman is Head Serials Librarian at the University of North Carolina, Greensboro, NC.

[Haworth co-indexing entry note]: "The New World Order: Serials Management of Electronic Resources and Document Delivery." Edelman, Marla. Co-published simultaneously in *The Serials Librarian* (The Haworth Press, Inc.) Vol. 25, No. 3/4, 1995, pp. 261-267; and: *A Kaleidoscope of Choices: Reshaping Roles and Opportunities for Serialists* (ed: Beth Holley and Mary Ann Sheble) The Haworth Press, Inc., 1995, pp. 261-267. Multiple copies of this article/chapter may be purchased from The Haworth Document Delivery Center [1-800-3-HAWORTH; 9:00 a.m. - 5:00 p.m. (EST)].

© 1995 by The Haworth Press, Inc. All rights reserved.

1993-1994, Duke University took the first steps in purchasing and providing electronic access across campus and for the main library, Perkins, and seven branches in the Perkins system—four science libraries; a Duke marine library 175 miles away on the North Carolina Coast; a divinity school library; a music library; and, on a separate campus, the Lilly Library containing art, philosophy, and media collections. There are also three separately funded and administered libraries: medical, law, and Fuqua School of Business.

Previously, Duke supplied traditional electronic access (in-library, mediated) to such sources as Dialog, Lexis/Nexis (L/N), University Microforms International (UMI), and interlibrary loan (ILL) for document delivery. As of summer 1994, the campus is fully wired with 7000 dormitory computer outlets and is simultaneously bringing up the DRA online catalog (PAC). Duke has decided to take a more proactive stance to deliver more information electronically. Van Goethem, along with the head of Collection Development and a team of bibliographers, looked at resources and decided what to buy based on: potential level of use, cost-effectiveness (base price and expected level of use), ease of use, and currentness of data. A variety of access modes were desirable so that the best could be determined. Criteria not measurable and factors not anticipated before this "learning experience" began were: computer infrastructure necessary to support the various databases, networkability of databases, lack of uniformity in search protocols between databases, and the degree of training needed.

Initially, the favored criterion was direct online access through the PAC. After they began to use DRANET to access Information Access Corporation's (IAC) Expanded Academic Index and Business Index and Company Profiles, along with UMI's Newspaper Index/Abstracts, they decided that IAC's InfoTrack search software better suited their needs. In 1994-1995, Duke will be using IAC search software to access directly the IAC database in Massachusetts from which users will be able to get full text. This will still be a menu item on the PAC. Duke also purchased six passwords to Dialog's Classroom Instruction Program, nine passwords to L/N's Academic Program, and 150,000 searches on FirstSearch. Since Dialog and L/N are restricted to student or faculty classroom instruction use only, front-end security software was written which required students to log in with a social security number. The most popular resource is UMI's full-text ProQuest file, although students must come to the library to use it. Vendor restrictions are the only obstacle in putting ProQuest on the network.

The Committee decided to purchase a CD-ROM jukebox to simultaneously run seventy-seven CD-ROMs. The jukebox has a 250-user fileserver for network access and eight telnet ports. The Library's wiring infrastructure could not accommodate this hardware and the systems office insisted on new network wiring. Additional electrical circuit wiring was also needed. Neither the complexities of getting the CD's to function via the network, nor the problem of Macintosh computer clusters attempting to connect to DOS-based CDs were anticipated. There is SilverPlatter software which would allow a connection, but only to SilverPlatter databases. Instead, the MACs must compete for the eight telnet ports, which will soon be increased in number. Other problems were caused by terminal emulation and command key inconsistencies between databases, and between telnet communication software.

The cancellation of print indexes began before their electronic counterparts were fully in place and problems arose when the CD-ROM tower was not functioning. Document delivery resources were funded because of an earlier guarantee for free documents to replace canceled journal subscriptions. This service is being expanded to include any journals not available locally. Ariel is available, but Duke still spends $10,000/year for traditional 'free' ILL and provides document delivery to users, with UnCover and FaxonFinder available on the PAC menu.

Van Goethem sees the acquisition of electronic resources as very time-consuming since one must negotiate license agreements which must be reviewed, altered (if possible), and signed. CD-ROM publishers are very careful about the use and control of their data and restrictions abound as the prices escalate. Most data are obtained through a lease. Superceded disks must be returned as must all data disks when a subscription is canceled. After telephone negotiations to determine price, license restrictions, and connectivity requirements, orders are placed and resulting CD-ROMs are checked-in on the acquisitions system. A form was devised to aid communication with library systems regarding: subscription status, installation instructions, 'help' phone number, license restrictions, return of old disks, and disposition of manuals/documentation.

CD-ROMs are cataloged but not analyzed for the PAC. For the full-text databases, the cataloging of individual journal titles is a possibility because the cancellation of corresponding paper subscriptions is being considered. This is problematic because titles are added or dropped, and coverage is inconsistent. In order for the electronic resources to be used well, coordinated publicity, good documentation and handouts, and one-on-one training are required.

Electronic resources will not rescue the budget because of rising costs of hardware, wiring, staffing, and support not previously needed with paper-based information. Questions for collection development arise because so much of the future of electronic resources is unknown. Is it wise to cancel paper subscriptions when the survival of the electronic counterparts is unsure? Will more genuine research titles become available digitally? It is also important to note that libraries may not be best served by these resources because titles indexed may be what are readily available, not necessarily what are needed. There is also a great deal of repetition between indexes. The industry is still evolving and libraries are paying a great deal for access with little fine-tuning to local needs. Another change caused by this mode of collection is that, instead of thinking in terms of specific collection needs, access purchasing must focus on technical issues such as network requirements, hardware, support, search protocols, user interface, and format. In the past, libraries bought books and journals, put them on the shelf, and shared them. Digital information and its concomitant restrictions bring a whole new meaning to 'sharing.' Should all campus libraries with access share the costs? Who doles out the slots on the CD tower, where they fill up fast, especially when changes are made and new titles require more space?

There are still many issues to be resolved on the frontier of the information highway, including copyright and its restrictions on the free flow of information, and the matter of leasing that information. A model for the electronic library has not been devised because the scene continues to shift and change, but libraries are learning from and sharing their experiences. There will not be a complete transformation of scholarly information without significant effort on the part of librarians.

Wiles-Young began her presentation with an overview of Lehigh University, a private coeducational institution with 4500 undergraduate and 3000 graduate students. There are three libraries: Fairchild-Martindale, with materials in science and social science; Linderman, with materials in the humanities and rare books; and Mountain Top, a satellite campus's library. Lehigh has been using GEAC 8000 since 1985, although they will be migrating (fall 1994) to a client-server platform on Unix.

Currently, there are no electronic resources in the online public access catalog. They are only available on the campus network. Wiles-Young distributed a list of 36 databases, dates and subject matter covered, where the databases are mounted, and how they are accessed. FirstSearch is available on the campus network. Lehigh acquired SiteSearch from OCLC and loaded two heavily used indexes: ERIC and Engineering Index. Uncover and Uncover Reveal are being used by faculty who bring the resulting citations to ILL for document delivery, rather than ordering the articles directly and at their own expense. To get the documents, ILL goes through Ariel which has been more heavily used since the number of Ariel sites has increased. The ILL function of FirstSearch has not yet been activated. The electronic resource used most frequently (7000 hrs./yr.) is Dow Jones News Retrieval. Also popular are L/N Academic (full text) and Adonis (image database of 500 biomedical journals). The latter was ordered because it included Brain Research, but Adonis will not be continued at Lehigh because the hardware is a problem.

The library gopher provides access to electronic texts, reference sources, and eighteen electronic journals. In the near future, a World Wide Web (WWW) server is coming up using Mosaic. The electronic journals mounted on their gopher have not been cataloged, but Wiles-Young believes that it is important for users to know that these journals are available since they are often cited and indexed. To assist users in getting to electronic resources, the Reference Department has created handouts and offers workshops and classes. There is also network training for faculty, although there have been delays for faculty who do not have the network software loaded on their office PCs. With the upcoming merger of the Library and Computer Center, there may be some changes.

Acquisitions has a separate budget for electronic resources which came from the monographs budget. Most orders originate in Reference. The Collection Development Team (consisting of the associate directors for public and technical services, and members from acquisitions and reference) decides which resources to purchase, reviews licensing agreements, and judges the cost-effectiveness of resources. At first, data regarding electronic resources was kept on a spreadsheet but it soon became apparent that information regarding receipt was needed by others outside acquisitions. The ordering and receipt of electronic resources was then put into the acquisitions system. Eventually, invoicing will have to be done through the system in order to keep better control of the budget.

The Collection Development Team began canceling the paper subscriptions but cataloging was reluctant to close the holdings without first providing users with the information that an alternative format was available. Reference requested that there be a single record for each title, so rather than adding a second record for the other format, a second holdings statement was included that contained the note, "Type DATABASES on network server." To help users find the 500 journal titles available on Adonis, cataloging wanted to add '246' fields (alternate title access) for each title but had difficulty including the years of coverage. Reference preferred that the Adonis record have a holdings statement: "Titles may be available from 1994."

Lehigh is a test site for attaching their union list local data records to FirstSearch via ISSNs. An "in library" message will show users that the information they seek is available locally. The use of the uniform resources locator will be a benefit to users of the future because it will take them from the online catalog directly to the full text article.

Some questions libraries should consider: What happens when the system that provides access to databases goes down and the paper backup is canceled? What happens when a CD-ROM LAN crashes? What happens when the database drops the indexing of earlier years or drops a title altogether, and the paper-copy has been canceled?

After the presentations, there were questions from the audience about coding, use statistics for databases and document delivery, database coverage, archiving data, hardware, software, security, cataloging individual titles within a database, and training provided by vendors.

Negotiating Contracts for Electronic Resources

Bill Kara
Ann Caputo
Trish Davis

Workshop Leaders

Nancy Gibbs

Recorder

SUMMARY. Serials in electronic formats often require contractual agreements governing their use. Librarians need to be educated consumers and understand the issues and concerns of the producer/vendor community to secure reasonable agreements for electronic access. Standard contracts often do not meet the needs of different libraries and may contain provisions that should be questioned or clarified. Database producers and vendors have their own contractual and legal obligations which must be considered when negotiating with individual libraries.

INTRODUCTION

Trish Davis, head of Continuations at Ohio State University, began the program with a quote from the most recent issue of the

---

Nancy Gibbs is Assistant Head, Acquisitions, North Carolina State University, Raleigh, NC.

[Haworth co-indexing entry note]: "Negotiating Contracts for Electronic Resources." Gibbs, Nancy. Co-published simultaneously in *The Serials Librarian* (The Haworth Press, Inc.) Vol. 25, No. 3/4, 1995, pp. 269-275; and: *A Kaleidoscope of Choices: Reshaping Roles and Opportunities for Serialists* (ed: Beth Holley and Mary Ann Sheble) The Haworth Press, Inc., 1995, pp. 269-275. Multiple copies of this article/chapter may be purchased from The Haworth Document Delivery Center [1-800-3-HAWORTH; 9:00 a.m. - 5:00 p.m. (EST)].

© 1995 by The Haworth Press, Inc. All rights reserved.

Journal *Library Administration & Management:* "As current licensing agreements are written, it is clear that some day soon a library will be the victim of a big, expensive lawsuit. Even if the library wins the suit, the cost in time and legal fees to the university or parent institution will be enormous."[1]

With this dire prediction as a beginning, Davis introduced the other workshop leaders: Bill Kara, head of Acquisitions, Mann Library, Cornell University, and Ann Caputo, manager of Academic Programs for Dialog Information Services. Davis outlined the program as a discussion of defining issues and users, the method of access for databases, and pricing structures. Leaders of this workshop hope this will raise everyone's consciousness about licensing agreements, and level the playing field to better understand each person's role in the licensing agreement arena. Each workshop leader has worked closely negotiating licensing agreements in their current positions in libraries or as an information vendor. Davis also reminded the audience of librarians and vendors that the discussion would center around those licensing agreements which must be signed as a legal document and in most instances must be returned to the vendor before the product is shipped to the library. The other most common type of licensing agreement is the shrink-wrapped passive agreement which arrives with a product and requires no acknowledgement from the library before using the information.

FUNDAMENTALS OF LICENSING AGREEMENTS

Licensing agreements are written in legalese and can be dull, boring, and no two agreements seem the same. Their main purpose is to define who is doing what; the licensor is the copyright holder, the licensee is the person acquiring the data. The importance of thoroughly reading the whole contract was stressed repeatedly by all workshop leaders.

A typical contract has:

1. definitions: detailing the parties involved, what is being purchased or leased, approved users and approved uses of the data, the technology needed to access the data, and the capabilities of that technology;

2. restrictions: defined in negative terms, delineating how information on the database can or cannot be used, modifications allowed by the software, and types and methods of access;
3. warranties/liabilities: written in negative terms outlining the limits from the licensor and the product, who is responsible for the accuracy of the information contained on the database;
4. general contractual clauses: discussing acts of God upon the database, state in which vendor may be sued, and the severability of the license.

Librarians are fully responsible for upholding these licensing agreements. Before the databases are placed on your campus or in your library, it is important to know and understand your role with each part of the licensing agreement. If a paragraph or portion of the licensing agreement is not understood by the library, an attempt can be made to ask the licensor to re-write that portion of the agreement into "plain English" so that each party can fully understand all provisions.

DEFINITION OF USERS

Bill Kara noted one of the most difficult parts of a licensing agreement is defining users and their capabilities. Users can include faculty, students, staff, public, graduate students, part-time extension faculty, on-campus users as well as off-site users. There can be simultaneous users who access the same information from different terminals on campus, users who dial-in from remote sites, or a single user who accesses the data from a simple, stand-alone workstation within the library. The library staff must know the capabilities of each of these user groups regarding printing, downloading, and viewing the information on the database in order to perform their role in monitoring and restricting use to particular functions or users in accordance with the licensing agreement.

SECURITY

Issues of security and the policing of users to adhere to security as defined by the licensing agreement is vitally important to both the vendor and the information provider. Ann Caputo noted vendors' fears include illegal downloading of information for potential re-sale and the lack of adherence to existing license agreements that allow "backdoor" access to mounted databases through the Internet. Neither the library nor the vendor wants to tackle this issue, but someone must take the responsibility to monitor access and make sure copyright is not violated by a user. Academic institutions are reluctant to take this role.

Vendors expect that the next best alternative is to have formal, but brief, copyright screens as the opening message when accessing a database. Further, vendors hope that a question or two must be answered by the user before access to data is available. Vendors have concerns about access through the Internet and predict that encryption devices will become a big business as access to the Internet continues to increase. If a library suspects problems with security violations, they should be in touch with the vendor at once. Each of these security issues can contain pitfalls of which the library must be aware in order to regulate security and abide by the restrictions signed in the licensing agreements. Understanding the issues surrounding these questions before negotiations begin will make this a much easier process.

NEGOTIATIONS

Negotiating for a database must be made in a collegial atmosphere, rather than an adversarial one, between the vendor and the institution. It is important to remember the database licensor may represent a third party who actually provides the data and holds the copyright to that data (known as an information provider IP) and the vendor with which you are negotiating is merely information in this format or on this search engine.

Vendors estimate that ninety percent of librarians do not review or question what they sign! No reputable vendor wants the library to be shocked when there are problems resulting from poorly negotiated licenses. Who signs these agreements varies from institution to institution. In some libraries it is the head of acquisitions, while on other campuses, the legal department or the purchasing department has the authority to sign for the institution.

PRICING STRUCTURES

Pricing by the vendor is usually done in one of three modes:

1. Data are purchased at the standard market value with no negotiating between either party. This is the most common pricing structure whereby libraries take the price the vendor sets or they do not purchase the data.
2. The vendor will state a given price that is not necessarily firm. Prices could vary depending upon consortia agreements, the large number or types of users, or a previously negotiated price between the vendor and an institution.
3. An instructional rate or give-away price is used by the vendor in hopes of reaching additional users with his product; the vendor might negotiate a pricing structure dependent upon future users.

Pricing is still being developed by vendors and is based on cost recovery of the data bought from the information provider and also accounts for database development, searching software development, and monitoring of security issues. Libraries must decide if they wish to purchase or lease the data they will access. Other variables which could impact the pricing of a database for a particular institution include: pricing by various users (limiting access to particular users, e.g., business students, graduate engineering fellows); additional fees for bundled equipment, purchasing of backfiles or just current information; how often that information is updated (quarterly, monthly), receiving a special edition of the information, and potential discounts because the library already subscribes to a print version of the same electronic data. Librarians need to know about their options before they agree to a firm price from a vendor; if that fee is not within their budgetary constraints they can reject the vendors' price and not purchase the item. On the other hand, librarians must remember that vendors have charges they must absorb in order to provide the data to the library and the vendor must make some form of profit on their product in order to stay in business. Many vendors are commercial operations and many are publicly owned companies with shareholders. Just as libraries need predictable pricing, vendors need predictable income in order to balance resources.

Negotiating the best price is important and libraries have ways to assist in getting a favorable pricing structure. They can consider flexible times to access the vendor's data; they can reduce the number of simultaneous users who can access the data at any one time; they can limit the types of users; they can provide offline search navigation in preparation for going online; and they can mount a pilot project while they finalize their negotiations.

Audience participants noted during this section of the program that pricing for the same datasets can vary for libraries in the United States and the United Kingdom. The workshop attendees thought this seemed unfair and unreasonable. Davis noted that several organizations within the national library groups of the UK and US are working towards a more standard user language to describe pricing, users, and access.

ACCESS

Types of access vary within institutions and on different applications with libraries demanding different pricing structures and licensing agreements. Network sites are different from single building sites which are different from stand-alone sites. Diskettes and CD-ROMs are different from Internet access or tape-mounted products. It is important to know the capabilities and future directions of your information system, and the limitations of your current licensing agreement. If changes occur in your types of access, this could necessitate a different or varying licensing agreement. The workshop leaders cautioned libraries not to be fooled by sales representatives saying "no other library does it this way." The number of configurations are endless among libraries and each needs to be addressed separately.

The relevant questions that need to be answered by the licensing agreement, the institution, and the information provider are:

1. What kind of access does the library want to provide?
2. What is the library able to support technologically and financially?
3. What is permissible/negotiable/available?

CONCLUSION

The workshop leaders concluded the program with the "mother of all disclaimers":

> This disclaimer is from Haventree Software's Easy Flow program: If EasyFlow doesn't work: tough. If you lose millions because EasyFlow messes up, it's you that's out the millions, not us. If you don't like this disclaimer: tough. We reserve the right to do the absolute minimum provided by law, up to and including nothing. This is basically the same disclaimer that comes with all software packages, but ours is in plain English and theirs is in legalese. We didn't want to include any disclaimer at all, but our lawyers insisted.[2]

NOTES

1. Edward A. Warro, "What have we been signing? A look at Database Licensing Agreements," *Library Administration & Management* 8 (Summer 1994): cover.

2. *Wired* 2 (January 1994): 35.

"Keep Them Doggies Rollin'," or, Using Series Authority Records to Improve Cataloging and Processing Workflow

Beverley Geer Butler
Beatrice McKay

Workshop Presenters

Kristine A. J. Smets

Recorder

SUMMARY. As libraries automate, paper files such as the card catalog, the shelflist, the order file, and authority files are also automated. To exploit the automated authority file and to help streamline the handling of titles in series, Trinity University Library has developed a method to store cataloging and processing information in the online series authority record. The issue of how to integrate the pure title authority function of the series authority record with the pragmatic aspects of processing titles in series is discussed. As a result of this integration at Trinity University, acquisitions staff, catalogers, and copy catalogers can easily obtain information about distribution and cataloging treatment of titles within series and analyzed serial titles. This procedure is adaptable to manual environments as well.

Kristine A. J. Smets is Serials Cataloger at the Center for Research Libraries, Chicago, IL.

[Haworth co-indexing entry note]: "'Keep Them Doggies Rollin'," or, Using Series Authority Records to Improve Cataloging and Processing Workflow." Smets, Kristine A. J. Co-published simultaneously in *The Serials Librarian* (The Haworth Press, Inc.) Vol. 25, No. 3/4, 1995, pp. 277-281; and: *A Kaleidoscope of Choices: Reshaping Roles and Opportunities for Serialists* (ed: Beth Holley and Mary Ann Sheble) The Haworth Press, Inc., 1995, pp. 277-281. Multiple copies of this article/chapter may be purchased from The Haworth Document Delivery Center [1-800-3-HAWORTH; 9:00 a.m. - 5:00 p.m. (EST)].

The use of the series authority records file as an effective tool to improve cataloging and processing workflow formed the main focus of this workshop. The presenters, Beverley Geer Butler and Beatrice McKay of Trinity University, showed that "branding" the series authority records correctly early on in the process allows for smooth processing, routing and cataloging, thus making work with titles in series more efficient and cost-effective.

Beatrice McKay, serials cataloger at Trinity University, introduced the topic of series authority work by examining the cost factors involved. She noted that although the Library of Congress estimates to save cataloging cost by reducing the amount of the series authority work done (as indicated in the proposal released by the Library of Congress to the library community in early December 1993), the cost savings will probably not outweigh the increased workload elsewhere in the library's operations and in libraries across the nation. While she could not judge the relative benefits and costs at the Library of Congress of instituting the proposed changes, she did demonstrate that decreased series authority work by the Library of Congress will result in cost increases at other institutions. If series authority work is diminished or abandoned, the result will be decreased efficiency and productivity as materials will be processed slower and duplicate purchases will increase. Furthermore, inconsistent treatment and loss of cross reference structure will result in incomplete searches on the part of bibliographers and patrons.

At Trinity University, a small private university with 2,500 students and a library collection of about 750,000 titles, series authority records are added to the integrated NOTIS online system for materials in all formats, including audio-visual materials and titles on CD-ROM. Acquisitions staff use series authority records at the point of ordering to determine how a title is treated and whether to download a new record and route it to monographs or serials cataloging. Cataloging staff consult series authority records to verify cataloging treatment and form of series tracing. Bibliographers at Trinity use the information in series authority records to avoid duplicate purchases and they are united in their desire to see consistent treatment of titles in series. Last but not least, patrons benefit from the collocation and cross reference structure that result from series authority work. Some faculty members are known to rely on the orderly display of titles in series to stay current with publications that interest them.

Beverley Geer Butler, head cataloger at Trinity University, continued the presentation by describing how Trinity University Library developed a method to store cataloging and processing information in the online series authority record file. When she arrived at Trinity in August 1992, she re-established series authority work which, for a variety of reasons, had been put on hold. At the same time, she decided to integrate the procedure into the NOTIS system, the latter having obvious advantages over the old manual card file as it allows for more efficient searching, multi-user access, and easy editing.

The workflows for standing order check-in and ordering staff were changed to include steps to identify series statements on the items and MARC records, as well as searching for series authority records in NOTIS. If the series title is not found in NOTIS, the book is sent to the Cataloging Department. In the Cataloging Department, series checking was also made part of the copy cataloging routine. If a series decision has not been made, copy catalogers are instructed to go through certain procedural steps, depending on what is found in NOTIS, the old card decision file and OCLC, and to prepare a packet of information, including pertinent printouts and photocopies of title pages. This packet is routed to the head cataloger. The instructions for the copy catalogers also include steps to arrive at a call number, so that the actual book, video, or CD-ROM can move on to the shelf as soon as possible.

The head cataloger at Trinity University reviews the series authority information packets and makes the series treatment decisions. The actual series authority records are either created locally (for those titles that are not represented in the Library of Congress's name authority file) or tapeloaded every month through MARCIVE's authorities service. Rather than having staff interpret MARC tagging, which at times can be a bit tricky, information regarding the treatment of the title at Trinity University is spelled out in the series authority records, using a local note (690 field). Six different series treatment possibilities were determined:

1. Cat/Class Mono: Monographs in these series are to be cataloged and classified as monographs. The materials are routed to monographs cataloging.
2. Cat Serial: Books in these series are to be cataloged as a serial (they are not analyzed). The materials are routed to serials cataloging.
3. Cat Mono/Class Series: Monographs in these series will get monographic cataloging, but all will be classified together. The materials are routed to monographs cataloging.
4. Government Document: Occasionally, government documents are received through acquisitions. All government documents are routed to the Government Documents librarian.
5. Cat Mono/Class Series If Distinctive Title; Cat Serial If No Distinctive Title: Any book in these series that has a distinctive title will get analyzed and those that do not will not go through copy cataloging. All volumes are classified together.
6. Monographic Set: Any new volumes are added to the monographic set bibliographic record in NOTIS and no records for the individual volumes are downloaded.

In addition to indicating the category of each title, the local note is used to include routing and processing instructions, as well as special tagging and cataloging information for the copy catalogers. Numerous examples were given to illustrate this practice at Trinity University. For example, when MARC tagging for a series is a bit unusual, a reference to an example bibliographic record in NOTIS is provided. When a series-like statement is to be given as a quoted note, rather than being traced as a series title, this is also made clear in the 690 field. Some series authority records at Trinity University have 690 notes explaining unusual publication patterns that might create confusion among staff, such as title changes, similar titles, subseries, changes in publisher, and numbering that is dropped or added. Changes in local treatment are indicated (because of certain circumstances, treatment of a series can change over time). At times, special cross references are added to the series authority record to aid in searching. For series that have to classified together (catmono/class series), the 050 field includes the call number that is to be used, and specific instructions on how to construct this call number at Trinity University. The series authority records that are created for government documents contain nothing more than processing instructions, making sure that these items get routed to the documents librarian.

Complicated cases, such as series that begin as consecutive volumes with a single serial title but later appear with distinctive titles (treatment possibility no. 5), are explained in detail. Series authority records for monographic sets are especially important because title pages often make it easy to miss the relationship with a monographic set. Bibliographers and ordering staff are instructed to search for every title that is present on the item and through this, locate the authority record that shows them to treat the individual volume as part of its set.

Another miscellaneous use of the series authority record at Trinity University is to add information about standing orders, which prevents duplicate ordering. At the present, staff are also contemplating using series authority records to record retention decisions. Finally, whenever confusion is noted among staff on a particular title, regardless of whether the title is a bona-fide monographic series or not, a series authority record is created with notes that help alleviate the problem.

Throughout the workshop, the presenters compared series work with cattle ranching: series are unruly, you have to rope, throw and brand 'em by adding series authority records that contain cataloging and processing instructions. If the cowboys and cowgirls in the cataloging department do their work well and pay attention to series authority work, they can "keep them doggies rollin'." The result is a fairly orderly and controlled herd that neatly follows the prescribed trail.

It was obvious from audience comments that this presentation provided ideas for workshop participants to improve series control at their respective institutions. The workshop provided an interesting demonstration of how series authority records can be improved, and used to facilitate efficient and cost-effective processing and cataloging of titles in series.

To Be Continued? Or, The Birth of a Series

Rita VanAssche Bueter
Vivian Buell

Workshop Leaders

Steve Oberg

Recorder

SUMMARY. The processes and perceptions that determine the development of a monographic series are discussed. The logic behind publishers' marketing strategies frequently seems at odds with the expressed needs and concerns of the library community. Through interviews with a cross-section of publishers (trade, scholarly, university, association/society), information was gathered that furthers the understanding of the goals, strategies, and problems involved with the publication of monographic series.

How do series come into being? What factors does a publisher consider when creating a new series? How do librarians manage acquisition of series? Answers to these and other questions are discussed in this workshop in the context of feedback from two surveys, one for publishers and another for librarians, conducted by the workshop presenters over a three month period.

Steve Oberg is Serials Cataloger at the University of Chicago, Chicago, IL.

[Haworth co-indexing entry note]: "To Be Continued? Or, the Birth of a Series." Oberg, Steve. Co-published simultaneously in *The Serials Librarian* (The Haworth Press, Inc.) Vol. 25, No. 3/4, 1995, pp. 283-287; and: *A Kaleidoscope of Choices: Reshaping Roles and Opportunities for Serialists* (ed: Beth Holley and Mary Ann Sheble) The Haworth Press, Inc., 1995, pp. 283-287. Multiple copies of this article/chapter may be purchased from The Haworth Document Delivery Center [1-800-3-HAWORTH; 9:00 a.m. - 5:00 p.m. (EST)].

Rita VanAssche Bueter, manager, Collection Development and Standing Order Services, Blackwell North America, and Vivian Buell, formerly manager, Approval Programs, Ballen Booksellers, addressed an audience which included several vendor representatives. Buell began with a brief overview of issues to be addressed in the workshop along with an explanation of the survey method used by the presenters. She explained that the workshop theme grew out of discussions at the end of their presentation on standing orders at last year's NASIG conference. Several librarians at that meeting expressed frustration with the way series are published and desired more information as to factors involved in publishing series. While conducting a survey of publishers to gather this information, the scope of the inquiry was widened to collect information on how librarians, as major players in the market for series, handled their acquisition. This was done at the urging of publishers who were eager to know more about libraries' management of series. The survey format was not designed to be a statistically significant research project; rather, it was chosen as a good framework upon which the discussion could be based. Results of the publisher survey included responses from twenty-two publishers, which included eight science, technology, and medicine (STM) publishers, seven trade firms, four societies, and three university presses. The survey of librarians was posted to NASIG-L and generated twenty-seven responses. Copies of this survey were handed out to the audience, and participants were encouraged to fill them out by the end of the presentation so that this information could be forwarded to publishers.

Buell then gave a brief overview of the publisher questionnaire and the rationale behind the questions included in it. The questionnaire has four main sections: I. The Librarian as Customer; II. The Origins of a Series; III. Control/Internal Communications; and IV. Bibliographics. The questions are Yes/No or multiple choice or a combination thereof; many include space for short essay answers as well. One sample question is: "How is a monographic series initiated within your organization? If this varies, can you rank the choices given, ranging from 1 as most likely to 4 as least likely?" Choices given for answering the question include In-House Editors, Outside Editors/Authors, Sales/Marketing, and Other (please specify). Section I was intended to reveal how tuned in the publisher is to the library market, while answers to questions in Section II indicate who is actually involved in decisions regarding series in a publishing firm and at what level. The third section deals with flow of internal information within the publishing firm, and the last section attempts to determine who makes the decisions which affect library record keeping, e.g., why titles are changed.

Rita Bueter followed with an in-depth discussion of responses to the first two parts of the publisher survey. Answers given by publishers provide several insights into the world of publishing and the role series play in that world. Publishers indicated, for example, that although libraries are important customers for series, they are only one segment of the publishing market. There is often an inherent conflict between publishers' desire to maximize sales of series and librarians' desire to control them. For instance, the question of numbering is a touchy one for publishers, since some believe that the presence of series numbering on a monograph discourages sales to individuals while it encourages sales to libraries. For those firms who seek the broadest possible market for a book, inclusion of series numbering may be an unattractive option. Numbering presents other problems for publishers, such as when production is interrupted for some reason, resulting in a volume or volumes issued out of sequence. New series are generally created when a critical mass of information builds up in a particular subject field, or when there is a perceived need for more monographs in a certain area. The idea for publishing a new series starts with an editor. Input from sales and marketing is also crucial at this point, and their role in the process is growing in importance. Bueter also noted that launching a series involves a large number of staff within the organization, from the editor on up to the head of the firm. Sales/marketing, finance, and production staff are also involved in the editorial board. The editorial board process may have to be repeated for each book published in the series. What future do publishers see for series? Interestingly, half of those surveyed believe there will be fewer series published in the future, while the other half believe the opposite will occur. One publisher firmly believes that series will become more common due to increased subject specialization. A majority of STM publishers are looking for more favorable publishing formats due to the relatively slow publication process for monographs in series, among other reasons. On the other hand, responses from society and university press publishers showed that they consider series a growth area.

Responses to the last two sections of the survey were then analyzed. This part included sections on control/internal communication and bibliographics. It is standard for editors to be the most knowledgeable about a series within a particular publishing firm. The survey brought to light potential weaknesses in the security of information about series located in publisher databases. Buell and Bueter found that for some firms, anyone with planning input can access and change this information. An obvious concern, therefore, is that accuracy and completeness of series information may be compromised. Furthermore, questions from outside a firm regarding series often cannot be answered by a single, well defined contact person. Buell closed this part of the presentation with some reasons given by publishers for creating title changes, as well as why some series are labeled "inactive" instead of "dead," even though nothing has been published in the series for years. Decisions about title changes are made by the editorial board and are often tempered by sales/marketing staff. One reason given for a title change is that a publisher may acquire a series from another publisher and the original title of the series is too descriptive of the old publisher. Reasons for labeling a series "inactive" range from relatively simple ones, for example indecision on the part of the publisher, to more complex issues. A good example of the latter is when a publisher is constrained by certain legal and contractual obligations. A contract for a series may be signed "in perpetuity." If the publisher cannot find a market for a scholar's works and yet cannot legally cease publication due to this type of contract, the publisher may simply reject every manuscript submitted for publication in the series.

In summarizing the results of the publisher survey, Buell wondered out loud whether we are back where we started. Lines of communication (within publishing firms and between librarians and publishers) still look haphazard; publishers do not seem to be ready to give up this publishing format; and many of the decisions regarding series which make no sense to librarians seem more understandable when seen from the publishers' viewpoint. Decisions made by publishers regarding series will always primarily be based on how many books they can sell. Improving control of series, while important and worthwhile, remains a secondary consideration.

For the last section of the presentation, Bueter focused on feedback from the librarian survey. The survey consists of eleven questions for gathering information on whether series are still being purchased by libraries, how libraries budget for and make decisions about series, and what suggestions librarians may want to communicate to publishers. Most libraries are acquiring the same amount of series this year as last year. A majority of the respondents favored receiving information about series either direct from the publisher or through accessing on-line vendor databases. The monographs budget or a separate series budget were the two most common funding sources in libraries. Bueter also read some of the suggestions from librarians to improve publishing of series, for example: be consistent with titles and numbering–do NOT change titles; do not issue a monograph as part of more than one series; abandon unnumbered series; and get ISSNs for all series and display them prominently on each piece.

Several members of the audience provided thoughtful comments on the presentation, or asked questions for further discussion. One publisher representative stated his belief that publishers need to move beyond the idea of libraries as just another customer. Instead, they should seek to develop partner relationships with libraries, out of which much needed standards would be more likely to develop. The need for further dialogue between librarians and publishers was affirmed by participants. Examples of useful information gathered from interaction between publishers and librarians at conferences such as this one were also given. Suggestions for improving or clarifying questions in the librarian survey were made. A librarian wanted to know how publishers substantiate the belief that unnumbered series sell better than numbered series. Is this a facile assumption? Series remain a crucial, yet complex and often frustrating link in the relationship between those who seek to control and provide access to them–libraries–and those who create and market them–publishers. Comments and questions from those who attended the workshop provide further evidence of interest in working to improve the future for series. Communication, the central theme of this presentation, is a crucial step toward that goal.

Integrating Documents Processing into Traditional Technical Services

Susan Davis
Deanna Iltis
Workshop Presenters

Judy Chandler Irvin
Recorder

SUMMARY. The experiences of two libraries incorporating federal documents processing into the traditional technical services workflow are examined. Oregon State Library automated its documents processing in a PC environment, while the State University of New York at Buffalo processes documents using the NOTIS integrated library system. Reorganization, staffing, and workflow changes, including labeling, shelflisting, check-in, and bibliographic control procedures are discussed.

This workshop dealt with the transfer of government documents processing from a separate documents division to regular technical services departments. The presenters came from two very different types of libraries. Susan Davis is head of Periodicals, University at Buffalo (UB). Deanna Iltis is a cataloger and active leader in the automation of government documents at the Oregon State Library (OSL).

Judy Chandler Irvin is Head of Serials, Prescott Memorial Library, Louisiana Tech University, Ruston, LA.

[Haworth co-indexing entry note]: "Integrating Documents Processing into Traditional Technical Services." Irvin, Judy Chandler. Co-published simultaneously in *The Serials Librarian* (The Haworth Press, Inc.) Vol. 25, No. 3/4, 1995, pp. 289-294; and: *A Kaleidoscope of Choices: Reshaping Roles and Opportunities for Serialists* (ed: Beth Holley and Mary Ann Sheble) The Haworth Press, Inc., 1995, pp. 289-294. Multiple copies of this article/chapter may be purchased from The Haworth Document Delivery Center [1-800-3-HAWORTH; 9:00 a.m. - 5:00 p.m. (EST)].

© 1995 by The Haworth Press, Inc. All rights reserved.

Davis began her talk with a short description of her library and work situation. The University at Buffalo is the largest university in the New York state system with an enrollment of 26,000 students and a library collection of over two million volumes. The library has a central technical services department which handles acquisitions, cataloging, and central processing for material received by the general libraries. It has been a selective government depository since 1963 and selects at the rate of 87% of available items.

Prior to integration into technical services, all processing and access functions for government documents were under the umbrella of public services. Processing was a completely manual operation with access to records available only to staff and students in the government documents area. None of the materials were recorded in the union catalog and access was mainly through the *Monthly Catalog.* The majority of documents were housed separately and catalogued using the SuDoc classification system. With the anticipation of an online catalogue in the late 1980s, plans were formulated to incorporate government document records into the automated system.

During this time, a major reorganization took place in the library and several of the changes directly affected documents. The Serials Department was disbanded and its staff was dispersed throughout technical services. A documents processing department was established with the former Serials Department Head as its leader. This new team began work to convert current and retrospective holdings, and conduct an inventory for document serial holdings.

In July 1990, the NOTIS OPAC, called BISON, was ready for use. At that time, few records for government documents were in the system. This created a problem because the reference staff was advertising, "If it's not in BISON we don't have it–it doesn't exist!" UB had several options: (1) buy the cataloging tapes from the GPO and load them into the OPAC; or (2) devote more documents processing time to retrospective conversion activities. The last option was preferred, because of concern about the quality of GPO cataloging records. As a result, documents processing was given a high priority within the library and more energy and staff were devoted to this activity.

With a second reorganization, the documents processing unit was transferred to the acquisitions department. New staff members were assigned to work with document materials to prepare them for the OPAC. Simultaneously, a large retrospective conversion project began in the cataloging department. This was done with the assistance of public services staff, who prioritized a list of government agencies for conversion. Using this list, catalogers pulled items from the collection for each agency. Each title was searched on OCLC. When a title was determined to be a serial, it was sent to serials catalogers for processing.

One person was assigned to work with documents to sort and send materials into the proper workflow. Material was checked against the shipping list and marked to be routed to one of two locations: the Lockwood library or the Science and Engineering library. Materials were stamped and a computer generated label was placed on each document. Materials were then routed into the appropriate workflow area: periodicals, serials, or monographs. Document periodicals were treated very much like other periodicals in the library except they were not checked-in on the OPR record in NOTIS, but were recorded directly onto the holdings record. Completed materials were routed to the stacks. Serial materials were checked-in on the holdings screen, and item records and barcode labels were established to allow the materials to circulate. The library occasionally received items that were classed "exceptions" (e.g., decals) and a decision was made against providing full cataloging for these materials. For these items, SuDoc numbers were assigned, and materials were sent to public service areas for review and evaluation. Monograph government document materials were processed by the bibliographic control unit. Materials were held two weeks after receipt before searching OCLC for copy. If a title was found on OCLC, the record was downloaded. The item was processed, and released into the collection. If the title was not found in OCLC, a brief record was produced for NOTIS. The material was processed, and forwarded into the collection. The brief record was later rechecked for a record on OCLC and updated when a match was located.

UB purchased the Marcive tapes to help facilitate the retrospective conversion process. The material was loaded into the system so that staff could access the database for appropriate records and use it as a base for cataloging, but the public did not have access to the file. This allowed simple use with minimal additional OCLC costs.

Another project was a holdings inventory for documents. In order for records to be accurate, the staff would spend time in the stacks recording holdings. Codes were established to allow staff to know what was being done and ward off duplication of work. A large backlog of microfiche also needed attention. Some large monographic series on microfiche were identified for collection level record treatment. A record for each series and base SuDoc number was established. Complete cataloging would be done later during the conversion process. This allowed these materials to be available to the patron with the expectation of providing full cataloging for each title in the series at a later date.

In late 1993, another reorganization took place with the addition of a new position, Documents Coordinator. This new employee had experience and interest in working with government documents. The acquisitions department used library school students as a resource for government documents work. Students who expressed an interest in documents work were given a practicum through the library school or hired as regular student assistants.

Special problems encountered by the changes taking place at UB centered around the unique character of government documents, and the publishing patterns of the GPO. The mind-set of serials staff, that complete runs and sets of materials are required, had to be modified to deal with government documents. Applying American National Standards Institute (ANSI) level 4 for holdings statements for microfiche is difficult, and extra time and care are required for processing these materials.

The second presenter, Deanna Iltis, spoke to the group about documents integration and automation at the Oregon State Library. The most important force leading to change in documents processing at OSL has been the development of the local on-line catalog. OSL's OPAC was developed in the mid-1980s, and by 1988 the Documents Section had made major changes in order to participate. Documents staff began to create brief MARC records in the system for all serials, most monographs received in paper, and selective microfiche. Oregon-related publications received full OCLC cataloging.

By the early 1990s, several other factors caused radical changes in both the Documents Section and the library as a whole. These factors included a change in the mission and goals of the library, and a property tax limitation measure which resulted in significant cuts in budget and staffing. Knowing well over a year in advance that there would be a major personnel reduction, technical services staff planned to restructure along purely functional lines. All technical services tasks, including those relating to documents, were divided into acquisitions functions (acquiring, claiming, and check-in) and cataloging (bibliographic access and authority control). When the documents staff decreased in July 1993 from 3.5 employees to 1 full time employee, documents functions were integrated into the acquisitions and cataloging units. For example, the Acquisitions Coordinator is now responsible for federal depository item selection/de-selection decisions, while the Cataloging Unit has overall responsibility for depository document processing and bibliographic access.

Successful integration of documents functions in a time of staff reduction would not have been possible without the simultaneous automation of functions. The Oregon State Library was the first user of the University of California at Riverside's (UCR) USDOCS automated depository documents system, created by Margaret Mooney, head of the UCR's Government Publications Department. This system automates processing functions, while providing electronic shelflisting for depository documents. A special adaptation by the library provides computer-generated brief MARC records in the OPAC (for all monographs) at the time of receipt of the documents. A final automation step is nearing completion–the overlay of these brief records with full MARC records.

The foundation of the USDOCS system is the GPITEMS database, which provides for electronic profiling of each SuDocs class. The elements of the profile include: the library's selection status, format of the class, status (active or inactive), classification number, class type (serial or monograph), special processing instructions, agency, title, local OPAC record number for serials, and notes.

The basic component of the USDOCS system is the electronic shelflist service currently provided by two vendors: Marcive and Bernan. Both services provide brief records which correspond exactly to the documents listed on GPO's depository shipping lists. The data are available weekly on diskette, or in the case of Bernan, electronically via Telnet. When the library receives a weekly batch of records, they are loaded into the USDOCS system where they are stored in a holding file until needed.

The actual processing of depository documents begins with the manual procedure of opening cartons, arranging publications in shipping list order, checking them against the GPO shipping list, and date stamping them. Then the USDOCS system takes over. After logging in, the technician is prompted to enter the shipping list number, and the system responds by gathering the appropriate shelflist records from the holdings file. Errors, such as mismatched SuDoc classification and item numbers, are identified by the program and are corrected before check-in begins. Next, labels are printed, material is checked-in using a single keystroke, special processing instructions are completed, and the records are added to various electronic shelflists.

The family of electronic shelflists at OSL includes a file for issue-specific serial records. There is a temporary file for monographs which are batched twice a week, translated by Data Magician software from dBase to MARC format, and added to the OPAC. Claimed/non-claimable records go into the CLAIMS file where some may be processed and removed at a later time if the publication is received. Another shelflist file called LIMBO stores records for errata sheets, update pages, and other odd records which are not suitable for addition to the OPAC. Finally, there is a temporary file for problems, e.g., records for new SuDoc classes which need matching GPITEMS records. Such problems are handled on an individual basis at a later time. The electronic shelflists can be searched by SuDoc classification number, title, and keyword in title.

Approximately a hundred people attended the first session of the workshop, and approximately fifty attended the second session. It was the general consensus of the audience that staff in technical services can learn to adapt to the differences between government documents and regular library material. The result will be better and faster access to documents for the library patron.

Ethics in Action:
The Vendor's Perspective

Mary Devlin

Workshop Leader

Heather Miller

Recorder

SUMMARY. Ethical questions ask: What should be done? What is right behavior? Real (but anonymous) situations which vendors have encountered and which may pose ethical problems are discussed. Through the presentation of a number of case studies, workshop participants explored a variety of issues relating to vendor-librarian encounters and attempted to understand more about ethical boundaries in these situations.

Using the Association for Library Collections and Technical Services (ALCTS) *Statement on Principles and Standards of Acquisitions Practice* [Draft, 2/5/94] as a framework, Mary Devlin provoked discussion by describing actual, but anonymous, situations experienced by a number of vendors in which they perceived the behavior of librarians to be possibly unethical. Devlin announced at the outset that this was to be a "participatory" workshop and the people in attendance were both thoughtful and articulate in discussing their views of the situations described.

Heather Miller is Head, Acquisitions Department, State University of New York Albany, Albany, NY.

[Haworth co-indexing entry note]: "Ethics in Action: The Vendor's Perspective." Miller, Heather. Co-published simultaneously in *The Serials Librarian* (The Haworth Press, Inc.) Vol. 25, No. 3/4, 1995, pp. 295-300; and: *A Kaleidoscope of Choices: Reshaping Roles and Opportunities for Serialists* (ed: Beth Holley and Mary Ann Sheble) The Haworth Press, Inc., 1995, pp. 295-300. Multiple copies of this article/chapter may be purchased from The Haworth Document Delivery Center [1-800-3-HAWORTH; 9:00 a.m. - 5:00 p.m. (EST)].

Case #1: A librarian seeking bids from library materials vendors received a bid that was later shared with a second vendor. The second vendor submitted a lower bid and received the contract. The librarian justified this by stating "anything for a lower price."

Discussion: Although some members of the audience felt that this was completely unethical and no one condoned such behavior, there was some discussion about the librarian's motivation (was the librarian trying to "punish" the first vendor?) and whether the quality of service had been considered. There was also discussion of formal bids versus informal requests for proposals (RFPs) and an acknowledgement of the differences between the two processes.

It was noted that *American Libraries* had published an article on how to handle RFPs. It was also stated that clarity on both sides is essential. The vendor must clearly understand the ground rules at the outset and the library must not change the rules. Librarians should state exactly what services they need and should not include services they do not intend to use, because a specific price will be attached to each service. If it is critical for a library to receive a certain service charge, that should be stated. One participant noted, "It is not honest to put in things you do not intend to use." The library must also be clear as to whether this is a formal bid or an informal process.

Bidding is very time-consuming and expensive for vendors. Libraries should think carefully about whom they invite to respond. Some libraries include lists of specific series titles, requiring the vendor to check each title. This is an extremely time-consuming and costly exercise for vendors.

In an informal process, it is acceptable to go back to a vendor and say that a better response is required. For example, a library might state that there are concerns about the vendor's electronic data interchange (EDI) capabilities and ask them to address the issue.

Two of the ALCTS guidelines address this situation: number three (grants all competing vendors equal consideration insofar as the established policies of his or her library permit, and regards each transaction on its own merits); and number six (uses only by consent original ideas and designs devised by one vendor for competitive purchasing purposes). Adherence to these mandates would have prevented the incident.

Case #2: A book vendor was asked to visit a library and to leave book covers and a catalog. The library used these items to select materials, but placed the orders with another vendor.

Discussion: There was a mixed decision on this case. It is common for order slips to be provided by a vendor. Because order slips are usually customized for specific libraries, vendors may expect to receive resulting orders. One member of the audience described efforts to make sure that orders go to the vendor who originated the source of information, but noted that it can be difficult to ensure that this information remains with an order, especially in large libraries with complex ordering processes. Another participant described her inability to stop slips, even when she told vendors that orders might go to other vendors.

Case #3: A selector became head of a library's acquisitions department. At a conference, she stated that vendor X is the best, but, in fact, she had no experience with any other vendor.

Discussion: This behavior was deemed "foolish, but not unethical."

Case #4: A librarian negotiated a reduced service charge based on payment within fifteen days. It became apparent that the library could not meet this payment schedule, but the librarian demanded the reduced service charge.

Discussion: Participants wondered whether both the librarian and vendor were naive. One participant said that the vendor should know better and another felt that further clarification was also needed on the payment agreement because libraries themselves rarely make the actual payment. Other participants felt that there were implications for *any* negotiated agreement.

One participant wondered whether vendors pay attention to a library's ability to adhere to its part of an agreement. Several vendor representatives noted that they "put up with a lot because of *hope!*" and that it is the vendor's responsibility to "defend its position." For example, if a periodicals subscription list is trimmed, the vendor must go to the library and explain that the service charge may increase. Another participant noted that a vendor making an offer where it cannot make a profit is making a bad decision.

Case #5: Vendors were asked to contribute to a library's building fund and a vendor perceived it as a threat, i.e., contribute if you want our business.

Discussion: Many questions were generated, including: Is this different from the Development Office seeking partnerships? Why would a vendor decide to contribute? A request like this changes the relationship between vendor and library and was pronounced "suspect" and having a potential "snowball effect." It was noted that most vendors budget some funds for contributions and some have guidelines about what they will support. A vendor representative stated that vendors are becoming "cash cows" for library organizations and some vendors have chosen to support a more general cause, such as scholarship.

Case #6: Vendor selection was done by a library clerk who took the easiest course and always used the same vendor. If this vendor could not supply an item, the clerk told selectors that it was unavailable.

Discussion: Ethics was not perceived to be the problem here, but, rather, ignorance or work flow problems and definitely the lack of supervision.

Case #7: A library planned to consolidate book orders with one vendor. Two vendors bid on the list. Each believed the bid was on the entire list, although the library had split the list between the two vendors.

Discussion: Little discussion was required to determine that this was unethical.

Case #8: A library consortium projected an inflated spending figure and received bids on that amount, but ordered much less.

Discussion: Participants questioned whether the consortium inflated its figure on purpose or circumstances changed, making it unable to order as expected. In either case, the vendor has a right to ask for a change and the consortium is behaving unethically if it insists on the original discount.

Case #9: A library negotiated terms for a combination of firm orders and an approval plan. A new librarian was hired who redirected orders, but demanded that the vendor stick to its original terms.

Discussion: Participants pointed out that such behavior is unethical. The original terms must be adhered to by both parties or renegotiated, although it is possible that the new librarian did not know of the existing agreement.

Case #10: A vendor made an appointment to visit a library. When the representative arrived, he was told that there would be only ten minutes for the meeting.

Discussion: This was deemed unethical "if repeated or deliberate, but once, just rude." Vendors prefer the truth. One vendor representative said, "Be assertive and truthful" so the vendor receives an honest depiction of the situation. Librarians should tell vendors if they do not want to meet or prefer to have informational materials sent. The librarians in the audience noted that it is counterproductive to "hide away" and that useful information can be gleaned from vendor representatives.

The group of approximately thirty people at the second workshop session consisted mainly of librarians. Only about five materials vendor representatives and one systems vendor representative attended this session. Participants were largely in agreement about the behaviors described and were as critical of their unknown colleagues as were the vendors. Discussion did not focus heavily on the ALCTS guidelines, although participants sometimes referred to the guidelines and to their occasional inscrutability and lack of definition. Most of the discussion emerged from the participants' personal experiences and beliefs.

APPENDIX

Statement on Principles and Standards of Acquisitions Practice

[Draft, 2/5/94]

[NOTE: This statement deals with business practices and relationships only. For statements dealing with other issues (such as those relating to unbiased selection of library resources), refer to the ALCTS Guidelines for ALCTS Members to Supplement the American Library Association Code of Ethics.]

An acquisitions librarian:

1. Gives first consideration to the objectives and policies of his or her library.
2. Strives to obtain the maximum ultimate value of each dollar of expenditure.
3. Grants all competing vendors equal consideration insofar as the established policies of his or her library permit, and regards each transaction on its own merits.
4. Subscribes to and works for honesty, truth, and fairness in buying and selling, and denounces all forms and manifestations of bribery.
5. Declines personal gifts and gratuities.
6. Uses only by consent original ideas and designs devised by one vendor for competitive purchasing purposes.
7. Accords a prompt and courteous reception insofar as conditions permit to all who call on legitimate business missions.
8. Fosters and promotes fair, ethical, and legal trade practices.
9. Avoids sharp practice.
10. Strives consistently for knowledge of the publishing and bookselling industry.
11. Strives to establish practical and efficient methods for the conduct of his or her office.
12. Counsels and assists fellow acquisitions librarians in the performance of their duties, whenever occasion permits.

Cost Accounting for the Serials Librarian: Making Financial Decisions in Tight Times

Wil Harri

Workshop Leader

Barbara Shaffer

Recorder

SUMMARY. Key cost accounting concepts are discussed and descriptions of how to use these concepts in serials management decision-making are presented. Because serials are ongoing publications, cost assessment must look at past, present, and future costs to libraries. There are three ways to look at the value of a journal collection: depreciation costs, opportunity costs, and replacement costs.

In the workshop "Cost Accounting for the Serials Librarian," Wil Harri, periodicals librarian, Moorhead State University Library, Minnesota, provided a cost accounting "tool kit" with approximately a dozen applications. Wil's MBA degree and his CPA credentials provided a credible, and creditable, background for this presentation. His aim was to define key accounting concepts and how to use them in the decision-making process. He emphasized that there would be no references to dollars, nor any formulas in this presentation.

Barbara Shaffer is Serials Librarian, University of Toledo, Toledo, OH.

[Haworth co-indexing entry note]: "Cost Accounting for the Serials Librarian: Making Financial Decisions in Tight Times." Shaffer, Barbara. Co-published simultaneously in *The Serials Librarian* (The Haworth Press, Inc.) Vol. 25, No. 3/4, 1995, pp. 301-305; and: *A Kaleidoscope of Choices: Reshaping Roles and Opportunities for Serialists* (ed: Beth Holley and Mary Ann Sheble) The Haworth Press, Inc., 1995, pp. 301-305. Multiple copies of this article/chapter may be purchased from The Haworth Document Delivery Center [1-800-3-HAWORTH; 9:00 a.m. - 5:00 p.m. (EST)].

© 1995 by The Haworth Press, Inc. All rights reserved.

The workshop was presented in four parts and included a short quiz at the end. In the first part, costs were defined. This was followed by an explanation of past, present, and future costs and how they differ. Cost behaviors were included in the third part of the presentation. Cost analysis techniques were dealt with last. At each point, an attempt was made to relate the topic with library considerations and relevancy to librarians. The quiz gave substance to some familiar old proverbs and clichés.

To define cost, Wil turned to the *Oxford English Dictionary* definition: that which must be given or surrendered in order to acquire, produce, accomplish, or maintain something. He pointed out that this varies, somewhat, from the economist's definition of cost: the value of the factors of production used by a firm in producing or distributing goods and services engaged in both activities. The accountant's definition of cost is the simplest: an outlay of cash. The serials librarian must take into consideration, along with these definitions, the "time-is-money" aspect of cost, with one's time counting as a valuable commodity.

The presentation then moved to costs past, present, and future. All past costs are historical in nature and irrelevant in libraries. Historical cost refers to the original price paid for an item, and is relevant to a for-profit business. Another term for historical cost is sunk cost. This phrase emphasizes the finality of money already spent and the irrelevance of such expenditures for future decisions.

Depreciation has a dual meaning. In an accounting sense, it is allocating the cost of an item to several accounting periods as an expense item. Wil contrasted this definition to the popular notion of depreciation as a loss in value or usefulness. These are not relevant to library uses. However, replacement costing is relevant to libraries. Replacement costing is an attempt to price a product or service at a rate or level which will provide funding to replace the equipment when it has worn out, keeping in mind that in these days of computer purchases, some new equipment is cheaper than the original was. Life cycle costing also falls into the category of past costs. This is what an item costs over the life of the item, the entire period the equipment is in use. A classic example of this analysis technique is the buy-versus-lease decisions which require librarians to compare purchase and lease costs, with consideration for the length of time the item will be in use.

Opportunity cost, recognizing that implicit in each decision there is an alternative choice that could have been made, is an example of a present cost. By choosing one course of action, we forego the opportunity to pursue some other course of action. Basically, the decision is whether to purchase something today. Standards that cost accountants apply are essentially mini-budgets for one item being produced. Such standards may be used as benchmarks in evaluating the appropriateness of costs incurred. They also facilitate building an overall budget, which is simply a quantified statement of future plans, reflecting priorities.

Future cost includes budgets. Librarians are seeing these plans of action change after becoming accustomed to a lifestyle of obtaining funding for subscriptions. Some librarians must look to article copy services in place of purchasing serial subscriptions. Cost centers within a budget indicate what costs are accumulated or assigned to a specific department, considering size of the department and totality of costs incurred with an awareness of how the costs are aggregated. Included in such considerations are direct costs, those clearly attributable to a particular product or process; indirect costs, those costs incurred but not easily attributed to a particular product or process; and overhead, those costs incurred which cannot be directly attributed to a particular product, process, or department. Overhead is an incurred cost and is unavoidable over the short run. Transfer pricing is similar to value-added taxes. It deals with the notion of transferring costs with an item when the item moves to some other department. Discretionary costs are those over which one should have control. Sometimes librarians are responsible for discretionary costs, but do not have authority over them.

The third part of the workshop dealt with cost behaviors over time and at differing activity levels. Two types of costs, fixed and variable, were examined. Fixed costs are costs that are being incurred and cannot be avoided in the short run. These are relatively constant in amount and are viable for a certain period of time, therefore more easily controlled. Variable costs change directly in relationship to an activity level or production level. The higher the level of activity, the higher the variable costs.

Five cost analysis techniques of use in the kinds of decisions made by librarians were introduced. The first was the payback period, the length of time before the savings realized by the purchase of a piece of equipment or adoption of a process will equal the original cost of the equipment or process. This should be three years or less.

The second cost analysis technique described was elasticity. Elasticity describes the sensitivity of demand to changes in pricing. An item's price is said to be relatively inelastic if a percentage price increase is not matched by a corresponding percentage decrease in demand. In librarians' terms, if a price of a subscription increases 25% and purchases only decrease 10%, the publisher is ahead. The librarian's alternative is to choose not to purchase the title but to have a cooperative sharing agreement with another institution or to obtain the title through electronic delivery to provide it to the patron.

Marginal, or incremental, analysis emphasizes comparing only those costs which change between alternative proposals. This approach facilitates the evaluative process by excluding from consideration all costs which are constant between alternative proposals. In this analysis, the librarian can evaluate two alternative proposals by scrutinizing differences or changes rather than totality of costs.

Productivity, as an analysis technique, emphasizes the change in the relationship of resources used (input) to the product created (output). Because it is a quantitative technique, qualitative changes cannot easily be incorporated in the analysis. The librarian must temper quantitative factors with qualitative measures.

The final technique introduced was materiality and petty economics. The materiality concept emphasizes focusing one's analysis on only costs that are significant, ignoring minor cost items. In other words, if it costs more to keep track of an item than its purchase price, do not bother to keep track of it. Petty economics recognizes a very human tendency to focus on very small factors or costs, in turn ignoring or subordinating substantive items in analyzing a project or proposal. This should be resisted.

At the conclusion of the presentation, the question was asked, "How do we assess the value of our journal collections?" The discussion that followed indicated that there are three ways to look at the value of a collection: depreciation costs, opportunity costs, and replacement costs. In other words, consider depreciation in that volumes in the most recent three to five years of a journal are most highly used. Consider opportunity costs in that the journals can be used forever, and consider replacement costs if the volumes had to be purchased today. To the question, "Why bind?" came the observation that the bound volume is more cost effective in storage and retrieval convenience than handling loose issues.

Wil then presented a short quiz, asking what cost concepts various clichés illustrated, as follows:

Swallowing camels and choking on gnats.	Petty economics
Don't cry over spilt milk.	Sunk costs
Can't see the forest through the trees.	Incremental analysis
You get what you pay for.	Qualitative analysis
Penny wise, pound foolish.	Materiality
A bird in the hand is worth 2 in the bush.	Opportunity cost
The boss is always right.	Incremental analysis

Participants left this workshop armed with some key accounting concepts for a better understanding of costs, their behaviors, and techniques for cost analyses. This "tool kit" provided by Wil Harri gave librarians in attendance the opportunity to take advantage of the professional accountant's applications for understanding and analysis of costs in libraries.

Serialists on the Front Line: New Opportunities for Serials Professionals in Reference and User Education

Diane Grover
Blaine E. Knupp

Workshop Presenters

Katy Ginanni

Recorder

SUMMARY. Serials and technical services librarians are in a unique position to share valuable expertise in public service and bibliographic instruction settings. Skills learned in the organization of information and experiences with electronic resources such as e-journals, databases, and the Internet, translate well into the user services arena. Several serials librarians, who have worked in both technical and public service positions, discuss the professional and personal rewards of public services.

Diane Grover, University of Washington, and Blaine Knupp, Indiana University of Pennsylvania, provided a background about

---

Katy Ginanni is Account Services Manager, EBSCO Subscription Services, Birmingham, AL.

[Haworth co-indexing entry note]: "Serialists on the Front Line: New Opportunities for Serials Professionals in Reference and User Education." Ginanni, Katy. Co-published simultaneously in *The Serials Librarian* (The Haworth Press, Inc.) Vol. 25, No. 3/4, 1995, pp. 307-310; and: *A Kaleidoscope of Choices: Reshaping Roles and Opportunities for Serialists* (ed: Beth Holley and Mary Ann Sheble) The Haworth Press, Inc., 1995, pp. 307-310. Multiple copies of this article/chapter may be purchased from The Haworth Document Delivery Center [1-800-3-HAWORTH; 9:00 a.m. - 5:00 p.m. (EST)].

© 1995 by The Haworth Press, Inc. All rights reserved.

their serials responsibilities and motives for pursuing reference service. Both librarians spent time "in the trenches" providing reference and user education services at their libraries. Grover began her presentation by saying that as she and Knupp prepared for the workshop, they found that they drew similar conclusions from their reference experiences, although their approaches to reference services differed.

After describing her primary responsibilities as a serials librarian, Grover explained some of her motives for choosing to work five hours a week in reference at the engineering library at the University of Washington. Most of her reasons were personal. For example, she felt she had reached a plateau in her career and was looking for challenge and growth. She also believes that many of the changes occurring in the library are taking place in the public service areas (e.g., CD-ROM technology, document delivery, etc.), and she believes she was "falling behind" in learning about these new technologies. Grover also discussed some of the specifics of her training and some of the insights she gained during her tenure in the engineering library.

She then outlined some of the benefits of her reference experience. One benefit to the engineering reference unit and to the library system at large is enhanced relations between public service personnel and the serials unit. Other benefits to the engineering library are an increased flexibility in staffing the reference desk, and having a serials expert available to provide reference service. Increased credibility was a bonus for the serials unit. Grover also believes that she brought back a greater understanding of public service issues to her home unit. For the library system, she thinks that cross training creates a stronger, more cohesive staff, and helps develop better relationships between public and technical services staff. On a personal level, Grover enjoyed the "instant gratification factor" ("People say thank you!"), the change of pace, and a broader and deeper knowledge of the library system and changes occurring within it. While some of these benefits are somewhat intangible, both Grover and Knupp believe they are undeniable and desirable.

After taking a number of questions from the audience, Grover turned the floor over to Knupp, who also gave some background about his serials position and library. Unlike Grover, Knupp's approach to reference service came from professional necessity rather than personal aspiration. At Indiana University of Pennsylvania, the professional librarians must "wear several different hats." In addition to his primary responsibilities as a serials librarian, Knupp has duties which include automation, reference service, and bibliographic instruction. He does not view this as a handicap, but sees it as an opportunity for growth. He believes that many technical services librarians have valuable expertise that all too often is wasted in a back room in the library, rather than being shared with the primary constituency of the library. Knupp discussed some of the new technologies that are available (e.g., CD-ROMs, electronic journals, the Internet). Frequently, technical services librarians have expertise with these new resources, yet research and his own experience indicate that there is a "pressing need" for user education for these resources. The new technologies are available, user expectations and demand are increasing, but there is a lack of education from other sources.

There are a number of opportunities for serialists to participate in user education. Some of the options Knupp examined are one-on-one instruction, small group sessions, workshops and seminars, and even courses for credit. One especially effective method for educating patrons used by Knupp is collaborating with library colleagues and teaching faculty. He described several workshops and courses developed in the library to promote information literacy and electronic skills among students, faculty, and staff across the university.

Tying in with admonitions from several of the plenary speakers who advised the NASIG attendees to go out and teach library users, Knupp gave the workshop audience ideas on ways to get involved. He suggested that we make contacts across our communities, and establish partnerships with people who have similar interests and goals. Perhaps of more importance is seeking administrative support in the way of release time and grants.

When speaking of the benefits of being directly involved in user education, Knupp reiterated some ideas raised by Grover. Both received personal satisfaction from their experiences in public services. Both feel they experienced personal and professional growth. Again, an intangible yet definite benefit was the increased cooperation and understanding between technical and public service librarians, and between librarians and teaching faculty.

Many of the questions from the audience dealt with the logistics of spending time in another department or unit. For instance, people asked Grover, "How far did you have to walk to the engineering library?" "Were you allowed to choose your own hours at the reference desk?" "Could you swap your hours with other reference staff if you needed to?"

While both speakers acknowledged that there were frustrations involved in the reference and user education experiences, both agreed that their experiences were worthwhile. Questions and comments from the audience indicated that many people think participation in user education is a good idea. Not surprisingly, staff cutbacks have created the impetus for some members of the audience to accept responsibility for user education or reference service. While discontent was expressed about this state of affairs, most of the audience members seemed to view it as a positive experience. Other comments revealed that most audience members have yet to try reference duty, but are seriously contemplating the idea and appreciated hearing about some firsthand experiences. Knupp provided a course syllabus, a brief grant proposal, and copies of an article he co-authored with a teaching colleague. Both speakers supplied outlines of their talks.

Who Needs to Know What? Essential Communication for Automation Implementation and Effective Reorganization

Cynthia Coulter
Lola Halpin

Workshop Leaders

Rita Broadway

Recorder

SUMMARY. Effective channels of communication must be established and maintained during the process of reorganizing in technical services. Several librarians describe the impetus for reorganization in their libraries, and how the decisions for change were made and implemented. The importance of maintaining different levels of communication, and involving a wide spectrum of individuals from inside and outside technical services are discussed.

This workshop described the impetus for reorganizing technical services, focusing on decision-making, communication, and the

---

Rita Broadway is Head of the Periodicals Department, Memphis State University, Memphis, TN.

[Haworth co-indexing entry note]: "Who Needs to Know What? Essential Communication for Automation Implementation and Effective Reorganization." Broadway, Rita. Co-published simultaneously in *The Serials Librarian* (The Haworth Press, Inc.) Vol. 25, No. 3/4, 1995, pp. 311-318; and: *A Kaleidoscope of Choices: Reshaping Roles and Opportunities for Serialists* (ed: Beth Holley and Mary Ann Sheble) The Haworth Press, Inc., 1995, pp. 311-318. Multiple copies of this article/chapter may be purchased from The Haworth Document Delivery Center [1-800-3-HAWORTH; 9:00 a.m. - 5:00 p.m. (EST)].

involvement of staff in the reorganization. Lola Halpin, Serials Unit supervisor, Emory University, Woodruff General Libraries, began the workshop by discussing general principles of reorganization. Generally, there are four stages:

1. Determining the need for change
2. Determining what to change
3. Determining methods of change
4. Determining strategies for change

DETERMINING THE NEED FOR CHANGE

When destabilizing factors exist within the organization, then change becomes necessary. Destabilization factors can occur in several areas of the organization either simultaneously or separately.

1. *Procedural Changes:* Individual tasks can become vastly different. For example, converting from a manual to an online cataloging system requires different procedures, knowledge, and skills for the employee, often creating an impetus for change.
2. *Organizational Processes:* These destabilizing factors are similar to individual tasks but are broader in scope, influencing the organization or department as a whole. With change occurring on the organizational level, the answers to several questions are useful. What will be the methods of control? Who will measure quantity and quality of work? How will these measurements occur? How will information be transmitted? How will decisions be made? Will information be provided by memos, in group meetings, or face to face? Will decisions be edicts from top administrators or will groups participate in decision making?
3. *Strategic Direction:* For example, a major shift in strategic direction that indicates a need for change often occurs in public service areas. Since patrons can now access library databases remotely, there is a need for new services and structures. Reference services may need restructuring to meet these different patron demands.

4. *Organizational Culture:* Customs, ideals, rituals, and myths are part of the culture of an organization. A mutual culture creates an understanding of organizational expectations, direction, and values. Thus, a strong company is created when structured around shared stories, rites, language, and symbols.

DETERMINING WHAT TO CHANGE

What to change is closely associated with the destabilizing factors that indicate a need for change. This close association means that individual tasks, organizational processes, strategic direction, and culture may all be changed when the organization is restructured.

DETERMINING METHODS OF CHANGE

Often, methods of change include technological methods that enhance or alter materials, resources, or time. Examples include implementing or upgrading an online system or establishing employee flex time. Methods of change can also be structural, involving the modification, division, or coordination of the organization's employees. Examples include creating new jobs or establishing work teams. Another method of change is managerial. Examples include bonuses, rewards, and recognition for employees. Methods of change also include human resources. Examples include layoffs, downsizing, and retraining transfers. Any or all of these alterations can be the impetus for reorganization.

DETERMINING STRATEGIES FOR CHANGE

There are four strategies for change:

1. *Facilitative*–This strategy includes providing the means, resources, and time to accomplish change.
2. *Attitudinal*–This strategy uses communication with employees to modify attitudes causing them to "buy into" the restructuring of the organization, and to support and implement changes.
3. *Political*–This strategy involves competing for scarce or finite resources, whether it be printers for computers, personnel, or space.

4. *Informational*–This strategy communicates to staff facts about the reorganization necessary for rational decisions and actions.

The decision to reorganize technical services at Emory University was initiated for several reasons. New policies and procedures were necessary due to the implementation of an automated acquisitions system. There were several changes in top and middle management, including a new director of the general libraries, a new head of Acquisitions, and a new head of Monographic Cataloging. As a result of these changes, Collection Management, Monographs Cataloging, and Serials Cataloging became a single unit called Collections and Technical Services (CATS). Further change resulted when Monographs and Serials Receiving became one unit within the Acquisitions Department.

This restructuring proved beneficial to the library. Communication improved because all catalogers were in one department, using consistent procedures, sharing tools, and attending the same departmental meetings.

E-mail and voice mail became new channels for communication and were used to disseminate general information and to arrange meetings. Staff members in departments outside Cataloging were included in meetings and decisions that would impact them.

Individual employees were involved in the restructuring process from the beginning, participating in planning, decision making, and implementation. All employees were encouraged to make suggestions and ask questions. Efforts were made to actively involve them in the restructuring effort. Timely, accurate information was provided. Channels of communication, including face to face meetings, memos, group meetings, and e-mail were successfully used to create support for the reorganization. The reorganization improved work flow and access to the collections. Good communication created staff support for the changes that are gradually becoming a permanent part of the organization.

Cynthia M. Coulter, head, Acquisitions Department, Donald O. Rod Library, University of Northern Iowa, focused on human and organizational barriers to communication. Human barriers, as developed by Conroy include:[1]

1. *Perception.* Each person brings a different background and experience to the communication process, creating obstacles to understanding each other.
2. *Low self-esteem.* Individuals often block effective communication by not stating opinions or not asking questions because of a lack of self confidence.
3. *Attitudes about communication.* Nonproductive attitudes include hoarding information, using information as a weapon, or using it to impress others rather than to share ideas.
4. *Information overload.* Rapid change can produce more information than a person can process.
5. *Isolation.* Individuals can be physically distanced from others, cutting them off from communication. Or, they can intentionally avoid communicating by choosing not to participate in the exchange of information.
6. *Lack of communication skills.* Listening, speaking, reading, and writing are ways to communicate.

Different levels of expertise in these four areas affect the ability to communicate. Norman D. Stevens believes that these skills are learned in a particular order, with listening learned first, then speaking, then reading, followed by writing. People use listening most often, followed by speaking, reading, and writing. This hierarchy reverses when it comes to teaching. Schools teach writing most often followed by reading, speaking, and listening.[2] Managers can help improve the communication skills of their employees through workshops and other means.

Organizational barriers to communication include the assumption that respective departments within a library automatically know each other's functions and procedures without direct communication. This departmental structure can create a "we" versus "they" atmosphere and territorial attitudes can develop between departments. These attitudes are detrimental to the flow of information between departments. Effective communication depends heavily on the attitude of top administrators, who must create open channels of communication and must believe that the staff has the right to accurate and timely information. To be effective communicators, managers must want to communicate and must attempt to improve communication by using all available channels. For managers, the first choice of communication is the memo, which is often the least effective way to send information. Other channels available for use include staff newsletters, departmental meetings, workshops, brainstorming sessions, and grapevines. Library managers must learn to receive as well as send information. Library managers can evaluate the effectiveness of their communication channels by asking the person at the end of the communication chain if the message was received and understood.

According to Coulter, reasons for reorganization include: the need for improvements in efficiency of operations; reductions or changes in staff; the need for different employee skills; moving, adding, or modifying job tasks; rearranging the physical environment; changing organizational philosophy; and whimsy on the part of administrators.

There are three stages of reorganization: (1) planning, (2) implementation, and (3) analysis and revision. During all stages, communication with staff becomes important if the organizational changes are to be accepted. Ineffective communication can create low morale among staff and a lack of support for change. All staff should be involved in the three stages, although to differing degrees. For example, information about organizational restructuring for staff whose jobs are not changing can come from group meetings. But, if an employee will have a different job or a different supervisor, the information should be exchanged in a face-to-face meeting. Coulter believes that, whenever possible, the employee should have a part in decision making. During reorganization, managers should plan to be visible and should realize that repeating the same information again and again in as many ways as possible is necessary for understanding and acceptance of change.

Managers who want to promote the acceptance of change must avoid Head and Hickels myths of reorganization:[3]

1. What our employees do not know will not hurt them.
2. Before you communicate with your employees, you need to have all the answers.
3. Employees would rather not hear about reorganization until it is about to be implemented.
4. We do not need to involve our employees in the reorganization effort.

5. We do not need to tell anyone outside our area about our reorganization.
6. Let our employees think that outside forces are the primary force behind reorganization.

Coulter used some of the principles of good communication to help reorganize serials workflow at the University of Northern Iowa. The goals of this restructuring were to improve workflow and to process serials more rapidly for patron use. The departments most affected were Acquisitions and Cataloging. Problems with serials workflow were identified at meetings and brainstorming sessions among staff from the two departments. After problems were discussed, managers of the departments appointed a task force, composed of experienced staff from each department. Operating with a specific charge and clearly defined guidelines, this task force worked autonomously–setting an agenda, rotating the chair rather than appointing a permanent chair, and using minutes of the meetings to write work procedures reflecting workflow changes. The final report was presented to administrators, who made suggestions and revisions. The revised document was returned for discussion and approval.

During the restructuring, guidelines were written for improving the serials workflow between Acquisitions and Cataloging. These guidelines were:

1. *Forward always forward:* Processing of material should proceed linearly. Reversals to a previous point for corrections should be kept to a minimum.
2. *Do not handle the merchandise too much:* Avoid as much as possible handling the piece more than once.
3. *Do not have too many people handling the merchandise:* As much as possible, let one staff member process the material.
4. *Move 'em up, move 'em out:* Process material as quickly as possible from point of receipt to shelves.
5. *Help the computer pay for itself:* Do not have staff doing what the computer can do.

Good communication that promotes active staff participation is crucial to effective reorganization. From the comments made by the audience, Coulter and Halpin chose a timely topic with several people speaking about reorganization within their own work places.

NOTES

1. Barbara Conroy and Barbara S. Jones, *Improving Communication in the Library* (Phoenix, AZ: Oryx Press, 1986), 23-26.
2. Norman D. Stevens, *Communication Throughout Libraries* (Metuchen, NJ: Scarecrow Press, 1983), 18.
3. Joel H. Head and James K. Hickel, "Restructuring? Avoid the Myths," *IABC COMMUNICATION WORLD* 6 (1989): 18-20.

Document Delivery: Staffing, Technology, and Budgeting Implications

Anthony Ferguson
Margaret Price

Workshop Leaders

Lucy Duhon

Recorder

SUMMARY. Today's fiscal realities encourage libraries to experiment with document delivery as an alternative mode of information delivery. Columbia University recently completed their Scientific Information Study, a segment of which compared the costs of ownership and access. Several other Columbia studies examined researcher acceptance of online indexes and document delivery as alternatives to ownership. The Woodward Biomedical Library at the University of British Columbia has a number of new technologies, including Ariel, Aviso, Docline, and a local online document delivery request system. The experiences of these libraries with document delivery are discussed.

Anthony Ferguson, Associate University Librarian at Columbia University, began the workshop by reviewing a scientific informa-

---

Lucy Duhon is Assistant Serials Librarian at the University of Toledo, Toledo, OH.

[Haworth co-indexing entry note]: "Document Delivery: Staffing, Technology, and Budgeting Implications." Duhon, Lucy. Co-published simultaneously in *The Serials Librarian* (The Haworth Press, Inc.) Vol. 25, No. 3/4, 1995, pp. 319-325; and: *A Kaleidoscope of Choices: Reshaping Roles and Opportunities for Serialists* (ed: Beth Holley and Mary Ann Sheble) The Haworth Press, Inc., 1995, pp. 319-325. Multiple copies of this article/chapter may be purchased from The Haworth Document Delivery Center [1-800-3-HAWORTH; 9:00 a.m. - 5:00 p.m. (EST)].

© 1995 by The Haworth Press, Inc. All rights reserved.

tion study conducted at his institution. Its purpose was to find alternative ways of providing information in the face of declining materials budgets. Could access to information easily substitute for physical ownership? Ferguson focused on two questions: (1) is access as cost-effective as ownership? and (2) under what circumstances would users find access acceptable?

Like most other institutions, Columbia University (CU) fell on hard times in the late 1980s. By 1989, the University, always heavily dependent upon private gifts and federal grants, had begun borrowing money to balance its budget. In 1990, as part of a creative solution, the provost applied for a grant from the Council on Library Resources. This grant made possible the study of alternative ways of meeting library user needs. Although Columbia had traditionally been a humanities institution, the University decided to study the sciences, since this was where cost increases had been most dramatic, and where the most urgent need for alternative information resources existed. Clearly, there was a need to develop new strategies for providing information.

Ferguson described information needs as three concentric circles of increasingly general categories: (1) citation needs, (2) browsing needs, and (3) retrospective research needs. Citation needs are the most specific, whereas retrospective research needs are the most unpredictable. CU chose three departments on which to focus its study. It chose Biology for its laboratory emphasis; Electrical Engineering for its perceived openness to new strategies; and Physics for its extensive retrospective literature.

To set the stage for the Scientific Information Study (SIS), faculty and students in the three departments were surveyed about where they obtain their information. Of the five sources that they rated highly, three had nothing to do with the library. Many relied on colleagues and conferences for their information, and then on their own personal libraries, with information only an "arm's reach" away. Researchers generally consulted the institutional library only after other sources failed to satisfy their information needs.

From 1991 to 1992, three studies were conducted, all focusing on periodicals. A citation needs study analyzing all publications by CU faculty for the year 1988 concluded that 137 periodical titles satisfied over 80 percent of citation needs, while 15 of these titles satisfied 50 percent of citation needs. Thus, a low number of journal titles satisfied most citation needs. A browsing needs study across several CU libraries found that of 629 current periodicals, 522 were used at least once and 410 were used at least 25 times. There was no direct correspondence between citation needs and browsing needs. A third study found that retrospective information needs form the greatest subset of all information needs. Of the 844 titles studied (both current and ceased), 619 were used. What does this mean for document delivery? Citation needs are the most predictable type of information need, and may be most easily satisfied by document delivery. On the other hand, large numbers of periodicals are needed for browsing and retrospective research needs. It is important to know what type of information is being sought before trying to reformat its delivery.

To answer the question, "is access as cost-effective as ownership?" Ferguson explained that at CU, the seven science libraries had been using book money to fund their own document delivery for some time. The Association of Research Libraries' Interlibrary Loan (ILL) cost study figure of $37.50 was used as a basis for figuring the average cost to borrow an item in three scientific disciplines. Eighteen months' worth of transaction cards made it possible to figure the cost of borrowing versus subscribing for one year in Biology, Electrical Engineering, and Physics. Ferguson's handout showed that Biology, for example, would have spent $343,900 on subscriptions per year for 1,062 items, while those same items would cost only $28,600 to borrow. For items not too heavily used, it is apparently more cost effective to borrow than to own.

Under what circumstances would users find access acceptable? Various departments were asked how they would allocate acquisitions funds if given a choice. Exactly 50 percent would spend almost all funds on books and journals, whereas only .8 percent would allocate more money to interlibrary loan. Another 38 percent would allocate more money to books and journals and 11 percent would divide the money evenly between books and journals and interlibrary loan. So, there was a significant preference overall for spending money on physically owned items. Knowing this, what factors would be necessary for researchers to prefer access over ownership? Since browsing is so important to users, it is important to find out how electronic browsing might successfully compete with physical browsing.

In 1993, an indexing plus document delivery service was studied. UnCover, developed by the Colorado Alliance of Research Libraries (CARL), was made available to humanities, sciences, and social sciences clientele. Selected users were given accounts and trained to use the system, using their own fax machines. Most users were impressed with UnCover's accessibility and speed, but were disappointed with its image quality and expense (average cost–$10 per article). Also, it was difficult to determine remotely whether an article was worth ordering. UnCover did prove useful when tracing an author's work, when working in a new field, or when the library was closed. Its coverage tended to be incomplete, however. Electrical engineers noted that title-level access was not enough, and that abstracts and full-text were necessary.

In 1994, another experiment was conducted at CU's business library with University Microfilms International's Business Periodicals on Disc (BPOD) workstation. Users were pleased with its indexing abilities, its printing capabilities, and the availability of full text. Many users were willing to pay 25 cents per page for the convenience. However, BPOD only covered 400 titles, its updating was rather slow, and with only one terminal, accessibility was difficult. Ferguson's handout, however, showed that 68 percent of users were very pleased with the service as an indexing tool, and 42 percent felt it was a good substitute for print copy. In this case, full-text access was almost as acceptable as ownership.

What were the consequences of the SIS? What needs to be considered if document delivery is to be as successful as information ownership? Some considerations include ongoing user needs analysis (with faculty, researcher, and student needs studied separately), the facilitation of electronic browsing (which is so important to users), the speeding up of interlibrary loan transactions, electronic information training, and the focus on serials priced $1,000 and higher. Access is generally more cost-effective than ownership; nevertheless, title-by-title decisions are necessary. For users to be satisfied with access as an alternative to ownership, they have to be given maximum information and as much control as possible over their searching and retrieving abilities.

What are the implications for staffing, technology, and budgeting? Ferguson stated that document delivery is basically an acquisitions function; therefore, staffing should more closely match that of a typical acquisitions unit, rather than that of an ILL department. In terms of technology, speed is critical. Libraries need to keep experimenting with newer access and delivery methods, and minimize bureaucratic interference. With regard to budgeting, money needs to be shifted from the tradition of anticipating user needs to one of responding to real needs. All of these areas need to be examined seriously if libraries are to remain in the forefront of providing the new world with information.

Margaret Price, head of the Document Supply and Delivery Centre at the Woodward Biomedical Library (WBL) at the University of British Columbia (UBC), then explained some of the specific document delivery methods being used at her institution. Price explained that shrinking budgets have caused librarians to think in terms of restructuring, merger, technological change, cost recovery, and customer service–terms not ordinarily associated with the library profession. She continued by describing the challenges her institution encountered when document delivery was instituted.

In 1982, the UBC Health Sciences Network was established. It consists of the Woodward Biomedical Library and three off-site affiliated teaching hospital libraries. This free service has grown considerably. In the first year there were 27,000 requests, and in 1993, that figure more than doubled. Requests, formerly faxed in, are now registered online via UBCLIB, the university's online catalog. Items are delivered by truck.

In 1991, the operation moved from the WBL basement to the main floor, where it could be given better attention. Merged with serials and interlibrary loan, it became known as the Document Delivery and Orders Unit. With a 24-hour turnaround commitment and widely varying numbers of requests, cross-training among the student workers in the three participating libraries is a necessity. Price supervises the three units and explained that although the student workers are not inexpensive, the library benefits from a large number of frequently rotated workers, thereby avoiding occupational injuries and low morale.

The UBC Libraries experienced budget cuts of $200,000 in each of two recent years, and is anticipating a cut of $400,000 in 1994/95. Because of this, resource sharing networks are becoming increasingly important. In 1993, UBC became involved with several consortias. They include, for example, the Canadian Association of Research Libraries (CARL), and the Council of Prairie and Pacific Libraries (COPPUL). UBC's philosophy on resource-sharing is that it should be free among reciprocal borrowers. This is not always possible, so fee schedules should be kept as simple as possible.

Docline and Aviso are two of the major document delivery services used at UBC. Docline, developed at the National Library of Medicine, was only recently introduced to Canada. A sophisticated system, it can route ILL requests automatically using an accession number. Aviso is an automated ILL software package which facilitates the Docline operation. It also serves as a valuable collection management tool. UBCLinc is a service covering zoology and other biology-related disciplines not covered by Docline. Ariel, developed by the Research Libraries Group (RLG), offers electronic image transmission and is able to scan articles, photographs, and tables. It is optimized for Internet transmission, and is faster, cheaper, and more reliable than faxed images.

In April 1994, a new fee-based document delivery service started at UBC. Items can be ordered online and either sent to the requestor, or picked up at the library. Price distributed brochures listing the various costs for this service, by book or by article. In 1994, another fee-based service began, involving British Columbia health-related libraries and institutions. Medical faculty can access *Medline* and scan *Current Contents* from their offices. The WBL services package provides corporate cards and document delivery cards to ease payment concerns. To keep costs to a minimum, users are asked to anticipate their needs and are billed with one annual invoice. Price explained that this helps provide ready capital for the service. A handout showed the various delivery methods used at UBC, including Ariel, fax, mail, campus delivery, hospital delivery, and courier pick-up. The delivery times for these services range from two hours to bi-weekly.

Price closed her presentation by pondering who will deliver the document in the future. Will libraries or commercial vendors be responsible? She asked whether librarians have the will to continue mastering the complex issues surrounding resource-sharing, copyright, and technological change. Will libraries eventually be overtaken by the faster, more profit-oriented commercial suppliers? Price noted that as libraries begin charging to cover costs for these services, and vendors begin relying more on libraries' collections, the distinction between the two will become "murky." Libraries must "question old loyalties and forge new alliances" to keep resource sharing and document delivery manageable.

Questions after the workshop focused on the cost and quality of the new technology, the complexity of fee structures, who would be responsible for providing access to what, and whether the conflict with publishers would eventually carry over into the electronic medium. The workshop leaders assured the audience that these issues would be handled in much the same way as libraries have handled issues in the print medium.

Methods for Collecting, Processing, and Providing Access to Electronic Serials

Beth Weston
Christa Reinke
Eric Lease Morgan

Workshop Presenters

Paula Sullenger

Recorder

SUMMARY. The issues surrounding methods for collecting, processing, and providing access to electronic serials are discussed. Weston debates the access versus ownership issues of electronic journals, and discusses the changing roles of systems and acquisitions librarians in the provision of access to these journals. Reinke outlines the University of Houston's acquisitions process, an approach paralleling traditional serials acquisitions methods. Morgan describes an automated serials acquisitions process developed at the North Carolina State University.

Beth Weston, coordinator of Serials Acquisitions at the University of Delaware, began the workshop by querying the audience

---

Paula Sullenger is Serials Cataloger at the Auburn University Libraries, Auburn, AL.

[Haworth co-indexing entry note]: "Methods for Collecting, Processing, and Providing Access to Electronic Serials." Sullenger, Paula. Co-published simultaneously in *The Serials Librarian* (The Haworth Press, Inc.) Vol. 25, No. 3/4, 1995, pp. 327-331; and: *A Kaleidoscope of Choices: Reshaping Roles and Opportunities for Serialists* (ed: Beth Holley and Mary Ann Sheble) The Haworth Press, Inc., 1995, pp. 327-331. Multiple copies of this article/chapter may be purchased from The Haworth Document Delivery Center [1-800-3-HAWORTH; 9:00 a.m. - 5:00 p.m. (EST)].

© 1995 by The Haworth Press, Inc. All rights reserved.

about their use of electronic journals. Approximately half the audience said that their libraries access some type of electronic journal and less than half that number catalog them in some way.

Weston said that there are some questions that must be asked before a library decides to acquire an electronic journal. First, what is its importance to local users? Next, what is the quality of access via remote sites? Third, are there site licenses? Weston believes site licenses may be the wave of the future for electronic journals. Fourth, what staff and computer resources are available at the library? The answers to these questions will probably determine whether the library will provide access to the electronic journal or archive locally.

Weston discussed some of the formats and standards libraries may be asked to support, such as ASCII, Standard Generalized Markup Language (SGML), Postscript, bitmapped images, etc. She then listed some advantages and disadvantages of each. As these may use different hardware and software, how can libraries try to support each? Weston then added that while electronic journals are "free" now, more sophisticated features such as graphics may drive up the price.

Once libraries acquire electronic journals, what links should be made to the online catalog? Can/should libraries provide full cataloging for something the library does not "own?" She next mentioned some of the work being done to facilitate cataloging of electronic journals. The American Library Association committee on representation in Machine Readable Bibliographic Information (MARBI) has added the 856 field to the MARC record which tells users where to go for access. There has been some progress on using a Universal Resource Locator (URL) which would require a unique identifier similar to the ISSN.

Weston concluded her presentation by mentioning some features of electronic journals which make them attractive: low cost (probably will not last); universal access from outside the library and which allows simultaneous access; physical volumes cannot be mutilated; and finally their fast publication time.

Christa Reinke, assistant serials librarian at the University of Houston, next told the audience of an ongoing project at the University of Houston for processing electronic journals. This project began in late 1993 and the first electronic journal became available in February 1994. The electronic journals are currently processed by a librarian, but as the process is stabilized and refined, the task will be given to a paraprofessional.

After an electronic journal is selected for acquisition, the Systems Department reviews the system requirements and if it is compatible with the library's hardware and software, the request goes to the Serials Department, which initiates the electronic subscription, usually by subscribing to a listserv. Any back issues are retrieved and the title is cataloged. As new issues are published, they are downloaded into the staff network, then transferred to WordPerfect to remove headers and review for errors. This copy is loaded onto the public network and indexed. The original is deleted from the staff network and the issue is checked-in.

Reinke listed some of the advantages of the project: There are no claimed issues; it has been an excellent opportunity to learn about the Internet; and the library receives the issues immediately. The disadvantages she mentioned are that the Serials Department must rely heavily on the Systems Department and changes in the local computers or networks can cause problems.

Reinke closed her presentation by asking some questions. What are the real costs of this program? Will gopher access or World Wide Web (WWW) access eliminate the need to archive locally? Most importantly, is this value-added service being used enough to warrant the large investment of time?

The last speaker, Eric Morgan, systems librarian at North Carolina State University (NCSU), described Mr. Serials, a pilot project he developed for handling electronic serials at NCSU. He told how Mr. Serials handles each of the following five functions: selection, storage, organization, access, and acquisitions.

Morgan selected Charles Bailey's list of library-oriented electronic journals to test and refine Mr. Serials. He set up "Mr. Serials" as a user name for subscribing to the titles. For storage and archiving, Morgan decided to use file transfer protocol (FTP). He set up a directory for each title that contains all issues received for that title. Each issue is given a unique name by condensing the name of the journal, and the issue's volume and number into a short code. For example, all issues of *Citations for Serial Literature* begin with "csl." Volume 1, number 22 of that journal would be named "csl-v1n22" and Volume 2, number 3 would be named "csl-v2n03."

Morgan next created gopher and WWW pointers to the FTP site. When a user selects an issue through the gopher, the server transparently opens an anonymous FTP connection to the NCSU libraries and retrieves the desired article as an ASCII file, closes the connection, and displays the file to the user. The WWW server works in a similar manner. FTP, gopher, and WWW are useful when the user knows which article is needed. For keyword access, a Wide Area Information Server (WAIS) index is created for each title and entered into the appropriate gopher or WWW directory. Once a day the entire NCSU collection of electronic journals is reindexed so that the WAIS index is never more than one day old.

By using a programming language called "perl," Morgan developed an automated acquisitions program for Mr. Serials which he calls AC. AC reads the e-mail message which contains an electronic journal issue, removes the header, extracts the name of the file to the message and adds a URL, and saves the file in an FTP directory. It next creates and saves a gopher link file or WWW document, deletes the original e-mail message, and then repeats the process for each issue received. This process uses a minimum of Morgan's time each day.

Morgan described some problems with Mr. Serials. The first drawback is that it is supported by only one person. The next problem is that AC, the automated acquisitions program, works only if the formatting of each issue of a title is entirely consistent. An extra space or line is all it takes to prevent AC from being able to accurately perform.

As Morgan described the various features and functions of Mr. Serials, he gave a demonstration of them through a computer. This gave the audience a chance to see Mr. Serials in action and an appreciation of its ability to perform with little human intervention.

After the presentations, there were some questions from the audience. A librarian wanted to know how to provide users with access. Should we use the OPACS? What is the best method for showing the user where to go? Morgan advised to skip setting up a gopher and to go straight to WWW. Another librarian asked why should librarians do this when faculty can use e-mail themselves? Morgan replied that libraries provide archives and indexing features that may not be available otherwise.

An academic society publisher expressed concern about the variety of formats and standards mentioned by Weston. He said publishers need to know which ones the libraries want to support. Neither libraries nor publishers can afford to support all formats and platforms.

Is It Tweaking or Cataloging Enrichment? Choices in Reshaping Serial Cataloging Copy

Carroll Davis
Kay Teel

Workshop Leaders

Phoebe Timberlake

Recorder

SUMMARY. Serial catalogers are required to balance the economy of taking standard cataloging copy "as is" against local demands to catalog apart from the standard. Two serial catalogers discuss examples of cataloging-enhancement practices from the viewpoint of their respective institutions. They examine each in terms of the following: impetus; problem solved or opportunity realized; stakeholders affected; costs, documentation needs, and new problems entailed; and factors shaping decisions to make changes.

In a lively workshop with frequent audience participation, two presenters invited their audience to analyze specific cases where the existing cataloging records had been judged to fall short of someone's expectations, and then to make their own judgments concern-

---

Phoebe Timberlake is Chair of the Library Resource Coordination Department at the University of New Orleans, New Orleans, LA.

[Haworth co-indexing entry note]: "Is It Tweaking or Cataloging Enrichment? Choices in Reshaping Serial Cataloging Copy." Timberlake, Phoebe. Co-published simultaneously in *The Serials Librarian* (The Haworth Press, Inc.) Vol. 25, No. 3/4, 1995, pp. 333-337; and: *A Kaleidoscope of Choices: Reshaping Roles and Opportunities for Serialists* (ed: Beth Holley and Mary Ann Sheble) The Haworth Press, Inc., 1995, pp. 333-337. Multiple copies of this article/chapter may be purchased from The Haworth Document Delivery Center [1-800-3-HAWORTH; 9:00 a.m. - 5:00 p.m. (EST)].

© 1995 by The Haworth Press, Inc. All rights reserved.

ing how to respond to those or similar requests for "enrichment" or "tweaking" of cataloging copy. Alternating in their presentations, Carroll Davis, serial cataloger, Columbia University Libraries, and Kay Teel, serial cataloger, Bobst Library, New York University, began by defining the issues most likely to generate requests to modify cataloging records.

They suggested that the impetus for local editing may come from the cataloger, as part of the usual check against national or local standards; from others, when problems arise; or from both. The context within which the records are viewed, including who created them, who will use them, and how they will be used, has implications for "tweaking." One sequence of events containing the possibility of actually reshaping cataloging practice was described as (1) a complaint or request for change in a cataloging record is received, such as adding an additional access point, (2) the cataloger agrees to take some action to remedy the situation, (3) the cataloger then repeats that action in similar situations, and (4) as a result, local cataloging practice may be changed. The cycle both shapes and is shaped by the cataloger's insight and experience. However, Davis cautioned the group that before any changes are actually made to records, other than the straightforward correction of obvious errors, the problem or "opportunity" must be clearly understood. Obviously, a change which does not address the real problem is not a solution at all.

Davis also stressed the importance of considering the stakeholders before modifying catalog records. Exactly who are the catalog's users? A working definition was offered as anyone who uses the record after the cataloger accepts it. In addition to patrons, that probably includes the staff of public service units, acquisitions, serials check-in, and interlibrary loan. Remote users, those sharing our utilities, networks, and other cooperative ventures are also stakeholders. Future users will also view these records, perhaps displayed by a different automated system with technical requirements as yet unknown. Seemingly simple "fixes" made in records now may in fact create serious access problems for those stakeholders of the future.

Another consideration is the cost involved in any cataloging "enrichment." The obvious concerns may be budgetary such as staff time, system capacity, and related supplies. However, there may be additional costs in terms of loss of record adaptability for other uses, slower or more stressful processing, and greater documentation needs.

Davis also described various forces which must be weighed and balanced when deciding whether to make changes. A management constant is the desire for increased productivity by "doing more, better, faster, and cheaper." At the same time, if the resources described by the cataloging records are not accessible because of problems with the records, then the records are not serving their purpose.

Ethical principles may also be a factor. Catalogers may adapt the popular minimal standard of professional conduct of "do no harm" to "do not misinform, misdirect, or mislead." There may also be an ethical dimension in our responsibilities to our stakeholders, our institutions, and, as professionals, to national standards. Our institution's identity, including its mission, goals, and principal clientele, should also play a role in our decisions.

Personality characteristics will affect how catalogers make decisions or approach problem situations. Being aware of these factors helps us guard against their influencing our cataloging in ways we neither want nor expect. Davis pointed out that our catalogs may, in fact, be shaped by our idiosyncracies with some catalogers being far more anxious to avoid conflicts and to accommodate requests.

Finally, the alternatives should be weighed carefully. Is the enrichment or recataloging response the only way to respond to a perceived problem? User education measures might be a more appropriate and less expensive solution. Are we attempting to make the catalog provide all of the answers? If we view the catalog as simply one source among many, are we being careful not to duplicate other already available means of access?

Keeping these issues and factors in mind, Teel and Davis each presented several cases from their own experience, first setting the stage by describing their institutions and the specific impetus for change or "tweaking" in each instance.

In the first case described by Teel, a title cataloged for the library's archival collection had incomplete frequency information. While less a concern for some collections, she believed that a more detailed frequency history would be useful to this particular library's staff and patrons, so she both revised and added 3xx (current and former frequency) fields. In this instance, her own concern had provided the impetus for enhancing the record.

In another case, 246 (alternate title access) fields were utilized to assist patrons in locating a pre-AACR2 record with a title proper of "Bulletin." The audience agreed that even without having the issues in hand to perform major recataloging of the title, Teel's decision to add several more descriptive titles which might fit the label "commonly known as: . . . " should increase access while doing no harm. She did, however, mention that another alternative to retrieving the issues in order to upgrade cataloging copy to AACR2 might be to search a database like OCLC for a current record.

One other example from Teel's experience related to a Japanese journal with an English parallel title. When a section split into a new title, the public service staff asked that titles in the linking fields be given in English rather than Japanese. Although her local system does not currently index 780/785 fields, the next system will. She decided that a compromise of including the English parallel title in a 580 along with the title proper might enhance identification without creating indexing problems in the future.

The first case discussed by Davis was an annual directory which had changed title twice. The business library, with holdings for the first title (Directory A) and third title (Directory C), wanted the existing "Continues:" and "Continued by:" notes on those titles to link directly to each other rather than to the second title (Directory B), which was not owned by the library. The audience agreed that complying with this kind of request misinforms the user. In addition, if the second title is ever acquired, both of the other records would have to be unlinked and relinked. One member of the audience wondered if the business library might consider simply withdrawing the earliest title. Someone else suggested utilizing bibliographic instruction to help users interpret serial cataloging records.

In another case, the local system indexed the title proper and other title information all together, resulting in the record for *Man* appearing many screens beyond where users would look for it. Following numerous complaints from reference staff, Davis decided to create a 246 field to index just the title proper, a fairly harmless solution at the time, but one which might be confusing if the system changes or enhances its indexing capability, essentially generating duplicate entries. While participants agreed this was the most effective step in the short term, they believed the cataloger should also, for the long term, pursue corrections to the systems indexing protocols, the real seat of the problem.

As each situation was described by the presenters and viewed against the context in which it had occurred, members of the audience were guided through the decision-making process unique to the presenter's library as well as given the opportunity to reflect upon similar situations in their own libraries. The results of this workshop should enable the participants to provide increased access, satisfied stakeholders, and enhanced, yet economical, catalogs at their home institutions.

The Journal Pricing Season: The Publisher, Subscription Agent, and Librarian's Viewpoint

John W. Breithaupt
Tina Feick
James Mouw

Workshop Leaders

Debbie Madsen

Recorder

SUMMARY. This workshop provides behind the scenes information on how and when journal pricing is determined by publishers, is handled by subscription agents, and is recorded and analyzed by librarians. The effects of "firm pricing," currency exchange rates, budgetary considerations, and other issues are discussed in relationship to the 1994 changes in the journal pricing season.

The two workshop sessions, attended by approximately two hundred librarians and vendors, described how publishers, subscription agents, and librarians set and cope with journal pricing.

John Breithaupt, director-general, Marketing and Association Management Services for Allen Press, described the process through

---

Debbie Madsen is Chair, Acquisitions Department, Kansas State University, Manhattan, KS.

[Haworth co-indexing entry note]: "The Journal Pricing Season: The Publisher, Subscription Agent, and Librarian's Viewpoint." Madsen, Debbie. Co-published simultaneously in *The Serials Librarian* (The Haworth Press, Inc.) Vol. 25, No. 3/4, 1995, pp. 339-343; and: *A Kaleidoscope of Choices: Reshaping Roles and Opportunities for Serialists* (ed: Beth Holley and Mary Ann Sheble) The Haworth Press, Inc., 1995, pp. 339-343. Multiple copies of this article/chapter may be purchased from The Haworth Document Delivery Center [1-800-3-HAWORTH; 9:00 a.m. - 5:00 p.m. (EST)].

which publishers establish journal prices. Breithaupt began with an explanation of how Allen Press, which is a printing company rather than a publisher, offers publishing services to its customers. Working primarily with non-profit associations and societies, Allen Press offers services, such as market analysis and pricing recommendations, to its customers to assist them in competing with commercial publishers.

For this presentation, Breithaupt surveyed eleven nonprofit, society-based organizations representing thirteen publications. He indicated that pricing decisions for society and association journals must generally be approved at the organization's regular meeting. It is the timing of this meeting that determines when prices become available, rather than vendors' or libraries' needs. Prior to the meeting, existing prices must be reviewed and a recommendation made. Since they are largely staffed by volunteers, and operate with review committees and executive boards made up of geographically dispersed academicians or subject specialists, these publishers generally do little in terms of market analysis. They may contract with for-profit companies, such as Allen Press, for this kind of journal pricing analysis.

Breithaupt commented that the primary goal of nonprofit societies and associations is to disseminate information, and further science and research in their discipline. Because profitability is of lesser importance, these publishers set prices which will cover costs and not take money away from other membership areas. The primary criteria used to determine journal pricing are the production and distribution costs in relation to income and financial health. Due to their membership being comprised of academicians and researchers, nonprofit societies and associations clearly understand university budget situations and strive to keep their publications affordable.

Breithaupt noted that for-profit publishers use many of the same pricing evaluation criteria as their nonprofit counterparts, including current publishing budget and revenues, production costs and projected increases, and delivery costs and projected increases. The for-profit sector, however, takes the process even further. To maintain a favorable competitive status, their publishers do research to determine the journal's ranking in terms of citation reports, the price per page history of the title, review the subscription agents' discount, and often conduct telephone surveys to assess the existing market conditions.

Tina Feick, senior serials specialist, Blackwell's Periodical Division, summarized journal pricing and payment timetables and discussed some of the related difficulties. Feick prefaced her remarks by noting that she had obtained input from several different subscription agents in preparation for this workshop. Journal pricing is a very complex issue. Vendors handle an immense quantity of material, and both timing and accuracy are critical.

In late May, vendors ask publishers to supply title-specific price and bibliographic information for the next year, including information about title changes; volume numbers; frequency; effective date of pricing; payment currency; variable pricing for individuals, institutions, foreign markets; postage; and definition of the subscription year. Publishers' responses vary in completeness and often require additional follow-up by vendor staff. At times, vendors must actually calculate the prices based upon publishers' information and such factors as postage to different geographical locations, shipping methods, currency exchange, and their own discount.

Scientific, technical, and medical (STM) publishers and university presses generally return their price lists to vendors by August or mid-September. Trade publishers' lists (popular titles and newspapers) are received throughout the year and often change prices several times per year. Vendors generally pay publishers in late October to December. As a result, vendors have very little time to receive, verify, and enter pricing information before payment must be made.

Concurrent with obtaining price information from publishers, Feick indicated that vendors are working with libraries to send out renewal lists (mid-May to August), receive returned renewals (June to December) and issue invoices (July to December). This concurrence results in a very complicated timeline. Feick noted that vendors prefer to receive cancellations from libraries by September first so they can forestall payment to the publisher.

Feick commented that the issue of firm pricing arose because libraries wanted to know prices before canceling journals. Viewed within the context of the timelines described above, it is apparent that, given the short time period, libraries generally cannot cancel before the vendors must pay the publishers.

Finally, Feick commented that within the next three years, pricing information should be transmitted via electronic data interchange (EDI) using X-12 standards. The International Committee on EDI for Serials (ICEDIS), made up of publishing and vendor representatives, is actively working on this and other goals.

James Mouw, head of Serials, University of Chicago, provided a view of how one library plans and conducts a year's business. The University of Chicago has four discrete segments in its serial planning cycle: predict and protect, monitor, correct, and analyze. In the initial phase, library staff predict journal costs for the up-coming year so the remaining budget can be allocated to serials, binding, and monographs. Generally, vendors' predictions are used for this purpose. Mouw cautioned that foreign currency changes are included in vendors' projections so libraries should be careful not to include this calculation twice. Next, the journal budget is protected through prepayments to vendors. Since vendors handle prepayments and associated currency conversions differently, Mouw encouraged librarians to investigate their vendors' policies carefully.

To monitor expenditures throughout the year, the University of Chicago produces detailed ten-year summary and comparison reports of foreign exchange rates and expenditures by country of publication. These reports, produced both in tabular and graphic form, provide detailed management data for use in projecting expenditures for the remainder of the year, and are extremely useful in illustrating changes and trends. As the projections are compared with actual expenditures, corrections are made as needed. Finally, prediction and expenditure data are analyzed to assess the accuracy of projections and whether or not alterations need to be made for the next year.

Mouw reported that obtaining firm prices from vendors about two months earlier than previously, allowed the library to make budget adjustments earlier. Firm pricing was not very useful for cancellations, however, because the University of Chicago's consultative process with bibliographers and faculty takes about four to six months. Thus, decisions still cannot be made for next-year cancellation.

These three presentations provided the audience with a greater understanding of the various factors associated with journal pricing as seen from three different perspectives. Librarians' desire to obtain firm journal prices earlier in the year must be viewed in the context of publishers' and vendors' activities. Although many publishers have made an effort to provide prices a month or two earlier, often this difference has not helped libraries cope with the difficult issues of budgets and cancellations. It is also true that, in many cases, publishers simply cannot guarantee a firm price.

... And Then It Happened: Effect of Changes in the Serials Information Environment on the Small-to-Medium Size Academic Library

Gale Teaster-Woods
Martin Gordon
Kathleen Sweet

Workshop Leaders

Elaine Jurries

Recorder

SUMMARY. Employing three institutional case studies, veteran academic serialists engage in a discussion of positive methodologies for harnessing the various forces at play within the scholarly information environment. Concentration is placed upon both personal and organizational strategies to successfully cope with the geometric rapidity of changes, both at the library and institutional level.

In this workshop, three case studies of the effects of change on the small-to-medium size academic library were presented. The

---

Elaine Jurries is Coordinator of Serials Services at Auraria Library, University of Colorado at Denver, Denver, CO.

[Haworth co-indexing entry note]: "... And Then It Happened: Effect of Changes in the Serials Information Environment on the Small-to-Medium Size Academic Library." Jurries, Elaine. Co-published simultaneously in *The Serials Librarian* (The Haworth Press, Inc.) Vol. 25, No. 3/4, 1995, pp. 345-347; and: *A Kaleidoscope of Choices: Reshaping Roles and Opportunities for Serialists* (ed: Beth Holley and Mary Ann Sheble) The Haworth Press, Inc., 1995, pp. 345-347. Multiple copies of this article/chapter may be purchased from The Haworth Document Delivery Center [1-800-3-HAWORTH; 9:00 a.m. - 5:00 p.m. (EST)].

© 1995 by The Haworth Press, Inc. All rights reserved.

three institutions discussed were Winthrop University, Franklin and Marshall College, and Phoenix College.

Gail Teaster-Woods began with a description of the process of restructuring at Dacus Library, Winthrop University. She stressed that although restructuring has many negative connotations, it can be handled in a positive manner and has been viewed positively at Dacus Library.

Historical, present, and future descriptions of change in the serials environment at Winthrop University were given to illustrate points made by Teaster-Woods. The usual catalysts for organizational restructuring of serials at Dacus Library have been, and continue to be, technological and personnel changes. Whether to organize by process or format has also been an issue. Recently, the entire campus was restructured to cut costs. Workflow in the Serials Department was analyzed and a number of serials cancelled. This cancellation of serials may result in future restructuring in the Serials Department. For example, the relocation of some serials personnel to other areas such as interlibrary loan and document delivery may occur. Also, a vacancy in technical services provides an opportunity for more restructuring and the process of change continues.

Martin Gordon of Franklin and Marshall College reflected on the unique effects change has on an academic institution steeped in long traditions. Franklin and Marshall College was established in 1787 and competes for the highest intellectual caliber of student. Showing a series of slides of campus scenes, an image of a serene, stable, and strongly traditional institution emerged. Behind this image, fundamental changes have occurred in the library. A decline in useable endowment funds, the high cost for tenured faculty, the need for a scholarly workstation to serve their clients, the advent of the Internet, competition for students, and the rise in periodical prices were all events that forced internal changes at Franklin and Marshall College Library.

Through a strategy of refinancing, reorganization of the management level, out-staffing, de-staffing via promotion, image adjustment to broaden appeal, and positivism, the library has managed to keep pace with the institution's "tradition in transition" plan.

Gordon provided some advice on dealing with change on a personal level. He suggested the following strategies: get angry and then get over it; assess your assets; redefine your parameters; set your priorities; discover your boss; sing your own song BUT join the choir, too; actualize; solicit feedback; and above all, water your staff by keeping them informed.

Kathleen Sweet of Phoenix College, presented the view of the paraprofessional on change in the library. Phoenix College is the second largest community college system in the United States.

Her message to the audience was: plan for change from the bottom up; allow employees to be a part of the decision-making and goal-setting process; consider every suggestion; and develop real teams, not just groups of people working together. The need for efficient communication; clear, positive statements; participative management; and a mechanism for measuring success were also discussed.

In conclusion, Sweet re-emphasized the importance of communication, saying that even if you cannot give your staff a definite answer, respond to their question. It is better to hear that you do not know the answers, then to hear nothing at all.

The workshop covered the spectrum of the effects of change on three libraries from the personal, serials department, library, and institutional levels. It succeeded in generating a lively sharing of thoughts from the audience.

Workstation Ergonomics and Computer Calisthenics

Frances C. Wilkinson

Workshop Leader

Amira Unver

Recorder

SUMMARY. As nearly every aspect of serials work becomes automated, we must select workstation furniture and equipment with human comfort, health, and efficiency in mind. A checklist for planning a new workstation or evaluating the "people ergonomics" of an existing one is provided. Exercises that can be completed at the terminal, with no special equipment, clothing, or athletic ability required are discussed.

This workshop provided a short history of ergonomics, guidance on establishing an ideal working environment for anyone who works with computers, and current and past trends in calisthenics.

Ergonomics seeks to find a happy blend of working environment, equipment (specifically computer and computer related equipment), and the worker. There were three key aspects emphasized throughout the workshop: (1) the need for worker friendly equipment, (2) an environment designed around workers using

---

Amira Unver is Serials Librarian at George Washington University Medical Center, Washinton, DC.

[Haworth co-indexing entry note]: "Workstation Ergonomics and Computer Calisthenics." Unver, Amira. Co-published simultaneously in *The Serials Librarian* (The Haworth Press, Inc.) Vol. 25, No. 3/4, 1995, pp. 349-351; and: *A Kaleidoscope of Choices: Reshaping Roles and Opportunities for Serialists* (ed: Beth Holley and Mary Ann Sheble) The Haworth Press, Inc., 1995, pp. 349-351. Multiple copies of this article/chapter may be purchased from The Haworth Document Delivery Center [1-800-3-HAWORTH; 9:00 a.m. - 5:00 p.m. (EST)].

© 1995 by The Haworth Press, Inc. All rights reserved.

computers, and as supplements to the first two aspects, (3) simple exercises that can be performed sitting or standing.

Fran Wilkinson, head of Serials at the University of New Mexico, Albuquerque, presented the workshop. She began by providing a brief definition and history of ergonomics, emphasizing the need that workstation and working environments should be adapted to workers, not the reverse.

Initial ergonomic studies, which began in the 1970s, primarily focused on the visual and musculoskeletal effects of work on employees. Present studies take into account many more factors, even though there is still much evidence that little training and proper attention to ergonomics actually occur in the workplace. This is despite the fact that it is estimated that by the year 2000, there will be 100 million video display terminals (VDT) in use in the United States.

One of the first things to check in looking at the working environment is to look at the position of a worker to the computer workstation. Body placement is an important factor: posture, eye-level, and use of cupped fingers over the keyboard can make extended time at the keyboard less of a strain. Wrists should not drop down, but should be kept straight, and feet should be flat on the floor.

Wilkinson provided a check-list for assessing whether a given workplace offers the most comfortable and ergonomically sound work environment. The list addressed the general environment, lighting, video display terminals, workstation tables, surfaces or desk space, and chairs.

Major points from each category include: (1) the need for non-glare, non-reflective surfaces around computer terminals; (2) lighting should be dimmed in area of VDT use, task lights are recommended; (3) video display terminals should have adjustable screens, the print on the screen should be clear, the top of the screen at eye level; (4) desktops should be at ideal height for operator (27-29 inches); (5) table tops should be adjustable; (6) chairs should be adjustable, comfortable, and should have lumbar support; and (7) footrests and wristrests should be provided, if needed.

Wilkinson noted that if only one investment can be made for

improving the working ergonomics, it should be a proper chair which can run $400-$500.

The benefits to be derived from attention to proper ergonomics can include increased productivity, reduced absenteeism, and better health and comfort for each worker. With an increase of workers being disabled from carpal tunnel syndrome and other repetitive stress injuries, some companies have found it less expensive to address the issues of ergonomics as a preventive measure, than to cope with disabled workers later. Prevention of health problems should be one of the employer's major goals.

The latter portion of the workshop addressed calisthenics, basic exercises which anyone can do to stretch and exercise overused or tensed muscles. The intent of the exercises is to gently stretch but never strain muscles. The choice of exercises should be made among those that are recommended by an exercise physiologist, a person who has training in the exercise field.

As both Wilkinson and the workshop participants noted, exercise trends come and go; so, it is advisable to keep abreast of the latest studies in those fields. When in doubt about a specific exercise, consult a doctor in the field, or someone knowledgeable in safety or exercise.

The exercises that were demonstrated concentrated on relieving eye strain, and neck and shoulder strain, as well as providing stretching and flexibility to hands and fingers. Tension reliever "toys" like squeezable balls can also act as strengthening tools for hands and fingers.

Wilkinson ended the workshop by encouraging participants to check their own workstations for improvement and to help spread the benefits of ergonomics through use of posters, brown bag lunches where ergonomics is discussed, and advice to co-workers as appropriate.

Problem Solving Workshop Based on Total Quality Management (TQM) Principles

Richard Lynch

Workshop Leader

Lawrence R. Keating II

Recorder

SUMMARY. While quality has long been an issue in libraries, total quality management (TQM) incorporates a structured approach to problem solving and has proven to be an effective vehicle for systemizing quality in libraries. Following a brief overview of the infrastructure required for TQM, systematic problem solving is discussed in depth. Examples illustrating the TQM seven-step problem solving process are presented.

The focus of the workshop was on the use of the structured Total Quality Management (TQM) approach to problem solving as an effective method of attaining quality improvements in library operations and services. Richard Lynch, director of Quality at The Faxon Company, began by surveying attendees on the reasons for their interest in the topic, the extent of their involvement with TQM

Lawrence R. Keating II is Head of the Serials Department, University of Houston Libraries, Houston, TX.

[Haworth co-indexing entry note]: "Problem Solving Workshop Based on Total Quality Management (TMQ) Principles." Keating II, Lawrence R. Co-published simultaneously in *The Serials Librarian* (The Haworth Press, Inc.) Vol. 25, No. 3/4, 1995, pp. 353-356; and: *A Kaleidoscope of Choices: Reshaping Roles and Opportunities for Serialists* (ed: Beth Holley and Mary Ann Sheble) The Haworth Press, Inc., 1995, pp. 353-356. Multiple copies of this article/chapter may be purchased from The Haworth Document Delivery Center [1-800-3-HAWORTH; 9:00 a.m. - 5:00 p.m. (EST)].

© 1995 by The Haworth Press, Inc. All rights reserved.

efforts, and, for those with TQM experience, the level of satisfaction both with the results and with the process. Among the trouble spots identified by the experienced audience members were the effort required simply to get the process started, sorting through the different parts of the process, and the attempt to do everything at once. Lynch then set three objectives for the workshop session: (1) identifying the seven steps in problem solving, (2) learning to write clear problem solving statements, and (3) diagnosing a problem solving story.

Problem solving is just one component of the larger TQM process. Lynch first provided a context for problem solving by presenting an overview of the key elements of the TQM infrastructure: setting specific goals for an organization; an organizational environment with the flexibility to set up task forces and quality improvement teams; learning and education; empowerment and promotion of improvements; diagnosing problems; monitoring solutions in discrete, measurable units; and provision of incentives and rewards which do not interfere with the TQM process. Before detailing the seven steps involved in TQM problem solving, he reviewed various alternatives to the systematic TQM approach, such as reliance on the inner self (gut feelings, intuition), copying solutions from others (imitation, consultation), avoiding solutions (delegation, negotiation, delay), and reliance on random methods (trial-and-error, guesswork, luck). Each of these alternatives entailed serious organizational drawbacks, such as diminished ownership of and commitment to a solution, the lack of a learning experience for determining successful solutions, and the failure to build an organizational ability to solve problems.

The seven steps of problem solving fall into the four general categories of planning (identifying the problem; collecting and analyzing data; determining the problem's root cause), doing (implementing the solution), checking (confirming that the solution worked), and acting (making sure the solution takes hold; reviewing the process and moving on to the next problem). Applying this process systematically offers a number of advantages. The seven-step methodology provides a common language for groups working on problems of a cross-functional nature and makes it easier for team members to communicate with minimal waste of time. When an organization moves from improvement to re-engineering (i.e., the fundamental re-thinking of the organization's core processes), the methodology offers a measure of stability while new systems and workflows are being put into place. Finally, the seven-step process rallies the employees around the goals of re-engineering and involves them in organizational learning in a new context.

The first of the seven steps is to identify the specific problem on which to work and to state the problem as a "theme," making sure that team members understand the importance of the problem and that the statement of the problem addresses a specific weakness or defect. The theme should be carefully selected to create a sense of urgency and to set challenging yet realistic goals: it should be clearly stated in terms that are neither too abstract nor too restrictive, and that are concrete and measurable. Once the theme has been stated, the team moves into the second stage of data collection and analysis. Here it is important that the team collect its own data rather than relying on historical data, that team members experience the problem firsthand and in context by going directly to the site, and that the data be examined from a variety of different perspectives. Lynch demonstrated the use of Pareto charts for displaying the data collected and for examining the data stratification.

Once data have been gathered and analyzed, the team moves into the third step of the process, that of determining the root cause of the problem. Lynch demonstrated the use of fishbone diagrams at this stage to determine the cause and effect patterns: the solutions then become the reversal of the root causes. After the team has determined what appears to be the most important root cause, it becomes necessary to verify this through further data collection and correlation analysis rather than simply accepting it by consensus. Focus groups or statistical tests can be utilized to confirm both the reality of the root cause identified by the team as well as the existence of a strong cause/effect relationship. In step four, solution planning, the team develops various alternatives to reverse the root cause, ranks the alternatives to determine the most effective solution, and then implements the solutions sequentially to determine what works and what does not work. Use of a pilot project at this point will often provide quick and valuable feedback.

In the fifth step, the team confirms after a period of time that the solution works by again gathering data on the problem and comparing the new data to the original. Making sure that the solution sticks is the sixth step and is accomplished by involving the workers affected by the solutions, by documenting procedures, establishing standards, and so on. The final step entails a team review of the process to determine whether the cycle was successfully completed as scheduled, whether the seven steps were followed and the tools used appropriately, and whether all team members were involved and committed to the process.

Throughout the workshop Lynch drew on the attendees' experience and interests to illustrate the various components of the TQM process. The analysis of the two case studies Lynch presented at the end of the workshop provided attendees with the opportunity to apply the TQM problem solving process to particular situations and to demonstrate the successful achievement of the workshop's three objectives.

Job Hunter's Workshop:
How to Find and Land the Right Job, and Survive the Transition

Rosanna O'Neil
Ann Vidor

Workshop Leaders

Carol MacAdam

Recorder

SUMMARY. One of the "strategies for adjusting to organizational change" is to start looking for another job, voluntarily or not! The workshop presenters review various job hunting skills and survival techniques for today's job market. Updating/tailoring resumes, cover letters, and aspects of the interview process are discussed.

Rosanna O'Neil, head of Cataloging at Pennsylvania State University, and Ann Vidor, head of the Catalog Department at Emory University, presented a lively slate of do's and don'ts for anyone thinking of looking for a new job. Calling upon their experience as employers and from serving as chair and/or members of many search committees, O'Neil and Vidor offered suggestions on how to apply and interview for a new job. With handouts that matched their

---

Carol MacAdam is Assistant Order Librarian at Princeton University, Princeton, NJ.

[Haworth co-indexing entry note]: "Job Hunter's Workshop: How to Find and Land the Right Job, and Survive the Transition." MacAdam, Carol. Co-published simultaneously in *The Serials Librarian* (The Haworth Press, Inc.) Vol. 25, No. 3/4, 1995, pp. 357-361; and: *A Kaleidoscope of Choices: Reshaping Roles and Opportunities for Serialists* (ed: Beth Holley and Mary Ann Sheble) The Haworth Press, Inc., 1995, pp. 357-361. Multiple copies of this article/chapter may be purchased from The Haworth Document Delivery Center [1-800-3-HAWORTH; 9:00 a.m. - 5:00 p.m. (EST)].

© 1995 by The Haworth Press, Inc. All rights reserved.

overhead projections, the two presenters provided many examples to illustrate their points on the job search process and specific pitfalls to be avoided.

O'Neil began by emphasizing the importance of periodic self-assessment to identify one's employment characteristics. She recommends, every five to six years, asking such questions as, What makes me tick? What makes me satisfied with my job? What am I good at? Exercises to focus this introspective process can be found in Richard Bolles' *What Color Is Your Parachute?*[1] These can help applicants identify the kind of position they should seek, based on self-gratifying skills and interests.

Vidor pointed out sources for position vacancy announcements, in general and specifically for people in the information industry. She included a list of sources in her handouts. She then discussed factors to be considered when deciding on whether or not to apply for a particular position. These include how desperate one is for a change and geographic mobility. She emphasized the importance of applying appropriately and not wasting your time or that of prospective employers. Applicants should be realistic, recognizing the salient skills in a position description. Internal applicants need to consider who their new colleagues would be, how they would handle a rejection, and whether they would feel obliged to leave if rejected for the new position.

Vidor went on to discuss the application process, and the importance of an appropriate cover letter. When a job posting results in a large pool of qualified applicants, a weak cover letter is a valid criterion for rejecting an application in favor of another with a strong cover letter. Vidor involved the audience in evaluating several examples of cover letters. She pointed out specific strengths and weaknesses, ranging from the general (length, appearance) to the specific (what to include or omit, spelling). Cover letters must be honest and consistent, and should make readers interested in your application. Searchers expect letters to complement and illustrate the contents of the resumé. A cover letter should state why the applicant is interested in the job, explain any anomalies in the resumé, such as gaps in employment history, changes of career direction, and apparent over-qualification for the position. An application should focus on illustrating how well-matched your skills are with those required.

Internal candidates should plan to write a complete letter of application, as not all colleagues may be aware of special projects and skills the applicant will bring to the new job.

O'Neil continued with advice concerning resumés. She recommended that applicants consult books on how to write resumés. Three types of resumés were identified and illustrated in the handouts: functional or competency cluster, focused or targeted, and chronological or work history. These were adapted from David Eyler's *Resumés That Mean Business*.[2] In the first type, applicants list all qualifications and skills, and in an overview, outline the kind of job of interest to them. This style resumé would be appropriate for an individual re-entering the work-force or changing careers. The focused resumé targets a specific job, eliminating skills and experience not directly related to it.

The type most candidates are likely to use is the chronological, which relates work and educational history. O'Neil suggested including all continuing education, special skills, languages (even those not required in the job description), and professional affiliations and activities. She described using a detailed analytical questionnaire as an exercise in self-examination and provided a sample outline in the handouts.

After her advice on what should be included, O'Neil listed items *not* to include in a resumé. Some of these are high school information, salary requirements, and personal information, such as marital status, number of children, age, health, and photographs. She reiterated that all her admonitions are based on applications she has seen, and many she has rejected.

References should be included only if they are required, in the number requested, and should be submitted, with complete names, titles, and addresses on a separate page. Applicants should send a copy of the job description, their cover letter, and their resumé to each person they are listing as a reference, for each job.

O'Neil offered further tips on presenting applications. Re-read the cover letter aloud and ask someone else to proofread it. Proofread and re-check the application package before mailing. Mail the package flat, not folded, and do not wait for the deadline. Do not send anything that has not been requested. Be sure the resumé is up-to-date and uses proper terminology for the profession. Use *white* paper and keep in mind how the resumé will photocopy for multiple search committee members. Never hire anyone to do your resumé. You must present yourself. She referred her audience to the list of action words found in Loretta Foxman's *Resumés That Work: How to Sell Yourself on Paper.*[3] O'Neil provided a bibliography that included sources on career choices, cover letters, interviews, and resumés.

The workshop concluded with both presenters offering suggestions about the interview portion of the job application process. Both emphasized that applicants should only agree to interview for jobs they really want. Before an interview, applicants should prepare a portfolio, and have questions ready for the search committee. Do background work on the institution to which you are applying and the area. Know the name of the local system and try it out before the interview.

The three "A's" of interviewing are attire, answers, attitude. In dressing for an interview, be aware of the climate where you are interviewing and dress appropriately. Prepare mini-presentations, including answers to standard interview questions, and practice them. O'Neil included a list of those questions in the handouts. Be honest in your answers and do not get too personal. Be careful of what you say at all times. Do not criticize your current employer. Listen a lot. Pretend you care, even if you do not.

After the interview, candidates should send a thank you letter to the head of the search committee. Inform the search committee immediately if you find it is necessary or advisable to withdraw your application. If you do not get the job, review your application process, and analyze it to discover weaknesses. An unsuccessful candidate may contact the personnel librarian to request comments and suggestions.

This very practical workshop had an attentive audience which came away with guidelines to direct them in making choices for change in their professional lives. The presentation by O'Neil and Vidor offered the challenge and encouragement to take on new opportunities in reshaping our individual roles in the serials industry.

NOTES

1. Richard N. Bolles, *What color is your parachute? A practical manual for job-hunters & career-changers,* 1994 ed. (Berkeley: Ten Speed Press, 1994).
2. David R. Eyler, *Resumes that mean business,* Newly revised and updated (New York: Random House, Inc., 1993).
3. Loretta D. Foxman, *Resumes that work: how to sell yourself on paper,* 2nd ed., ed. Walter L. Polsky (New York: John Wiley & Sons, Inc., 1993).

Ninth Annual NASIG Conference Registrants, University of British Columbia, June 1994

Conference Registrants *Institutions*

Aaron, Amira	Readmore Automation
Adrian, Philip	Rush University
Aiello, Helen M.	Wesleyan University
Aitchison, Jada A.	UALR/Pulaski County Law Library
Alessi, Dana	Baker & Taylor Books
Alexander, Adrian W.	Faxon
Algier-Baxter, Aimee	Santa Clara University
Allgood, Everitt	Birmingham Area Library Service
Altenberger, Alicja	Harvard University
Altimus, Joe	University of Oregon
Anderson, Amy F.	Southwestern University
Anderson, Elma	Marywood College
Andrews, Judy	Reed College Library
Anemaet, Jos	Ohio State University
Anspach, Karen	Data Trek Inc.
Antelman, Kristin	University of Delware
Aquila, Sam	University of Victoria, McPherson Library
Arcand, Janet	Iowa State University
Ashby, John	Faxon Canada
Ashton, Jonathan	Dawson Subscription Service
Atkins, Julie	Oxford University Press
Atkinson, Judy	University of British Columbia
Aufdemberge, Karen	University of Toledo

Badics, Joe	Eastern Michigan University
Baia, Wendy	University of Colorado
Baker, Carol	University of Calgary
Baker, Jeanne	University of Maryland
Baker, Mary Ellen	California Polytechnic University
Baker, Ruth	Blackwell North America
Baker, Theresa	University of Kansas Medical Center
Balaski, Dianne	Athabasca University
Baldwin, Nadine	University of British Columbia
Banas-Marti, Kathy	University of Connecticut
Banks, Jennifer	MIT Libraries
Barstow, Sandy	University of Wyoming
Bentley, Ronald W.	Canadian Argicultural Library
Bergholz, Donna C.	Duke University
Bernards, Dennis	Brigham Young University
Bick, Dawn	Texas Medical Center Library
Blixrud, Julia C.	Council on Library Resources
Bloss, Alex	University of Illinois - Chicago
Bloss, Marjorie	Center for Research Libraries
Bodner, Stewart	New York Public Library
Boguski, Dr. Mark	National Library of Medicine
Bolman, Pieter	Academic Press
Born, Kathleen	EBSCO
Borsman, Mary Linn	Treadwell Library, Mass. General Hospital
Bostick, Sharon L.	University of Massachusetts - Boston
Bozich, Steve	Baker & Taylor Books
Bracken, Lee	Baker Library, Harvard Business School
Bradley, Melissa	Denver Public Library
Breed, Luellen L.	University of Wisconsin, Parkside
Breithaupt, John	Allen Press, Inc.
Breton, Gabriel	National Library of Canada
Broadwater, Deborah H.	Vanderbilt University, Eskind Biomedical Library
Broadway, Rita	Memphis State University
Broering, Naomi C.	Georgetown University, Dahlgren Memorial Library

Bross, Valerie	California State Unversity, Stanislaus
Broussard, Camille	New York Law School Library
Brown, David	DBJ Associates
Brown, K. B.	IUP
Brown, Ladd	Georgia State University Law Library
Brown, Margaret	Kwantlen College Library
Bryant, Lee Ann	University of British Columbia
Bubber, Moninder	Simon Fraser University
Buckingham, Jeanette	University of Alberta
Buell, Vivian	Librarian-at-Large
Bueter, Rita	Blackwell North America
Bull, Greg	University of St. Thomas
Bunnell, Keith	University of British Columbia
Burgos, Mary	Columbia University Law Library
Burk, Martha	Babson College
Burks, Suzan K.	Ball State University
Busby, Joan	National Library of Canada
Bustion, Marifran	George Washington University
Cady, Sue	Lehigh University
Callaghan, Jean	Wheaton College
Cameron, Hazel	University of Victoria
Campbell, Larry	University of British Columbia
Caputo, Anne	DIALOG Information Services, Inc.
Cargille, Karen	University of California, San Diego
Carlson, Bobbie	Medical University of South Carolina Library
Casetta, Prima	Getty Center
Caskey, Elizabeth	University of British Columbia
Castle, Mary K.	University of Texas - Arlington
Celeste, Eric	MIT Libraries
Cenzer, Pam	University of Florida
Chaffin, Nancy J.	Texas A&M University
Champagne, Thomas E.	University of Michigan
Chang, Ling-li	Loyola University Chicago
Chatterton, Leigh A.	NELINET, Inc.

Choi, Yu-mei — British Columbia Institute of Technology
Chou, Charlene — Columbia University
Chow, Helen — University of British Columbia Woodward Library

Chressanthis, June — Mississippi State University
Clack, Mary Beth — Harvard College Library
Clark, Cynthia — University of California–Irvine
Clarke, Judy — Judy Clarke & Associates
Clarkson, Jane — Florida State University
Clay, Genevieve J. — Eastern Kentucky University
Cleary, Robert — University of Missouri
Clendenning, Lynda F. — University of Virginia
Cochenour, Donnice — Colorado State University
Collins, Dorothy — Readmore Academic Services
Condit, Nancy E. — Arizona Health Sciences Library
Congleton, Robert — Temple University
Conway, Cheryl L. — University of Arkansas
Cook, Eleanor — Appalachian State University
Copeland, Lynn — Simon Fraser University
Corbett, Gloria — CISTI
Coulter, Cynthia M. — Univeristy of Northern Iowa
Courtney, Keith — Taylor & Francis
Cousineau, Marie — University of Ottawa
Cox, Brian — Elsevier Science Limited
Cox, John — Carfax Publishing Company
Crump, Michele — University of Florida
Culotta, Wendy — California State University, Long Beach

Curry, Dr. Ann — University of British Columbia SLAIS

Curtis, Jerry — Springer Verlag
Czech, Isabel — ISI–Philadelphia

Dabkowski, Charles — Niagera University Library
Dane, Steve — Kluwer Academic Publishers
Darling, Karen — University of Oregon
Davidson, Joyce — University of British Columbia
Davis, Carroll Nelson — Columbia University
Davis, Susan — SUNY-Buffalo
Davis, Trisha — Ohio State University

Dawson, Julie Eng — Princeton Theological Seminary
Day, Nancy — Linda Hall Library
De Soignie, Ralph — Allen Press, Inc.
DeBuse, Judy — Washington State Library
Deeken, JoAnne — Clemson University
Degener, Christie T. — University of North Carolina–Chapel Hill Health Sciences

Devlin, Mary — Faxon
Di Biase, Linda — University of Washington Libraries

Dietch, Janice — University of Manitoba
Diodato, Louise — Cardinal Stritch College
Donovan, Bernard — A.L.P.S.P.
Donovan, Joanne — University of California, San Diego

Doran, Kelly — Weyerhaeuser
Douglass, Janet — Texas Christian University
Downs, Valerie — O.I.S.E.
Doyle, Ann — Univeristy of British Columbia
Drabek, Hilda L. — University of Connecticut
Drake, Paul B. — Roger Williams University
Duhon, Lucy — University of Toledo
Dupras, Rheba — University of Alaska Fairbanks
Duranceau, Ellen — Massachusetts Institute of Technology

Dykstra, Lorraine — Faxon Canada
Dykstra, Stephanie — University of British Columbia

Eadie, Tom — University of Calgary
Edelman, Marla — University of North Carolina
Edmunds, Sandra — Gallagher Law Library
Edwards, Jennifer L. — Kansas State University
Elliot, Maxine — Clemson University
Entlich, Richard (Rich) — Cornell University Mann Library
Entwistle, Steve — B.H. Blackwell
Estes, Marilyn — Gallaudet University

Fairley, Elaine — Simon Fraser University
Farwell, Anne — CANEBSCO Subscription Services

Faust, Dror — Puvill Libros

Feick, Tina	Blackwell's Periodicals Division
Ferguson, Tony	Columbia University
Ferley, Margaret	Concordia University
Field, Kenneth	Trent University
Fisher, Fran	North Dakota State University
Fisher, Heidi	Princeton University
Fitchett, Christine	Vassar College Library
Fletcher, Clare	Routledge Publishers
Fletcher, Marilyn	New Mexico Newspaper Project
Folsom, Sandy	Central Michigan University
Forbes, Jennifer	University of British Columbia
Forrester, David	Blackwell Publishers
Forrester, Jim	Ontario College of Art
Fortney, Lynn	EBSCO Subscription Services
Foster, Connie	Western Kentucky University
Frade, Pat	Brigham Young University
Frick, Rachel	Readmore
Friend, Fred	University College London
Gallilee, Patty	University of Regina
Galloway, Dr. James W.	Texas Women's University
Galloway, Margaret E.	University of North Texas
Gammon, Julia	University of Akron
Gasser, Sharon S.	James Madison University
Geer-Butler, Beverley	Trinity University
Geller, Marilyn	MIT Libraries
Gibbs, Nancy J.	North Carolina State University Libraries
Gick, Natalie	Burnaby Public Library
Gill, Linda	Middle Tennessee State University
Gillespie, E. Gaele	University of Kansas
Gimmi, Robert D.	Shippensburg University
Ginanni, Katy	EBSCO Subscription Services
Glasgow, Kay	Binghamton University
Gobin, Kip	University of Virginia Law Library
Godolphin, Jocelyn	University of British Columbia
Gordon, Martin	Franklin & Marshall College
Gordon, Mike	Dawson Subscription Service
Gordon-Gilmore, Anita	Fort Hays State University
Gormley, Alice	Marquette University Library

Goshulak, Ted	Trinity Western University
Grande, Dolores	John Jay College
Gray, Mavis	University of Manitoba
Green, Toby	Elsevier Science Ltd.
Greene, Phil	EBSCO Subscription Services
Grover, Diane	University of Washington
Grycz, Chet	University of California/Office of the President
Guernsey, Nancy	University of Wyoming
Guijt, Bas	Martinus Nyhoff International
Gurshman, Sandy	Readmore Academic
Haas, Ruth	Harvard College Library
Haest, Ruth	University of New Mexico
Hagen, Lin	University of Nebraska-Lincoln
Hall, Barbara	University of Southern California
Halpin, Lola	Emory University
Hamakawa, Marlene	University of British Columbia Woodward Library
Hamilton, Fred	Louisiana Tech University
Harcourt, Kate	Columbia University
Hardin, Barbara	Kennesaw State College
Hardy, Eileen	Wellesley College
Harmon, Amanda	University of North Carolina–Charlotte
Harris, Wil	Moorhead State University
Harris, Ava Nell	University of Texas at Arlington
Harris, Jay	University of Alabama at Birmingham
Harris, Jim	University of British Columbia
Harris, Mary L.	Simon Fraser University
Harris, Sandra	Linda Hall Library
Harris, Tom	U.S. Environmental Protection Agency
Harrison, Colin	Everetts
Hart, Tricia	University of Washington
Hasiuk, Anne Z.	University of Chicago
Hattink, Jan	Kluwer Academic Publishers
Hawks, Carol P.	Ohio State University
Hedberg, Jane	Wellesley College
Helinsky, Zuzana	BTJ Subscription Service

Hepfer, Cindy	Serials Review
Heras, Elaine	Watzek Library
Hermsmeier, Tomoko	University of British Columbia
Heterick, Bruce	Faxon
Hewitt, Laurie	Dynix Library Systems
Hill, Joan	National Research Council
Hillery, Leanne	Ball State University
Hinders, Tom	Oberlin College
Hinger, Joseph	Detroit College of Law Library
Hirning, Lorraine	Athabasca University
Hirons, Jean	Library of Congress
Ho, Yee-Ip	Hong Kong University of Science & Technology
Hodge, Stan	Ball State University
Holeton, Anna	British Columbia Institute of Technology
Holland, Jeffrey	University of Nevada-Reno
Holley, Beth	University of Alabama
Holley, Sandra H.	University of Texas Health Center
Holt, Tom	Stanford University
Hooks, Dr. James	Indiana University of Pennsylvania
Horiuchi, Linda	Washington State University
Horn, Maggie	University of California-Davis
Horner, Terry	University of British Columbia
Hoyle, Mary Sue	EBSCO Subscription Services
Hsieh, Jenny	University of Massachusetts-Boston
Hughes, Katherine	Loyola University Chicago
Hurst, Brenda	CISTI
Iljin, Kristina	University of Alabama at Birmingham
Iltis, Deanna	Oregon State Library
Impellittiere, Agnes J.	Elsevier Science Inc.
Irvin, Judy	Louisiana Tech University
Isabelle, Elizabeth	Rosary College
Iverson, Theresa	University of British Columbia
Ivins, October	Louisiana State University
Jaeger, Don	Alfred Jaeger, Inc.
Jakubowski, Kathi L.	University of Wisconsin, Milwaukee

James, John R.	Dartmouth College
Jarvis, Will	Washington State University
Jayes, Linda D.	University of Chicago
Jizba, Richard	Creighton University
Johnson, David L.	Princeton University
Johnson, Judy	University of Nebraska, Lincoln
Johnson, Kay	University of Pittsburgh, SLIS
Johnston, Judith A.	University of North Texas
Johnston, Lynda	University of British Columbia
Jones, Danny	University of Texas Health Sciences Center
Jones, David L.	Sci-Tech Library, University of Alberta
Jones, Mary Elizabeth	Williams College
Julian, Gail	University of South Carolina
Jurries, Elaine	Auraria Library
Kanter, Dorothy	University of Wisconsin, Center for Health Sciences Library
Kara, Bill	Cornell University
Kay, Mary H.	Humboldt State University
Keate, Heather	University of British Columbia
Keating, Lawrence	University of Houston
Keen, Sherry	Brandeis University
Kennedy, Kit	Readmore Academic
Kerr, Linda G.	University of Alberta
Kersey, Harriet	Georgia Tech Library
Khosh-khui, Sam A.	Southwest Texas State University
Kichuk, Diana	University of Saskatchewan
Kim, Sook-Hyun	University of Tennessee Libraries
Kirkland, Kenneth	DePaul University
Knapp, Leslie	EBSCO Subscription Services
Knupp, Blaine E.	Indiana University of Pennsylvania
Kobyljanec, Kathleen	Case Western Reserve Law Library
Krishan, Kewal	University of Saskatchewan
Kromann, Sonja	National Marine Mammal Lab
Kropf, Blythe	New York Public Library
Kuhn, Joanne	University of Waterloo

Kunz, Margarett N.	National Institutes of Health Library
Ladjen, Nadia	New York Public Library
Lai, Sheila	California State University, Sacramento
Lalande, Christine	Sport Information Resource Centre
Lamborn, Joan G.	University of Northern Colorado
Landesman, Betty	George Washington University
Lawrence, Jane	Harcourt Brace & Company
Leadem, Ellen	NIEHS
Leathem, Cecilia	University of Miami
Leazer, William	EBSCO -Biomedical Division
Lebron, Maria L.	American Physical Society
Lee, Maureen	University of Toronto
Lee, Sul	University of Oklahoma Libraries
Lennie, Mike	Current Science Ltd.
Lenville, Jean	University of Richmond
Lester, Mark	San Diego State University Library
Levin, Fran	Houston Public Library
Lewis, Susan	Johns Hopkins University Press
Lindquist, Janice	Rice University
Long, John	Institute of Physics
Long, Nigel	Faxon Canada
Lucas, John	University of Mississippi Medical Center
Luebbe, Mary	University of British Columbia
Luther, Judy	Faxon
Lynch, Rich	Faxon
Ma, Anthony	University of British Columbia
MacAdam, Carol	Princeton University
Macklin, Lisa A.	Georgia Institute of Technology
MacLennan, Birdie	University of Vermont
MacWithey, Mary	NOTIS Systems Inc.
Madarash-Hill, Cherie	University of Akron
Madsen, Debbie	Kansas State University
Magee, Elizabeth	University of Regina
Magenau, Carol	Dartmouth College Library
Malawski, Susan	John Wiley & Sons, Inc.

Malinowski, Teresa	California State University
Mann, Margi	National Library of Medicine
Marill, Jennifer	Washington Research Library Consortium
Markley, Susan	Villanova University
Markwith, Michael	Faxon
Marsh, Corrie	NOTIS Systems Inc.
Martin, Robert S.	Louisiana State University
Martin, Sylvia	Vanderbilt University
Masri, Dalene	Information Access Co.
Matthews, Kathleen	University of Victoria
Mauch, Joe	Blackwell's Pacific
Mauldin, Peggy	MUSC Library
McAdam, Tim	University of California
McDermand, Bob	San Jose State University
McGlinchey, Sean	Current Science
McGrath, Kat	University of British Columbia
McKay, Bea	Trinity University
McKay, Peter	Harcourt Brace & Co.
McKay, Sharon Cline	Dynix Marquis, Inc.
McShane, Kevin	National Library of Medicine
McSweeney, Marilyn G.	MIT Libraries
Meiseles, Linda	Hofstra University
Melton, Sonja	Michigan Tech University
Meneely, Kathleen	Cleveland Health Sciences Library
Mering, Margaret	University of Nebraska
Merrill-Oldham, Pete	Acme Bookbinding
Middleton, Cheryl	Louisiana State University SLIS
Miller, Abby	Auraria Library
Miller, Heather S.	SUNY-Albany
Mills, Pam	University of Minnesota, Minneapolis
Minnerath, Janet	OU College of Medicine, Tulsa
Mitchell, Marilyn	University of Puget Sound
Moles, Jean Ann	University of Arkansas for Medical Sciences
Moore, Linda	TranSKILLS
Moran, Sheila	Massachusetts General Hospital
Morgan, Eric Lease	North Carolina State University Libraries
Morgano, Susan	Faxon

Mouw, James	University of Chicago
Mullins, Teresa	UnCover
Murden, Steve	Virginia Commonwealth University
Myers, Carolyn	University of Nevada, Las Vegas
Naslund, Jo-Anne	University of British Columbia Education Library
Nelles, Marjorie	Simon Fraser University
Nelson, Carol	Ball State University
Nelson, Catherine R.	University of California
Nelson, Karen	University of Minnesota
Nelson, Katy	University of Victoria
Nesto, Mary Ann	University of Hartford
Nez, Ann	University of Washington Law Library
Nguyen, Hien	National Library of Medicine
Niblock, Pam	University of British Columbia Woodward Library
Nobles, Steve	University of Tulsa
Nordman, Alan	Dawson-US Operations
Norton, Geneva	Shoreline School District
Novak, Denise	Carnegie Mellon University
O'Neil, Rosanna M.	Pennsylvania State University
Oberg, Steve	University of Chicago
Ogburn, Joyce	Yale University
Okerson, Ann	Association of Research Libraries
Olson, Gretchen	Watzek Library
Olson, Stan	Trinity Western University
Osheroff, Shiela	Oregon State University
Packer, Donna	Western Washington University
Palm, Miriam	Stanford University
Palmiter, Sherry	University of Maryland
Pappas, Susan	Kluwer Academic Publishers
Paradis, Olga	Baylor University
Parang, Elizabeth	University of Nevada, Las Vegas
Parker, Laura	Elsevier Science
Perrotta, Lorraine	Getty Center

Perry, Sara — CISTI
Peters, Victoria M. — Northern Arizona University
Peterson, Brenda — University of British Columbia
Peterson, Jan — Academic Press
Petty, Mary — Gonzaga University
Phillips, Sharon — California State University, Hayward

Pintozzi, Chestalene — University of Arizona
Pitman, Ronnie — North Carolina State University
Pitman, Suzanne — North Carolina State University
Pitti, Daniel — University of California, Berkeley

Pleasant, Rosemarie — CGIC
Plutchak, T. Scott — Saint Louis University
Polakowski, Betsy — University of St. Thomas
Porter, Sherry — UNT Health Science Center
Power, Tony — Simon Fraser University
Presley, Roger — Georgia State University
Price, Margaret — University of British Columbia, Woodward Library

Prior, Albert — U. K. Serials Group
Proctor, David — Texas Tech University
Pullinger, Dr. David — Institute of Physics

Radbourne, Margaret — John Wiley & Sons
Raines, M. Diane — DYNIX, Inc.
Rakes, Ann — Innovative Interfaces
Ralston, Joan — Villanova University
Randall, Kevin M. — Northwestern University
Randall, Mike — University of California, Los Angeles

Rankin, Juliann — Cal State Chico
Rast, Elaine — Northern Illinois University
Ravinder, Sarita — Princeton Theological Seminary
Reid, Marion — California State University, San Marcos

Reinalda, Roy J. — Dawson Subscription Service
Reinke, Christa — University of Houston
Revas, Robert — University of Utah
Reynolds, Regina — Library of Congress
Rice, Karen — Western Washington University

Richard, Trina	F.L.I.S.
Rieke, Judy	University of North Dakota Medical Library
Riley, Cheryl	Central Missouri State University
Rioux, Maggie	MBL/WHOI Joint Library
River, Sandy	Texas Tech University
Roach, Dani	Macalester College
Roberts, Connie	University of Connecticut
Robischon, Rose	United States Military Academy
Robison, David F. W.	NorthWestNet
Roche, Tony	Universal
Rodell, Nancy Tento	Academic Book Center
Rodgers, David L.	American Mathematical Society
Roepke, Greg	University of Maryland
Rogers, Marilyn	University of Arkansas
Romaniuk, Elena	University of Victoria
Rose, Midge L.	Idaho State University
Rossignol, Lu	Smithsonian Institution Libraries
Rowan, Helen	Douglas College
Rumph, Virginia	Butler University
Russov, Olga	Kennesaw State University
Saint, Barbara	University of British Columbia
Sak, Ludmila	Rutgers University
Salk, Judy	Reed Reference Publishing/ R. R. Bowker
Salmond, Maggie	Priestly Law Library
Sanders, Susan	NIST
Sarazin, Georges	Readmore Canada
Saxe, Minna C.	CUNY Graduate School
Schaafsma, Carol	University of Hawaii Library
Scheer, Cheryl	University of South Dakota-Lommen HSL
Scheffler, Eckart A.	Walter de Gruyter, Inc.
Schein, Anna M.	West Virginia University
Schmidt, Kathy	University of Wisconsin, La Crosse
Scholl, Miki	Hamline University Law Library
Schreiner, Suzanne	University of Puget Sound

Schwartz, Marla	American University Law Library
Schwartzkopf, Becky	Mankato State University
Schwind, Penny	Bryn Mawr College
Scott, Sharon	University of Nevada, Reno
Sellberg, Roxanne	University of Washington
Settle, Huguette M. T.	University of Alberta
Shadle, Steven C.	NSDP/Library of Congress
Shaffer, Barbara	University of Toledo Libraries
Shearrer, Cindy	University of Missouri-Columbia, SLIS
Sheble, Mary Ann	University of Alabama
Sherman, Cynthia	Data Research Associates
Shropshire, Sandra	Idaho State University Library
Sievers, Arlene Moore	Case Western Reserve University
Signori, Donna	University of Victoria
Simpson, Pamela	Pennsylvania State University
Sinha, Reeta	Emory University Health Sciences Center Library
Sleeman, Allison M.	University of Virginia
Sleep, Esther L.	Brock University Library
Smets, Kristine	Center for Research Libraries
Smith, Alan	Blackwell's Periodicals
Smith, Dean	Chapman & Hall
Smith, Sue	Blackwell's Periodicals
Smith, Susan	Weyerhaeuser
Smith, Susan	University of Connecticut
Smithers, Anne B.	University of Alberta
Soper, Ellen	GSLIS University of Washington
Sorensen, Sally	Texas Christian University
Sozansky, Bill	University of Minnesota, Duluth
Stamison, Christine	Blackwell's Periodicals
Stankowski, Becky	Purdue University Calumet
Steele, Heather	Blackwell's Periodicals
Stephens, Joan	Georgia State University
Sterling, Harold	Dawson Subscription Service
Stevens, Julie	University of British Columbia
Stewart, Wendy	Portland State University
Stickman, Jim	University of Washington
Stretesky, Lola	Auraria Library
Su, Julie	IUPUI University

Sullenger, Paula	Auburn University
Sullivan, Kathryn	Winona State University
Sutherland, Laurie	University of Washington
Swanson, Jean	University of Redlands
Sweet, Kathy	Phoenix College
Swets, Ariane	Swets Subscription Service
Sylka, Christina	University of British Columbia, David Lam Library
Tagler, John	Elsevier Science
Talley, Kaye	University of Central Arkansas
Tallman, Karen	University of Arizona
Taylor, Kay	University of Minnesota, Minneapolis
Taylor, Wayne	Simon Fraser University
Teague, Elaine	Burroughs Wellcome Co.
Teaster-Woods, Gale	Winthrop University
Teel, Kay	New York University
Tenney, Joyce	University of Maryland Baltimore County
Terry, Ana Arias	MCB University Press
Terry, Nancy	Grand Valley State University
Teskey, John	UNB
Testi, Andrea R.	University of New Mexico
Thomas, Suzanne	University of Pittsburgh
Thompson, James	University of California
Thomson, Sarah	University of Massachusetts Amherst
Thorne, Kathleen	San Jose State University
Timberlake, Phoebe	University of New Orleans
Tong, Dieu V.	University of Alabama at Birmingham
Tonkery, Dan	Readmore
Toussaint, Jo Ann	University of St. Thomas
Tribit, Don	Ganser Library, Millersville University
Trish, Maggie	University of Arizona
Tseng, Sally	University of California
Tumlin, Markel	University of San Diego
Turitz, Mitch	San Francisco State University
Tusa, Sarah	Lamar University

Tuttle, Marcia	University of North Carolina
Unver, Amira	George Washington University Medical Center
Van Auken, Gayle	Linda Hall Library
van Dyk, Jacqueline	North Vancouver District Public Library
Van Goethem, Jeri	Duke University
van Reenen, Johann	University of British Columbia
Vanderhoof, Audrey	Texas Christian University
Vent, Marilyn	University of Nevada, Las Vegas
Vidor, Ann	Emory University
Vogt, Norm	Northern Illinois University
Waisman, Yail	Burnaby Public Library
Wakeford, Paul J.	University of California, San Francisco
Wallace, Pat	University of Colorado
Wallace, Sheila	Emily Carr College of Art & Design
Wang, Margaret K.	University of Delaware
Wang, Sophia	Baker Library, Harvard University
Ward, Jeannette	University of Central Flordia
Ward, Sharon	National Library of Canada
Weber, Robert	Northeast Consulting Resources
Weiss, Paul J.	National Library of Medicine
Weisser, Teresa	Lafayette College
Welsh, Ed	Academic Book Center
Weng, Cathy	Temple University
Westall, Sandy	Innovative Interfaces
Weston, Beth	Univeristy of Delaware
Westover, Keith	Brigham Young University
Whipple, Marcia	NCCOSC RDTEDIV Tech Lab
Whittaker, Martha	Uncover Co.
Whitehead, Martha	University of British Columbia
Wiles-Young, Sharon	Lehigh University
Wilhite, Marjorie	University of Iowa
Wilkerson, Judy	University of Oklahoma Health Sciences Center

Wilkinson, Fran	University of New Mexico
Williams, Gerry	Northern Kentucky University
Williams, Martha	Minot State University
Williams, Sheryl	University of Nebraska Medical Center
Williams, Sue	University of Colorado, Boulder
Williamson, Ed	University of Delaware
Williamson, Josie	University of Delaware
Willmering, Bill	National Library of Medicine
Willoughby, Patrick	University of British Columbia
Winchester, David	Washburn University
Winjum, Roberta	University of Hawaii
Wirtz, Terri	Yankee Book Peddler
Wise, Mary	Central Washington University
Witsenhausen, Helen	John Wiley & Sons
Wong, Joyce	Burnaby Public Library
Woodford, Barbara	EBSCO Subscription Services
Wurzbach, Janet	Vancouver Community College
Xu, Zhishan (Amanda)	MIT Libraries
Yates, Graham	Readmore Canada Ltd.
Yeaple, Jenn	Simmons College - GSLIS
Youmans, Mary	Western Carolina University
Zager, Suzan	University of British Columbia Woodward Library
Ziegler, Roy	Southeast Missouri State University
Zinnato, Diana	Thomas Jefferson University
Zuidema, Karen	University of Illinois at Chicago
Zuriff, Sue	University of Minnesota

Index

AACR2 228,238-239,244,250,336
Alice in Wonderland 44,134
America Online 22,63
American Association of University Presses (AAUP) 243
American Chemical Society 112-122
American Libraries 296
American Memory project 230
Anderson, Rachel 191
ANSI standards 292
Archie 19
archival cataloging 335-336
ARIEL 206,324
Ariel, Joan 211
artificial intelligence 225-226
ASCII 47,120,328,330
Association for Library Collections & Technical Services (ALCTS) 295-296,299-300
Association of American Publishers (AAP) 56,245,251
Association of Research Libraries (ARL) 28,159,206,243,321
authority control 226-227,278-281

Bailey, Charles 34
Baker, Nicholson 232
Bellcore 112-122
Berman 293
BISAC 138
Bitmaps 115-117,328
Bridges, William 150-151
British Columbia Library Association 6,8
Burne, Eric 102-104
Bush, George 135
Bush, Vannevar 231

California State University/ Northridge 218-221
CALS initiative 246
Canadian Association of Research Libraries 324
Canadian Library Association 6
cancellations 341-342
career paths 164-171
CARL 322
Carnegie Mellon University 139
CASPR, Inc. 166
Cataloging 77,121,223-233, 235-241,249-252,278-281, 333-337
Cataloging in Publication (CIP) 226
CD-ROM 58-59,71,75-76,166,180, 205,207,263-264,266,274, 278
Center for Electronic Text in the Humanities 251
Central & Eastern European Library Project 51
Cerf, Vint 58
change 43-72,96-109,133-145, 149-160,181-191,193-202, 210-211,311-318,345- 347
Chaos theory 154
Chemical Abstracts Service 112-122
citations 320-321
Citations for Serials Literature 329-330
classification 238-239
client-server computing 11-13,18,30
Coalition for Networked Information (CNI) 60
Columbia University 320-323
communication within organizations 314-318
Compendex 209

© 1994 by The Haworth Press, Inc. All rights reserved.

competencies 186-187
CompuServe 22,63
contracting 256-259,269-275
Coombs, Renear & DeRose 247-249
Cooperative Library Agency for Systems & Services (CLASS) 164-165,167
copy cataloging 333-337
Corbin, John 186-187
CORE Project 112-122
Cornell University 59,112-122
Corporation for National Research Initiatives 58
cost accounting 301-305
Council on Library Resources 183-184,320
Crichton, Michael 129,232
Current Contents 324
cyberspace 203-204

Data Magician 294
database homology searching 128-130
dBase 294
de la Peña McCook, Kathleen 216-217
de Pree, Max 159
Deming, Edwards 141
depository program (U.S.) 7
Designing Information 190
Dewey Decimal classification 227,239
Dialog 262-263
Digital envelopes 61-62
Dimitroff, Alexandra 229
Directory of Electronic Journals, Newsletters & Academic Discussion Lists 28-29,34
DNA sequences 126
Docline 324
document delivery 75-76,263,265, 319-324
Document Type Definitions 245, 250-251
Dow Jones 205,209,265

DRA 262
Drucker, Peter 142
Duke, John 250
Duke University 261-265
duplicate record detection 239
Dynix 165-166,169

e-mail 12,81-82,205,314,331
EBSCO 165-166
EDI 67,88,296,342
electronic data interchange. *See* EDI
electronic journals 29,76,112-122, 173-180,327-331
Electronic Letters Online 251
electronic serials. *See* electronic journals
Electronic Text Center & Online Archive of Electronic Texts 225
Elixir 139
Elsevier 139
Emory University 314
Enright, John 184
Entrez 128-130
Ercegovac, Zorana 226
Ergonomics 349-351
Ethernet 115
Ethics 295-300,335
Expert systems 225-228,235-241

Fattig, Karl 228-229
File transfer protocol. *See* FTP
firm prices 341-342
Flexiplace 256-259
Florida Center for Library Automation 229
Franklin & Marshall College 345-347
FreeNets 8-9
FTP 11,18,226,329-330

GEAC 204,265
Geller, Marilyn 228

GenBank 126-130
Georgetown University 77-87
Gibson, William 204,231
Gopher 12,17-26,112,121,228,
    329-330
government documents 289-294

Harris, Roma 183
Harvard College 150,155-159
Horton, Forest 164,171
Hogue, Maggie 229
HTML 31-32,226,248
HTTP 29-31
Human Genome Project 126
HyperLynx 229
Hypertext 28,229

IAIMS project 78-85,89
ICEDIS 67,342
ILL. *See* interlibrary loan
imaging technology 230-231
Index Medicus 78,257
Indiana University of Pennsylvania
    308-309
Information Access Corp. 262
information policy, governmental
    5-9
"information superhighway" 64,
    136,180,252
Intel 59
intellectual property rights 70,176
interlibrary loan 176,262,265,
    321-323
Internet 11-42,47,49-53,57-63,112,
    139,189,244,272,274
ISBD punctuation 226
ISSN 229,266,287,328

Jajko, Pamela 213-214
job hunting 357-360

Johns Hopkins University Press
    173-180
Joint Steering Committee (on
    AACR2) 238
Jughead 19-20
Juran, Joseph 141

Kahn, Bob 58
Kilgour, Fred 138
Knowbots 32,58,227
Kurzweil, Raymond 75

LANs 204,266
Larson, Ray 250
LCRIs 228,250
Legal Resource Center (Legal
    Services Society of British
    Columbia) 5-6
Lehigh University 204-209,261,
    265-267
Lexis/Nexis 209,262
"liberspace." *See* virtual library
Library of Congress 7,19,137-138,
    225-230,258,278
Library of Congress Classification
    239
Library of Congress Rule
    Interpretations. *See* LCRIs
*Library-Oriented Computer
    Conferences and Electronic
    Serials* 34
Library Services & Construction Act
    (LSCA) 135
listservs 33-42
local area networks. *See* LANs
Lynx 12

Mapper (expert system) 226
MARBI 328
MARC format 137-138,186,
    228-230,240,245-252,279,
    292-294

Marcive 291,293
May, Rollo 196
Mayo, Elton 140
Mead Data Central 64
MEDLINE 127-128,324
Microforms 57
Mintzberg, Henry 141
MIT 24,26,228
MLS degree 164-165,168,216-217
monograph series 283-287
Monthly Catalog 290
Mooney, Margaret 293
Mosaic 12,27-32,58,91
Mr. Serials 329-330
multiculturalism 216-217
multimedia 31,58

NASIG
 gopher 19
 home page 30-32
National Center for Supercomputing
 Applications (NCSA) 28
National Information Infrastructure 136
National Library of Medicine 78,
 126,236,256-259,324
National Science Foundation 63
National Union Catalog (NUC) 137
NCBI 126-130
Network service providers 62-63
Newby, Gregory 231
Newlon, Lorraine 218
Nintendo 71
NLM Classification 239
Noble, David 211
North Carolina State University
 329-330
Northeast Consulting 56
Northwestern University 226
NOTIS 226,229,278-280,290-291
NREN 89
NTIS 229

OCLC 112-122,138,205,227,245,
 251,279,291-292,336

*Online Journal of Current Clinical
 Trials* 251
*Online Journal of Knowledge
 Synthesis for Nursing* 251
OPACs 46,205,229,262-263,
 290-292,330
Oregon State Library 289,292-294
OS/2 226
Oxford English Dictionary 225,302

PALINET 208
Penniman, David 183-184,190
periodicals use studies 320-321
perl 173,330
personalization of information 58,60
Peters, Paul Evan 60
Peterson, Mary 217
Phillips, Gerald 217
Phoenix College 345-347
"phoenix fantasy" 197
Pixlook 117
Postscript 63,173,328
pricing 177-179,273-274,339-343
Print, preference for 117
Project MUSE 174-180
publishers 284-287,340-341
publishing, future of 48-53,55-64

Reagan, Ronald 135-136
Red Sage 139
Reference service 307-310
reorganization of technical services
 311-318
retrenchment 100,105
Rheingold, Howard 203-204
Riddle, Prentiss 183
rights management 61
Rodes, Barbara 51
Romania 49-50

San Jose State University 165
Scepter 116

Schiff, Jackie 102
SEGA 71
Senge, Peter 184
Serials
 cataloging 333-337
 pricing 61-62
series. *See* monograph series
SGML 63,117,186,224,226,228, 243-252,328
shelflisting 240
SISAC 67,138
Stacey, Ralph 152-153
Standard Generalized Markup Language. *See* SGML
State University of New York at Buffalo 289-292
Sterling, Bruce 8
Stevens, Norman 315
STM journals 68-69,71,118-119, 284,341
Strawn, Gary 226
subscription agents. *See* vendors
subscriptions 68

Taylor, Frederick 140
TCP/IP 50
Technical vs. public service 188
Technology
 and vendors 66-72
 and change 45-48,210-211, 213-221
telecommuting 218-221
Text Encoding Initiative 246, 250-251
Toffler, Alvin 141
Total quality management (TQM) 141-143,353-356
training 86-87
transition (as opposed to change) 195-202
Trinity University 278-281
TULIP 139

U.S. National Center for Biotechnology Information *See* NCBI
U.S. Postal Service 210
UMI 262,322
UnCover 265,322
Universal Resource Locator. *See* URL
University of British Columbia 182, 323-324
University of California, Berkeley 250
University of California, Los Angeles (UCLA) 226
University of California, Riverside 164-165,167,293-294
University of Chicago 342
University of Florida 229-230
University of Houston 328-329
University of Illinois, Urbana-Champaign 28,231
University of Milwaukee 229
University of Nebraska, Lincoln 228
University of Northern Iowa 317
University of Virginia 225
University of Washington 308
UNIX 12,23,34,204,265
URL 16,24,29,31-32,328
user acceptance of electronic journals 118-120

Vaill, Peter 150
van Goethem, Jeri 262-263
van Houweling, Douglas 150
vendors 65-72,164-171,295-299, 341-342
Veronica 19-20,22,112
video conferencing 59
video display terminals (VDTs) 356
Virginia Commonwealth University 250
virtual library 70,74-92,204-211, 213-221
virtual reality 231
voyageurs (metaphor for personal exploration) 96-109

Wade, Nicholas 210
WAIS 11,91,121,330
Werman, Bob 217
Wheatley, Margaret 153-155
Winthrop University 345-347
Wolfram, Dietmar 229
WordPerfect 246-247,329
workstations 66-67,76-77,81-84
World Wide Web (WWW) 11-14,
    22-23,27-32,58,91,121,130,
    208,265,329-330

X-12 138,342

Ziff Publishing 64
Z39.50 13,88,205,246